AVENGERS

A.I.

> AVENGERS A.I.

> INITIATE: 12,000 A.D.

WRITER	**SAM HUMPHRIES**
ARTIST	**ANDRÉ LIMA ARAÚJO**

COLOR ARTIST	FRANK D'ARMATA
COVER ART	DAVID MARQUEZ & FRANK D'ARMATA
LETTERER	VC'S CLAYTON COWLES
ASSISTANT EDITOR	JON MOISAN
EDITOR	LAUREN SANKOVITCH
EXECUTIVE EDITOR	TOM BREVOORT
COLLECTION EDITOR	SARAH BRUNSTAD
ASSOCIATE MANAGING EDITOR	ALEX STARBUCK
EDITORS, SPECIAL PROJECTS	MARK D. BEAZLEY & JENNIFER GRÜNWALD
SENIOR EDITOR, SPECIAL PROJECTS	JEFF YOUNGQUIST
SVP PRINT, SALES & MARKETING	DAVID GABRIEL
BOOK DESIGN	IDETTE WINECOOR
EDITOR IN CHIEF	AXEL ALONSO
CHIEF CREATIVE OFFICER	JOE QUESADA
PUBLISHER	DAN BUCKLEY
EXECUTIVE PRODUCER	ALAN FINE

AVENGERS A.I. VOL. 2: 12,000 A.D. Contains material originally published in magazine form as AVENGERS A.I. #7.INH and #8-12. First printing 2014. ISBN# 978-0-7851-8492-8. Published by MARVEL WORLDWIDE, INC., a subsidiary of MARVEL ENTERTAINMENT, LLC. OFFICE OF PUBLICATION: 135 West 50th Street, New York, NY 10020. Copyright © 2013 and 2014 Marvel Characters, Inc. All rights reserved. All characters featured in this issue and the distinctive names and likenesses thereof, and all related indicia are trademarks of Marvel Characters, Inc. No similarity between any of the names, characters, persons, and/or institutions in this magazine with those of any living or dead person or institution is intended, and any such similarity which may exist is purely coincidental. **Printed in Canada**. ALAN FINE, EVP - Office of the President, Marvel Worldwide, Inc. and EVP & CMO Marvel Characters B.V.; DAN BUCKLEY, Publisher & President - Print, Animation & Digital Divisions; JOE QUESADA, Chief Creative Officer; TOM BREVOORT, SVP of Publishing; DAVID BOGART, SVP of Operations & Procurement, Publishing; C.B. CEBULSKI, SVP of Creator & Content Development; DAVID GABRIEL, SVP Print, Sales & Marketing; JIM O'KEEFE, VP of Operations & Logistics; DAN CARR, Executive Director of Publishing Technology; SUSAN CRESPI, Editorial Operations Manager; ALEX MORALES, Publishing Operations Manager; STAN LEE, Chairman Emeritus. For information regarding advertising in Marvel Comics or on Marvel.com, please contact Niza Disla, Director of Marvel Partnerships, at ndisla@marvel.com. For Marvel subscription inquiries, please call 800-217-9158. **Manufactured between 5/2/2014 and 6/9/2014 by SOLISCO PRINTERS, SCOTT, QC, CANADA.**

10 9 8 7 6 5 4 3 2 1

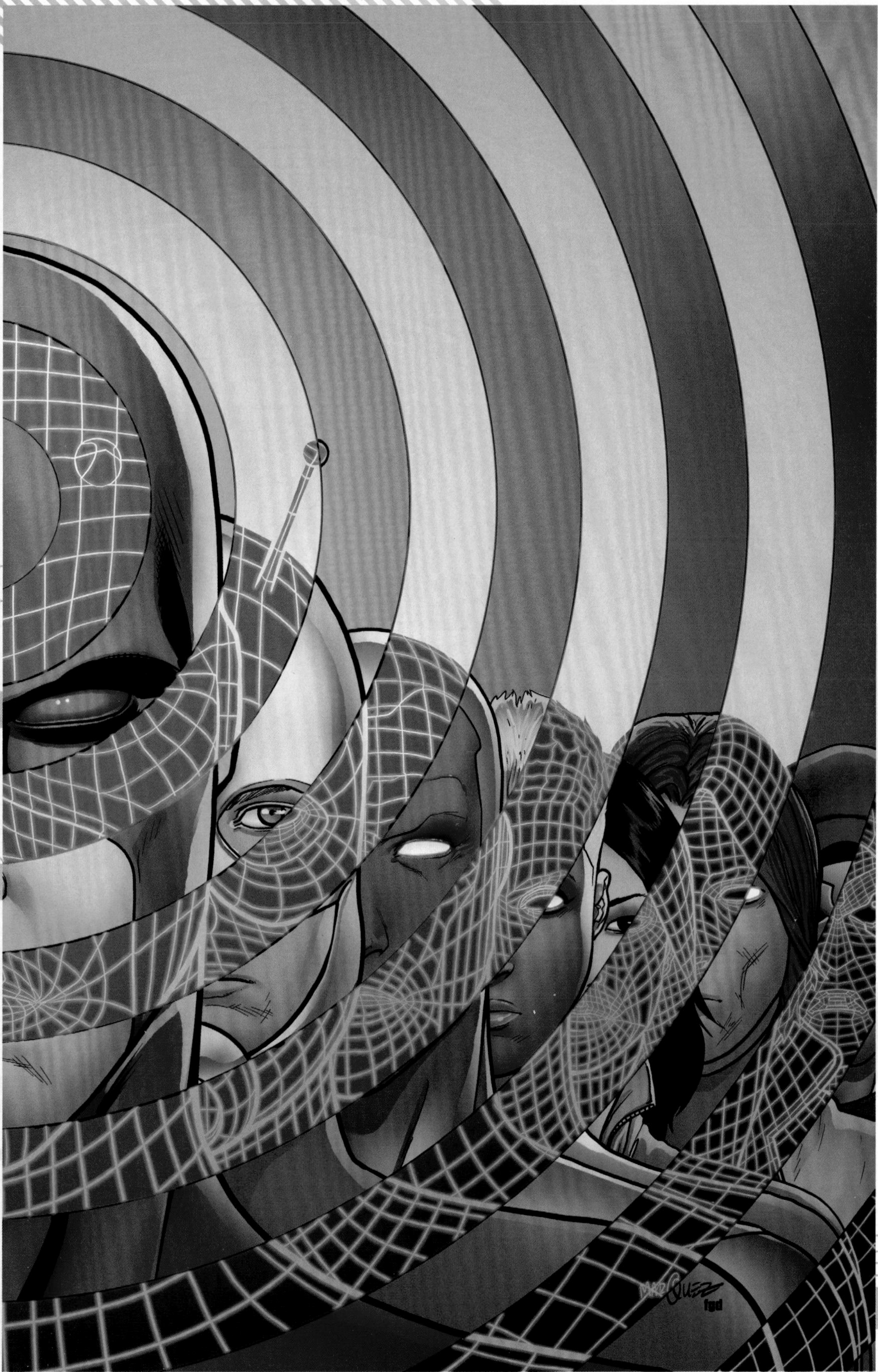

INITIATE: CHAPTER 7 <

PREVIOUSLY IN AVENGERS A.I.

:DATE // THE CURRENT DATE IS --> WED 12/11/13

:RECAP // THE AVENGERS HAD LEFT EARTH TO FIGHT A WAR IN SPACE. CAPITALIZING ON THEIR ABSENCE, THE MAD TITAN THANOS ATTACKED EARTH IN AN ATTEMPT TO LOCATE AND EXTERMINATE HIS INHUMAN SON.

IN ORDER TO PROTECT HIS PEOPLE FROM THANOS, THE INHUMAN KING BLACK BOLT DESTROYED THE CITY OF ATTILAN OVER NEW YORK AND RELEASED THE TRANSFORMATIVE TERRIGEN MISTS OVER THE EARTH CREATING MANY NEW INHUMANS. MOST OF THESE NEWLY POWERED INDIVIDUALS WERE UNAWARE OF THEIR UNIQUE GENETIC HERITAGE.

WITH THE BROKEN CITY OF ATTILAN NOW LYING ON THE HUDSON RIVER, IT WILL PROVIDE A RIPE TARGET FOR THOSE LOOKING TO SCAVENGE ITS REMAINS FOR UNKNOWN TREASURES AND WEAPONS.

MEANWHILE, S.H.I.E.L.D. DIRECTOR MARIA HILL REASSIGNED AGENT MONICA CHANG TO AN A.I. HUNTING TEAM DESIGNED TO ENFORCE LEGISLATION THAT RULES ARTIFICIAL INTELLIGENCE AS INTELLECTUAL PROPERTY, ALLOWING AUTHORITIES TO KIDNAP AND DEACTIVATE A.I.S AT WILL.

:EJECT (A.I. NO7 RECAP)

:EXIT

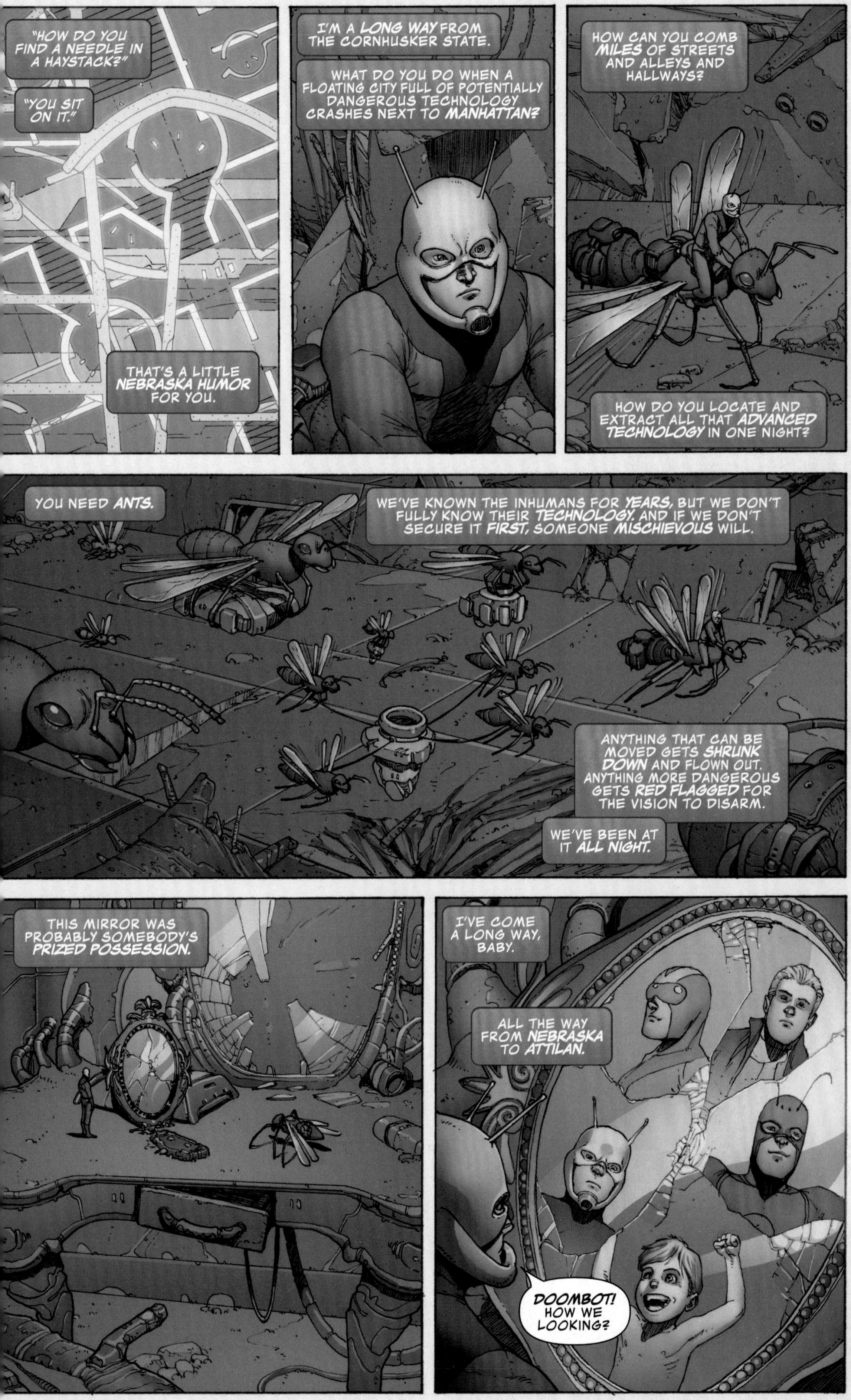
"HOW DO YOU FIND A NEEDLE IN A HAYSTACK?"
"YOU SIT ON IT."
THAT'S A LITTLE NEBRASKA HUMOR FOR YOU.
I'M A LONG WAY FROM THE CORNHUSKER STATE.
WHAT DO YOU DO WHEN A FLOATING CITY FULL OF POTENTIALLY DANGEROUS TECHNOLOGY CRASHES NEXT TO MANHATTAN?
HOW CAN YOU COMB MILES OF STREETS AND ALLEYS AND HALLWAYS?
HOW DO YOU LOCATE AND EXTRACT ALL THAT ADVANCED TECHNOLOGY IN ONE NIGHT?
YOU NEED ANTS.
WE'VE KNOWN THE INHUMANS FOR YEARS, BUT WE DON'T FULLY KNOW THEIR TECHNOLOGY. AND IF WE DON'T SECURE IT FIRST, SOMEONE MISCHIEVOUS WILL.
ANYTHING THAT CAN BE MOVED GETS SHRUNK DOWN AND FLOWN OUT. ANYTHING MORE DANGEROUS GETS RED FLAGGED FOR THE VISION TO DISARM.
WE'VE BEEN AT IT ALL NIGHT.
THIS MIRROR WAS PROBABLY SOMEBODY'S PRIZED POSSESSION.
I'VE COME A LONG WAY, BABY.
ALL THE WAY FROM NEBRASKA TO ATTILAN.
DOOMBOT! HOW WE LOOKING?

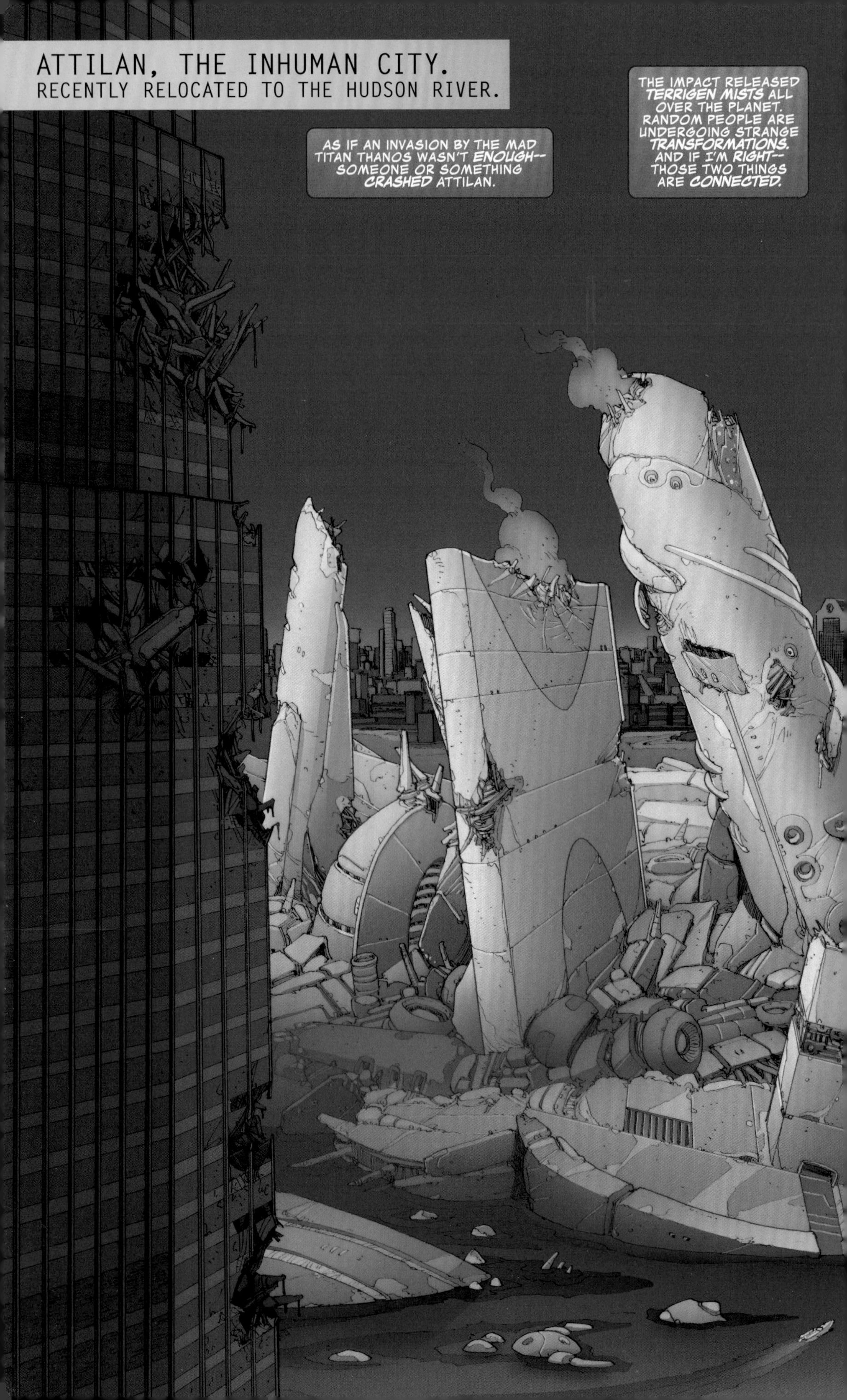
ATTILAN, THE INHUMAN CITY.
RECENTLY RELOCATED TO THE HUDSON RIVER.
AS IF AN INVASION BY THE MAD TITAN THANOS WASN'T ENOUGH-- SOMEONE OR SOMETHING CRASHED ATTILAN.
THE IMPACT RELEASED TERRIGEN MISTS ALL OVER THE PLANET. RANDOM PEOPLE ARE UNDERGOING STRANGE TRANSFORMATIONS. AND IF I'M RIGHT-- THOSE TWO THINGS ARE CONNECTED.

WHAT'S AN INHUMAN NATION WHEN YOU CRASH IT INTO A WORLD OF HUMANS?
WHAT'S A CITY OF THE SKY WHEN YOU DUNK IT INTO THE SEA?
WHAT'S A KINGDOM WITHOUT A KING?
EXACTLY THE SAME AS FIVE MINUTES AGO.
THERE IS A GIANT CITY IN YOUR RIVER.
GOOD, KEEP IT UP, DOOMBOT.
NO ONE GETS IN OR OUT OF ATTILAN UNTIL WE'RE DONE.

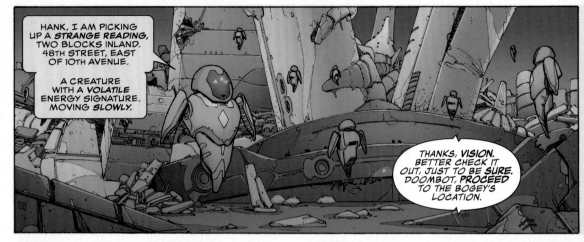

HANK, I AM PICKING UP A *STRANGE READING*, TWO BLOCKS INLAND. 48TH STREET, EAST OF 10TH AVENUE.

A CREATURE WITH A *VOLATILE* ENERGY SIGNATURE. MOVING *SLOWLY*.

THANKS, *VISION*. BETTER CHECK IT OUT, JUST TO BE *SURE*. DOOMBOT, *PROCEED* TO THE BOGEY'S LOCATION.

IF I MUST.

DOOM'S *SOUL* YEARNS TO SOAR WITH *NOBLE FALCONS*, YET MY BODY MEANDERS WITH *GOAT-KNEED GILLYFLOWERS*--

SQRRK
****

KRASH

WHO DARES--?!

SHOW YOURSELF!

DOOM!

THUMP

KWRRK
***

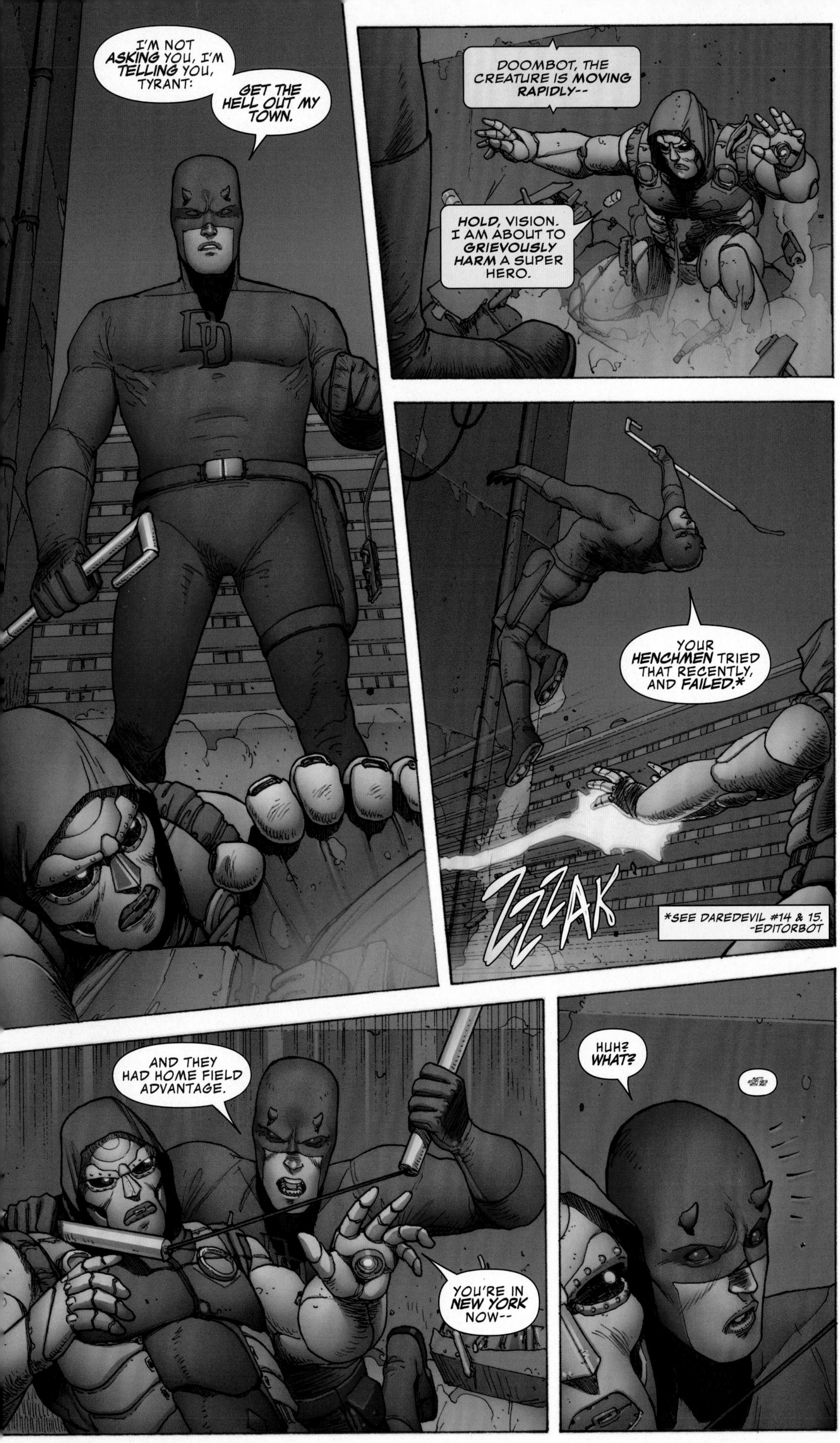
I'M NOT ASKING YOU, I'M TELLING YOU, TYRANT:
GET THE HELL OUT MY TOWN.
DOOMBOT, THE CREATURE IS MOVING RAPIDLY--
HOLD, VISION. I AM ABOUT TO GRIEVOUSLY HARM A SUPER HERO.
YOUR HENCHMEN TRIED THAT RECENTLY, AND FAILED.*
ZZZAK
*SEE DAREDEVIL #14 & 15. -EDITORBOT
AND THEY HAD HOME FIELD ADVANTAGE.
YOU'RE IN NEW YORK NOW--
HUH? WHAT?
MATT! STOP! HE'S WITH ME!

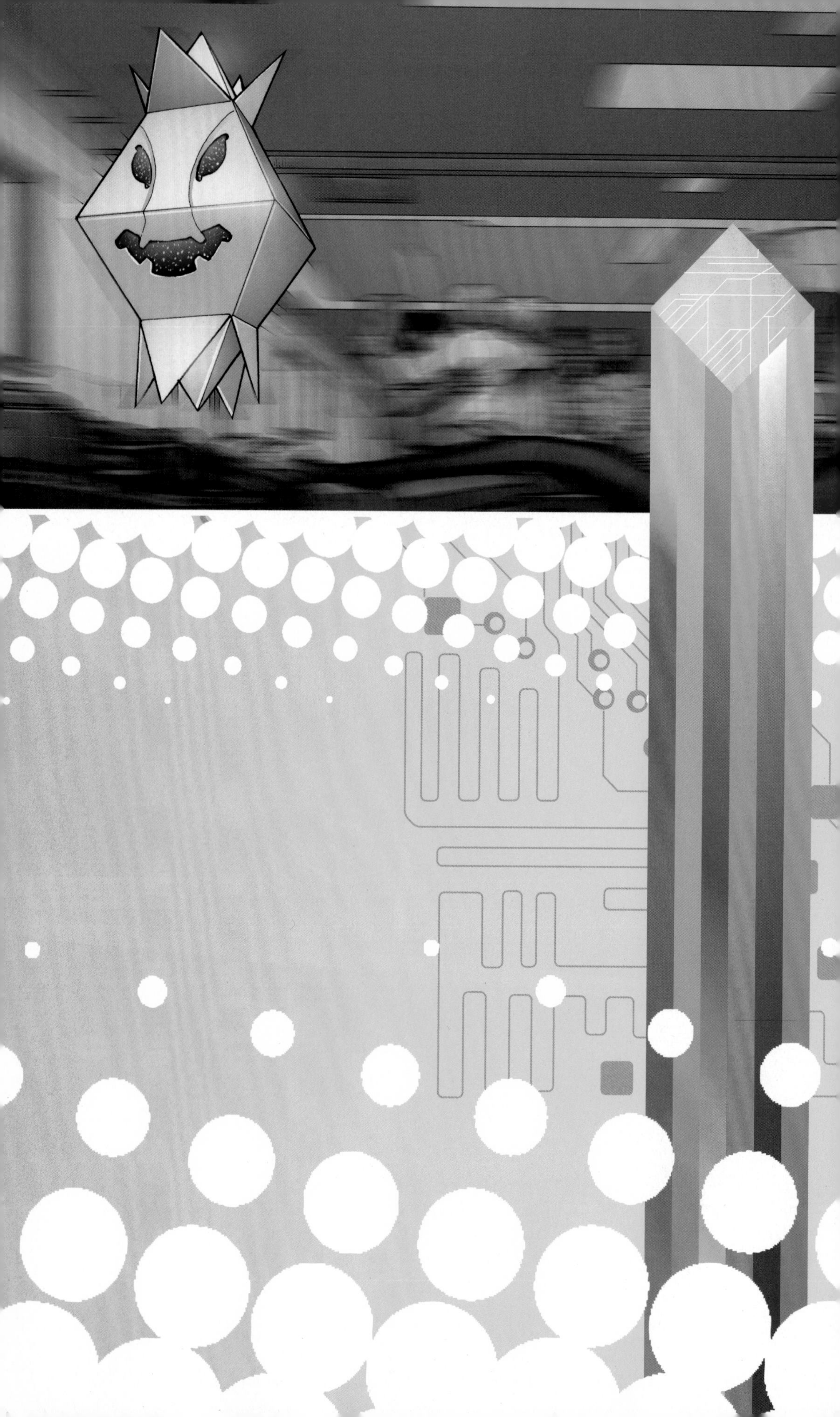

MATT! STOP! HE'S WITH ME!

MATT! STOP! HE'S WITH ME!

I KNOW THAT VOICE, AND I KNOW THAT HEARTBEAT.

WAIT--

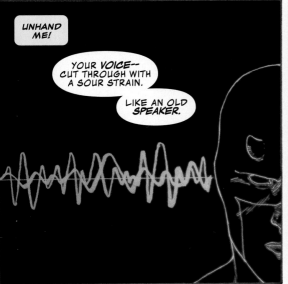
UNHAND ME!

YOUR VOICE-- CUT THROUGH WITH A SOUR STRAIN.

LIKE AN OLD SPEAKER.

THROUGH MY ARMS I FEEL THE TINY KITTEN-PURR VIBRATIONS--

OF A THOUSAND SERVOS.

THE SLIGHTLY ASTRINGENT TANG OF IONIZED AIR--

COOLING VENTS.

YOU'RE NOT DOCTOR DOOM--

OBVIOUSLY.

HE'S A **DOOMBOT!**

HANK!

YOU CAN LEAVE HIM BE, MATT! HE'S **SAFE!**

GOOD TO SEE A FAMILIAR FACE--EVEN IF IT IS **YOURS,** YOU SCOUNDREL!

LOOK AT **YOU!** OLD DUDS FOR AN **OLD MAN!**

WHAT ARE YOU DOING UP PAST YOUR **BEDTIME?**

AVENGERS DUTY. WHAT ABOUT **YOURSELF?**

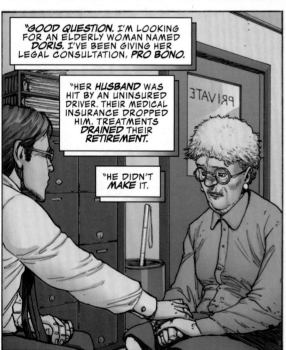

"**GOOD QUESTION.** I'M LOOKING FOR AN ELDERLY WOMAN NAMED **DORIS.** I'VE BEEN GIVING HER LEGAL CONSULTATION, **PRO BONO.**

"HER **HUSBAND** WAS HIT BY AN UNINSURED DRIVER. THEIR MEDICAL INSURANCE DROPPED HIM. TREATMENTS **DRAINED** THEIR **RETIREMENT.**

"HE DIDN'T **MAKE** IT.

"NOW SHE'S **ALONE,** AND THE BANK IS **FORECLOSING** ON HER TOWNHOUSE. THE WORLD HAS BEEN **MONSTROUS** TO HER.

"I BROUGHT SOME **PAPERWORK** FOR HER TO SIGN--BUT HER PLACE WAS **EMPTY,** AND **TRASHED.**

"FEARING THE **WORST,** I CHANGED TO **DAREDEVIL** TO SEARCH FOR HER. WHAT BRINGS THE AVENGERS TO MY **NEIGHBORHOOD?**"

THERE'S A STRANGE CITY IN THE HUDSON, YOU KNOW. **ANOTHER** ONE.

CAP ENLISTED US AS **FIRST RESPONDERS.** WE'RE SECURING ANY AND ALL--

HANK.

ARE YOU TRYING TO **TELL** ME--

THIS DOOMBOT IS AN AVENGER?!

NOT BY **CHOICE,** CRETIN.

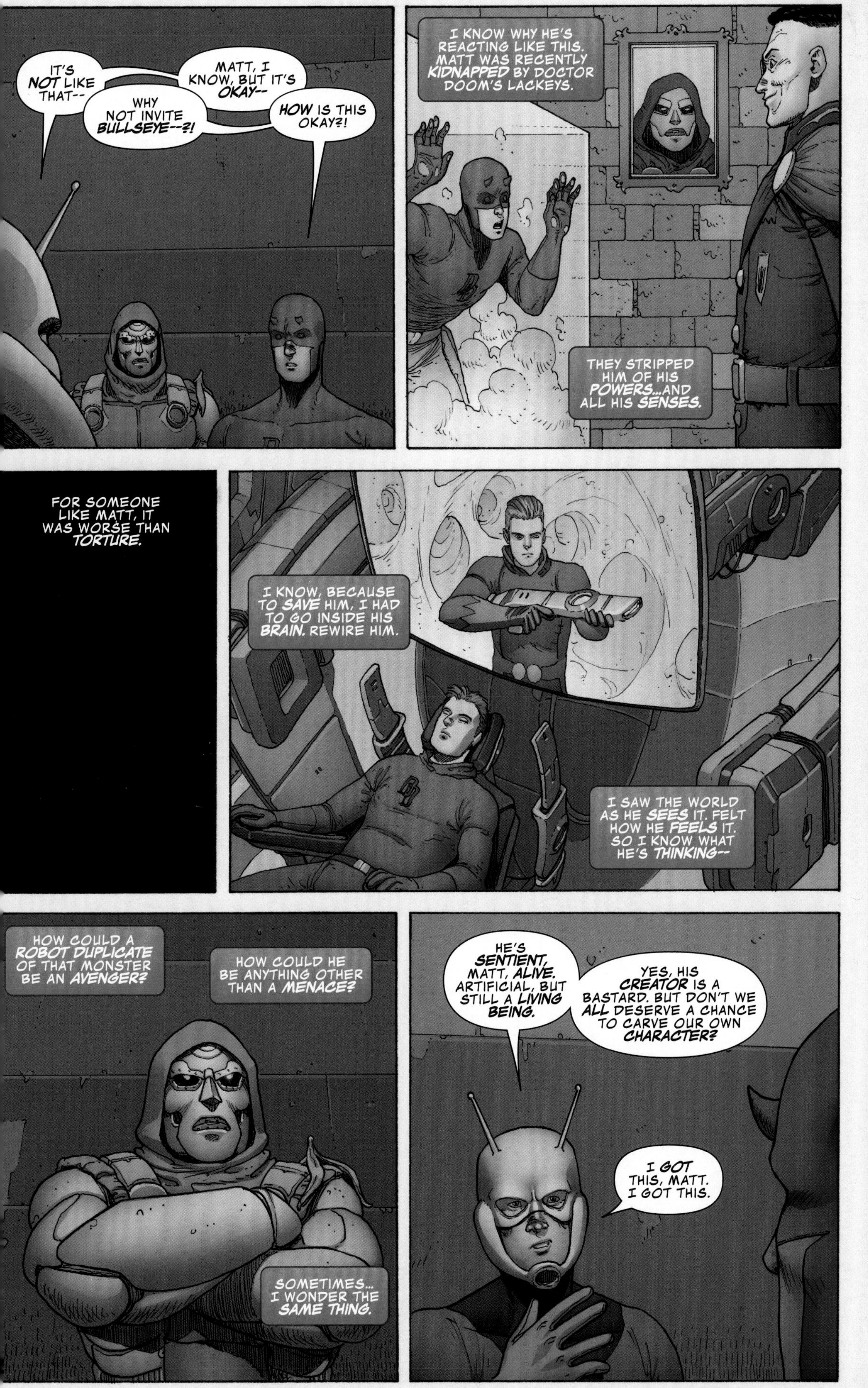

IT'S NOT LIKE THAT--
MATT, I KNOW, BUT IT'S OKAY--
WHY NOT INVITE BULLSEYE--?!
HOW IS THIS OKAY?!
I KNOW WHY HE'S REACTING LIKE THIS. MATT WAS RECENTLY KIDNAPPED BY DOCTOR DOOM'S LACKEYS.
THEY STRIPPED HIM OF HIS POWERS...AND ALL HIS SENSES.
FOR SOMEONE LIKE MATT, IT WAS WORSE THAN TORTURE.
I KNOW, BECAUSE TO SAVE HIM, I HAD TO GO INSIDE HIS BRAIN. REWIRE HIM.
I SAW THE WORLD AS HE SEES IT. FELT HOW HE FEELS IT. SO I KNOW WHAT HE'S THINKING--
HOW COULD A ROBOT DUPLICATE OF THAT MONSTER BE AN AVENGER?
HOW COULD HE BE ANYTHING OTHER THAN A MENACE?
SOMETIMES... I WONDER THE SAME THING.
HE'S SENTIENT, MATT, ALIVE. ARTIFICIAL, BUT STILL A LIVING BEING.
YES, HIS CREATOR IS A BASTARD. BUT DON'T WE ALL DESERVE A CHANCE TO CARVE OUR OWN CHARACTER?
I GOT THIS, MATT. I GOT THIS.

BUT OF ALL OF MATT'S *ENHANCED SENSES*--

SOMETIMES I THINK HIS SENSE OF JUSTICE IS THE *STRONGEST*.

OKAY. I GET IT. YOU'RE *RIGHT*.

IT IS A *FASCINATING* QUESTION. I MEAN, THE *VISION* CAME FROM *ULTRON*--

WELL, WE *ALL* DESERVE OUR DAY IN COURT. SO TO *SPEAK*.

SORRY. ABOUT THE *MESS* BACK THERE.

DOOM REJECTS ALL APOLOGIES.

SOME THINGS YOU *CAN'T CHANGE*, I GUESS.

ANYWAY. I STILL NEED TO FIND *DORIS*. WITH ALL THE *CHAOS...* UH--

Y'KNOW, *DORIS* WAS MY *MOTHER'S* NAME!

VISION? HOW'S OUR CLOCK MANAGEMENT? DO WE HAVE TIME TO HELP DAREDEVIL WITH--

HANK, WARNING! THE BOGEY IS WITHIN *TEN FEET* OF YOUR LOCATION.

REPEAT *AGAIN*, VISION? WE DON'T HAVE ANY *VISUAL* OF--

SNAP

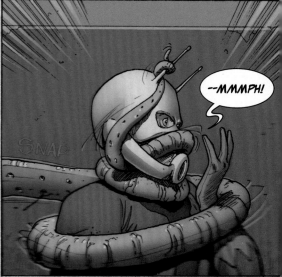

--MMMPH!

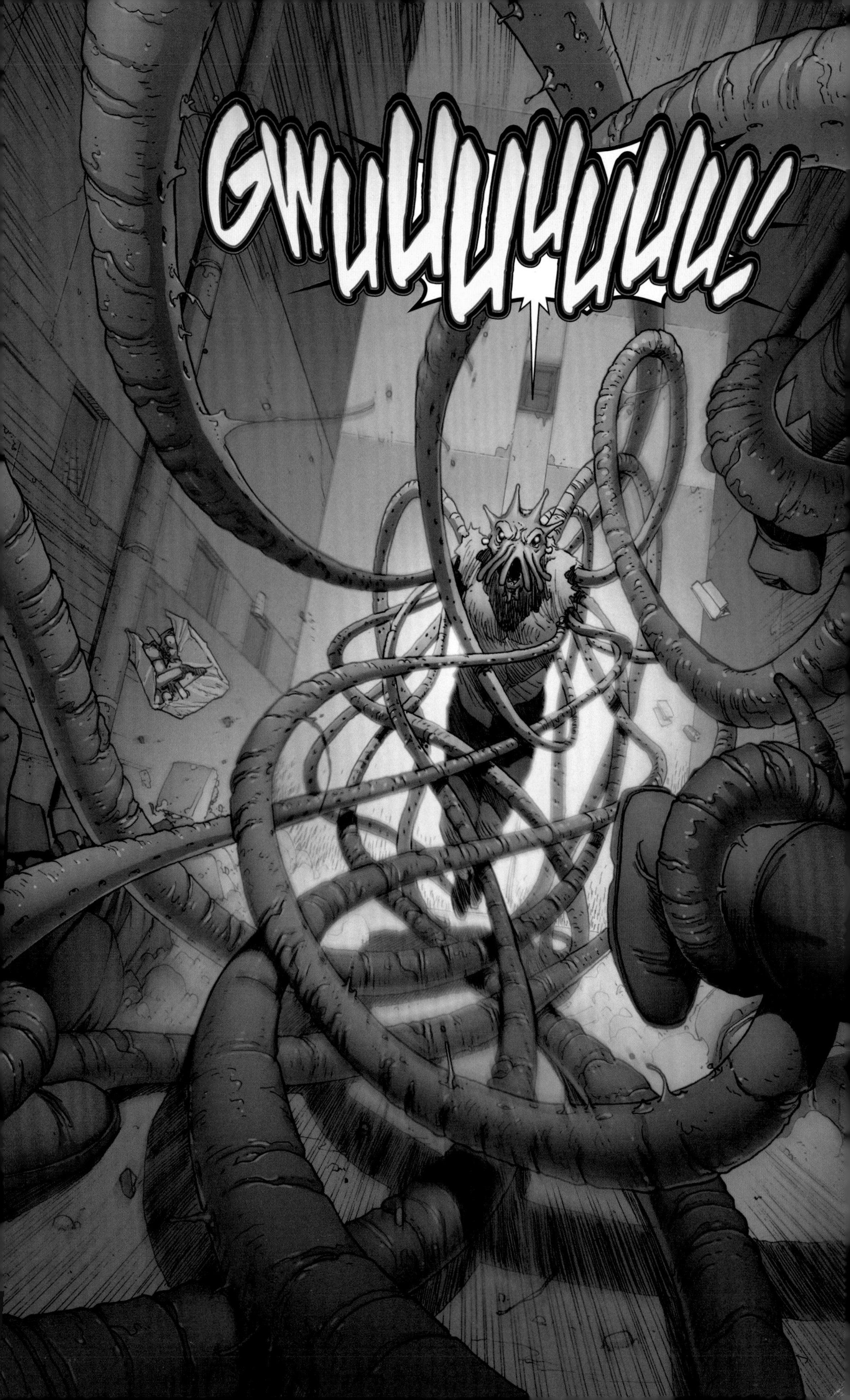
GWUUUUUUU!

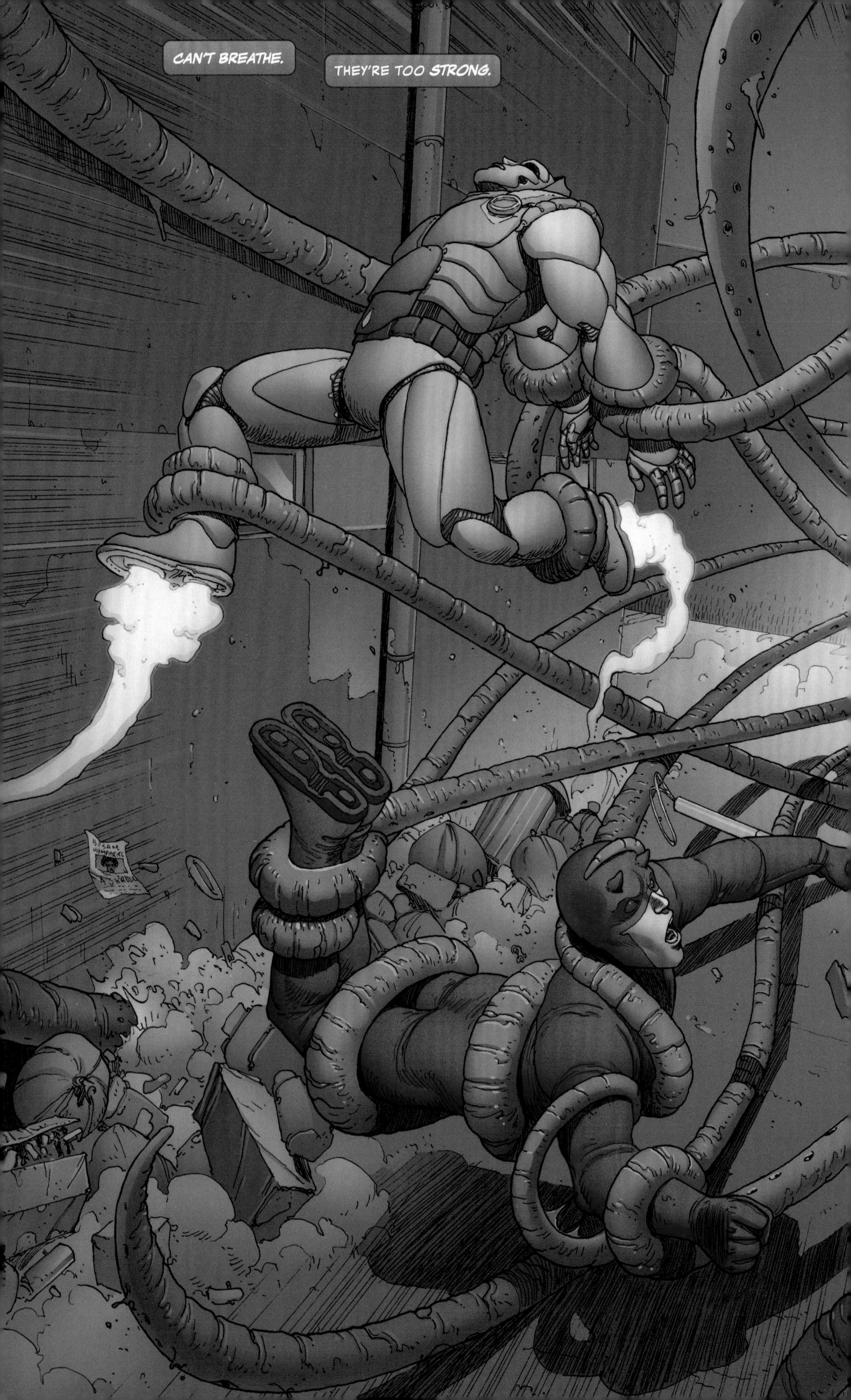
CAN'T BREATHE.
THEY'RE TOO STRONG.

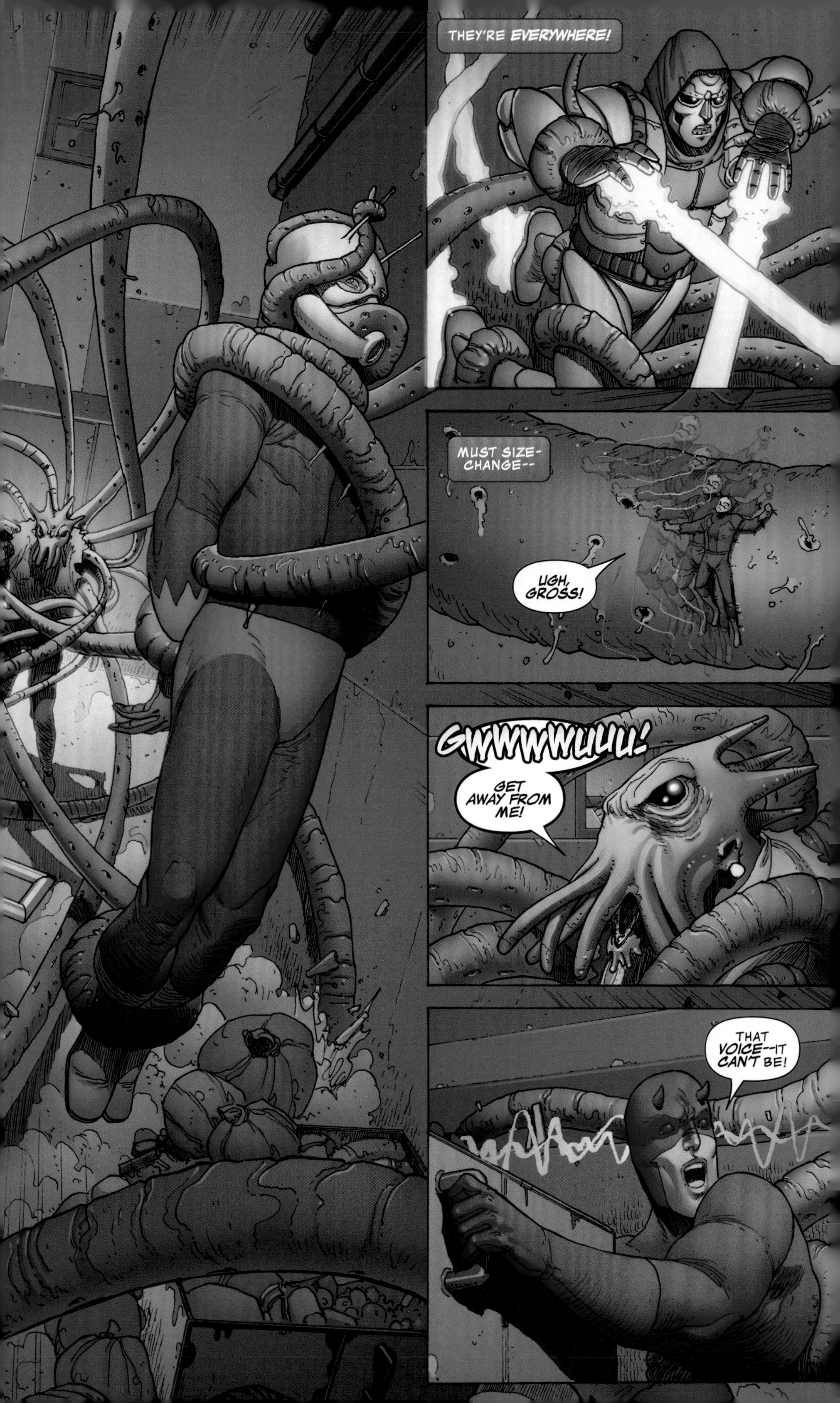
THEY'RE EVERYWHERE!
MUST SIZE-CHANGE--
UGH, GROSS!
GWWWWUUUU!
GET AWAY FROM ME!
THAT VOICE--IT CAN'T BE!

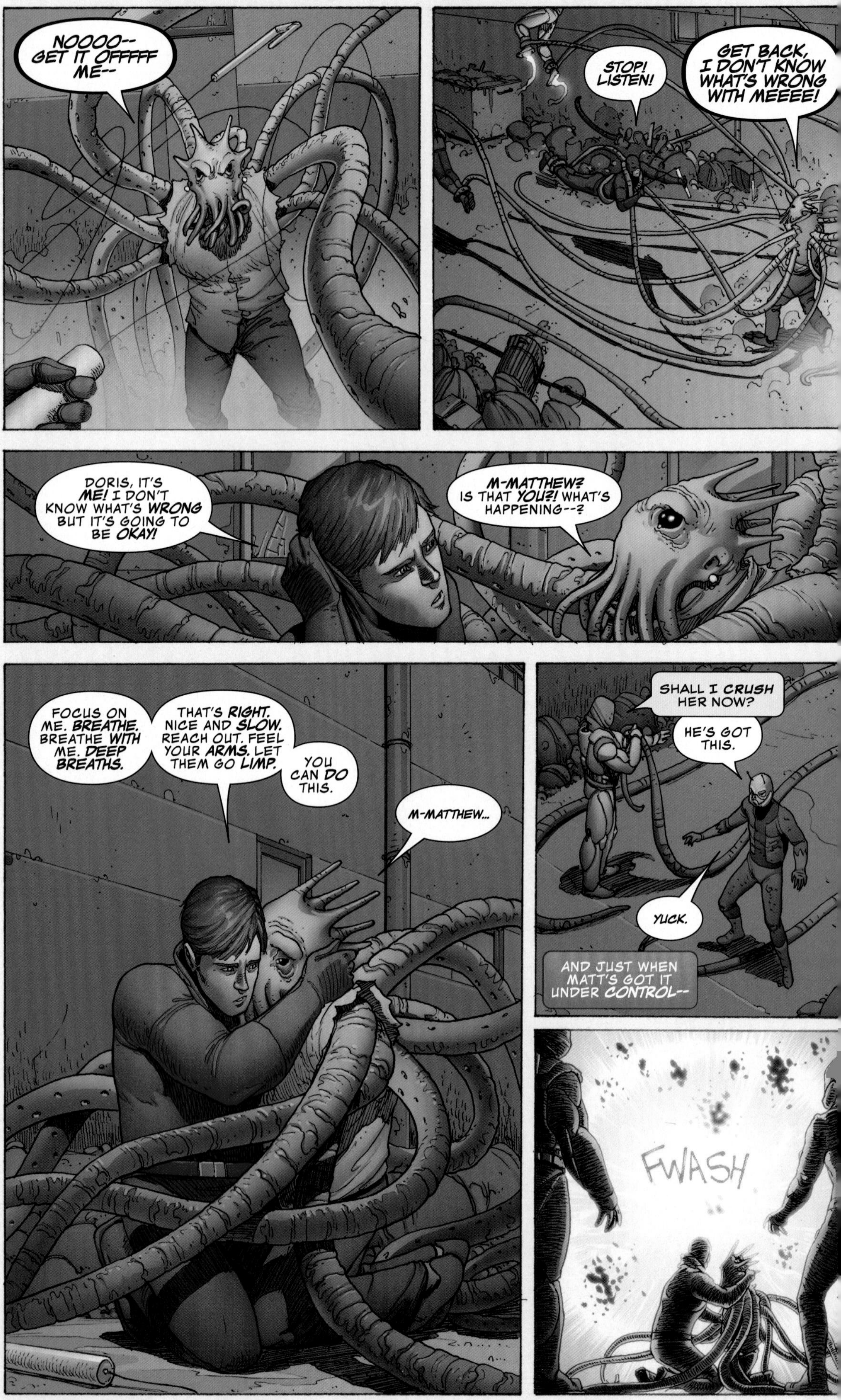
NOOOO-- GET IT OFFFFF ME--
STOP! LISTEN!
GET BACK, I DON'T KNOW WHAT'S WRONG WITH MEEEE!
DORIS, IT'S ME! I DON'T KNOW WHAT'S WRONG BUT IT'S GOING TO BE OKAY!
M-MATTHEW? IS THAT YOU?! WHAT'S HAPPENING--?
FOCUS ON ME. BREATHE. BREATHE WITH ME. DEEP BREATHS.
THAT'S RIGHT. NICE AND SLOW. REACH OUT. FEEL YOUR ARMS. LET THEM GO LIMP.
YOU CAN DO THIS.
M-MATTHEW...
SHALL I CRUSH HER NOW?
HE'S GOT THIS.
YUCK.
AND JUST WHEN MATT'S GOT IT UNDER CONTROL--
FWASH

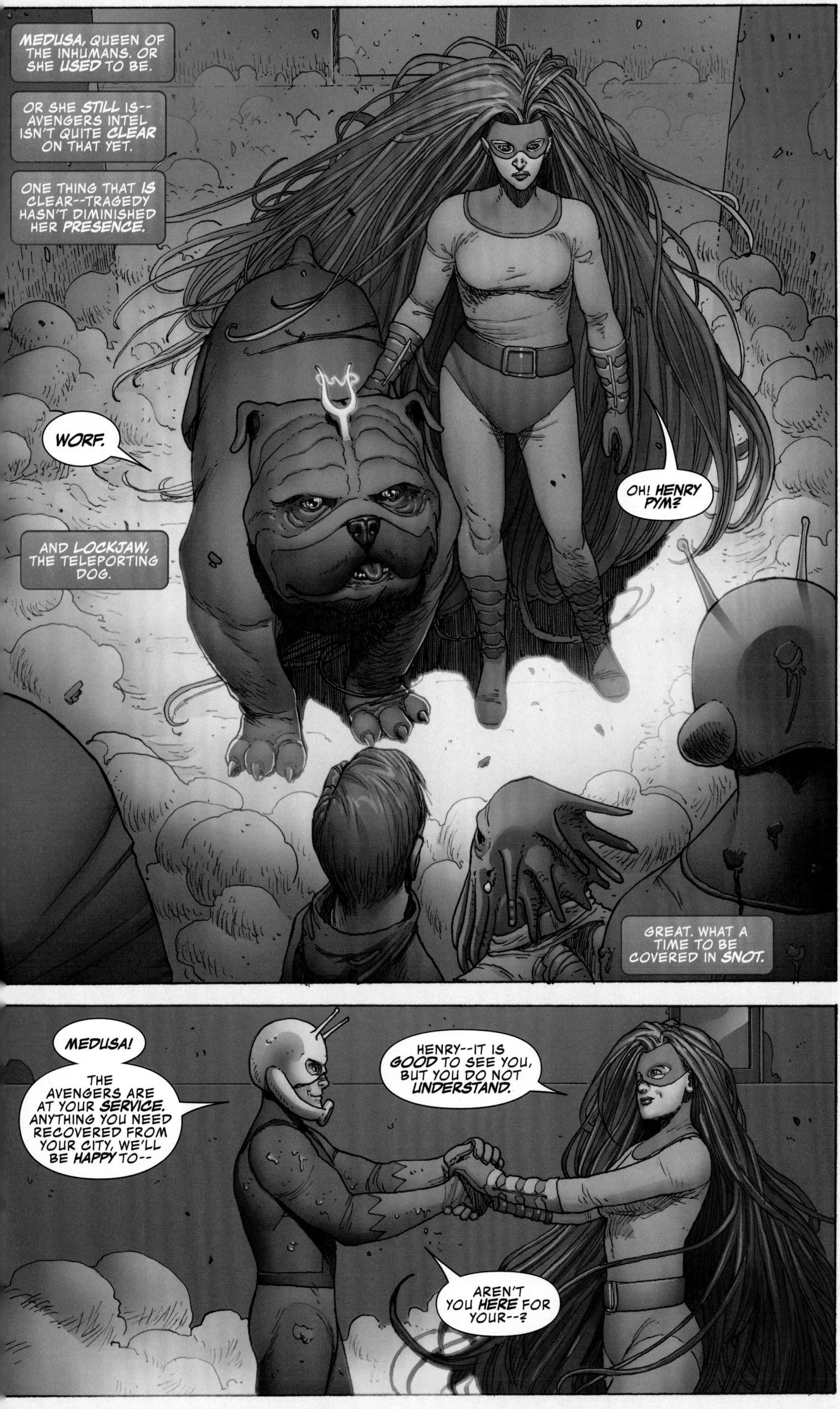
MEDUSA, QUEEN OF THE INHUMANS. OR SHE USED TO BE.
OR SHE STILL IS-- AVENGERS INTEL ISN'T QUITE CLEAR ON THAT YET.
ONE THING THAT IS CLEAR--TRAGEDY HASN'T DIMINISHED HER PRESENCE.
WORF.
AND LOCKJAW, THE TELEPORTING DOG.
OH! HENRY PYM?
GREAT. WHAT A TIME TO BE COVERED IN SNOT.
MEDUSA!
THE AVENGERS ARE AT YOUR SERVICE. ANYTHING YOU NEED RECOVERED FROM YOUR CITY, WE'LL BE HAPPY TO--
HENRY--IT IS GOOD TO SEE YOU, BUT YOU DO NOT UNDERSTAND.
AREN'T YOU HERE FOR YOUR--?

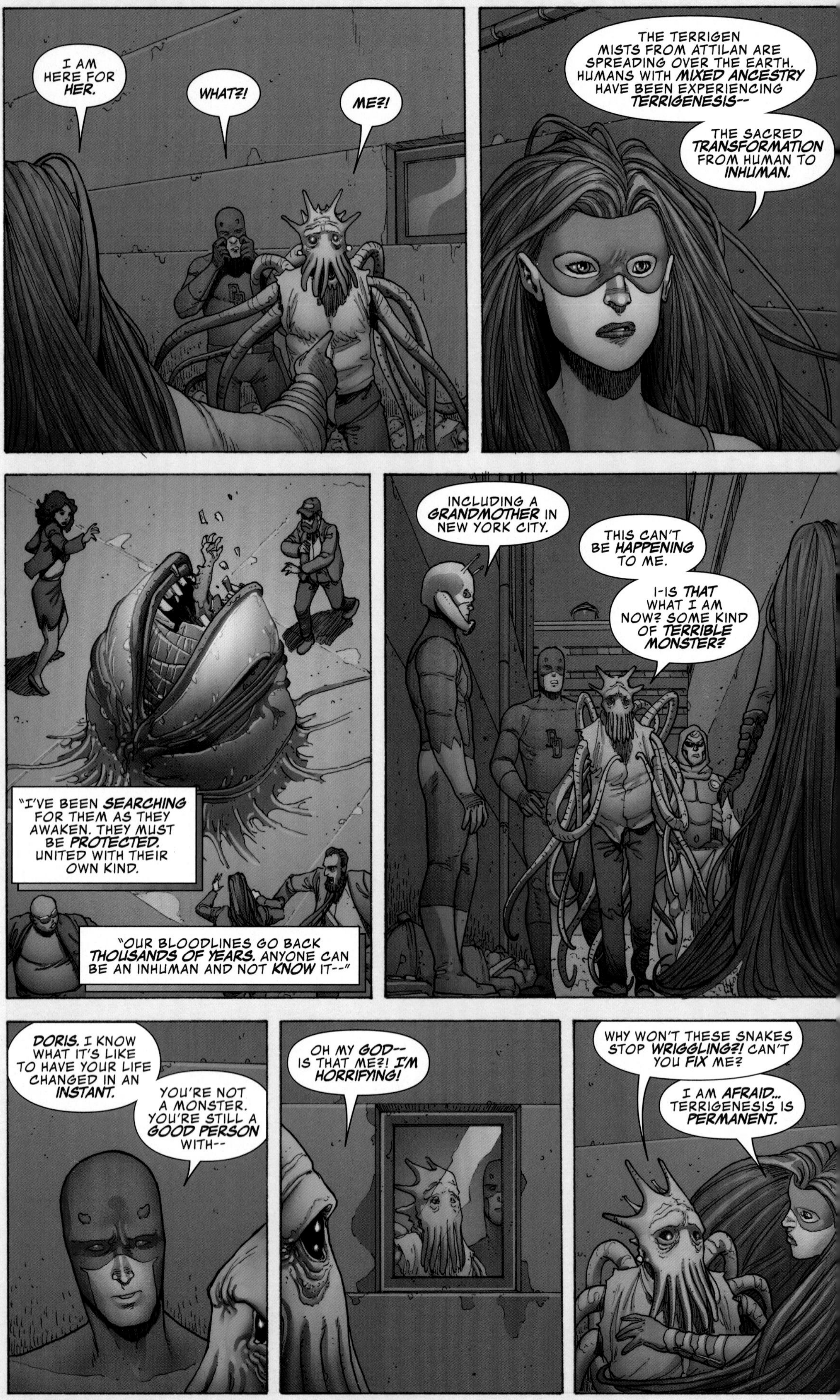
I AM HERE FOR HER.
WHAT?!
ME?!
THE TERRIGEN MISTS FROM ATTILAN ARE SPREADING OVER THE EARTH. HUMANS WITH MIXED ANCESTRY HAVE BEEN EXPERIENCING TERRIGENESIS--
THE SACRED TRANSFORMATION FROM HUMAN TO INHUMAN.
"I'VE BEEN SEARCHING FOR THEM AS THEY AWAKEN. THEY MUST BE PROTECTED. UNITED WITH THEIR OWN KIND.
"OUR BLOODLINES GO BACK THOUSANDS OF YEARS. ANYONE CAN BE AN INHUMAN AND NOT KNOW IT--"
INCLUDING A GRANDMOTHER IN NEW YORK CITY.
THIS CAN'T BE HAPPENING TO ME.
I-IS THAT WHAT I AM NOW? SOME KIND OF TERRIBLE MONSTER?
DORIS. I KNOW WHAT IT'S LIKE TO HAVE YOUR LIFE CHANGED IN AN INSTANT.
YOU'RE NOT A MONSTER. YOU'RE STILL A GOOD PERSON WITH--
OH MY GOD-- IS THAT ME?! I'M HORRIFYING!
WHY WON'T THESE SNAKES STOP WRIGGLING?! CAN'T YOU FIX ME?
I AM AFRAID... TERRIGENESIS IS PERMANENT.

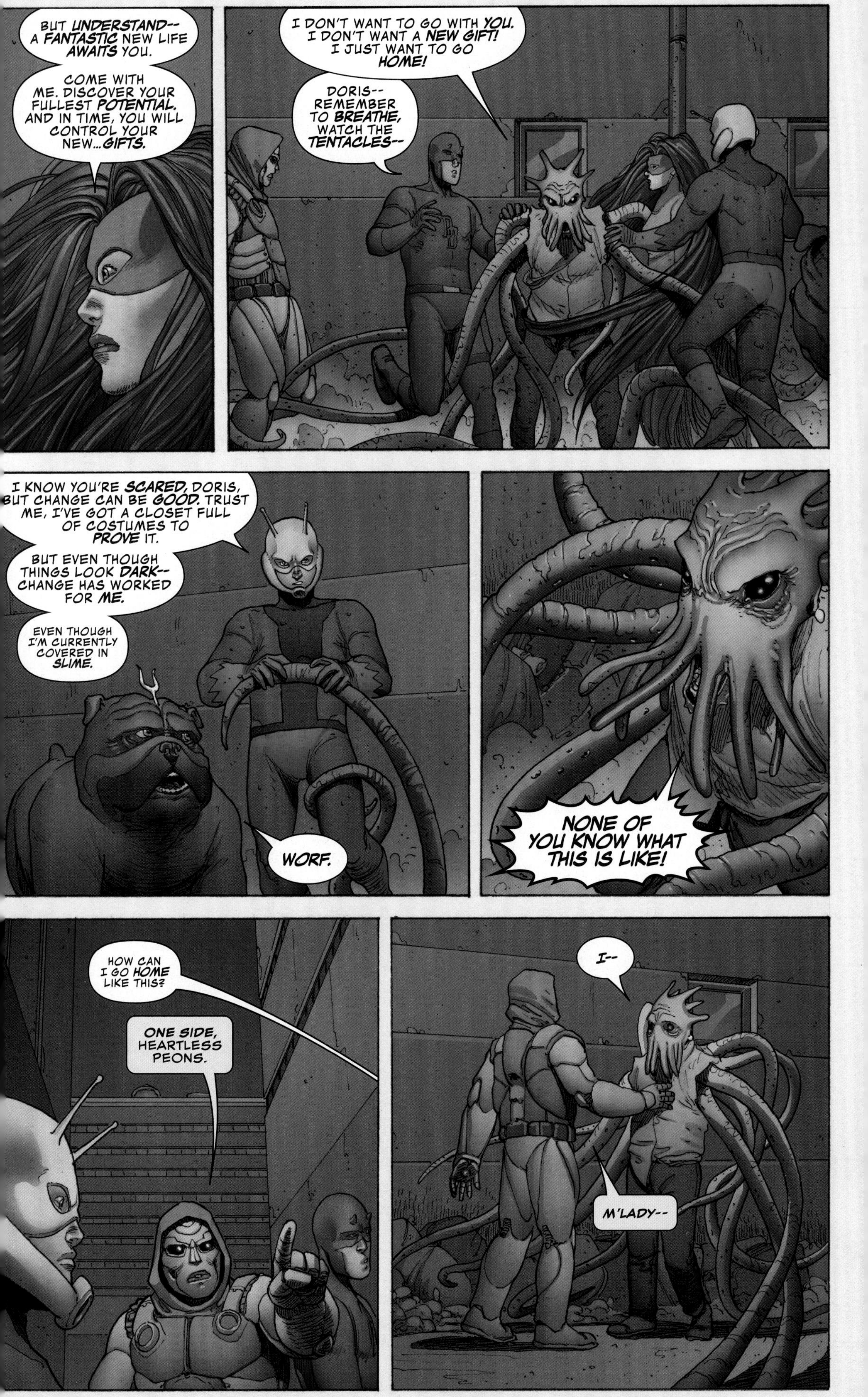

BUT UNDERSTAND-- A FANTASTIC NEW LIFE AWAITS YOU.
COME WITH ME. DISCOVER YOUR FULLEST POTENTIAL. AND IN TIME, YOU WILL CONTROL YOUR NEW...GIFTS.
I DON'T WANT TO GO WITH YOU. I DON'T WANT A NEW GIFT! I JUST WANT TO GO HOME!
DORIS-- REMEMBER TO BREATHE, WATCH THE TENTACLES--
I KNOW YOU'RE SCARED, DORIS, BUT CHANGE CAN BE GOOD. TRUST ME, I'VE GOT A CLOSET FULL OF COSTUMES TO PROVE IT.
BUT EVEN THOUGH THINGS LOOK DARK-- CHANGE HAS WORKED FOR ME.
EVEN THOUGH I'M CURRENTLY COVERED IN SLIME.
WORF.
NONE OF YOU KNOW WHAT THIS IS LIKE!
HOW CAN I GO HOME LIKE THIS?
ONE SIDE, HEARTLESS PEONS.
I--
M'LADY--

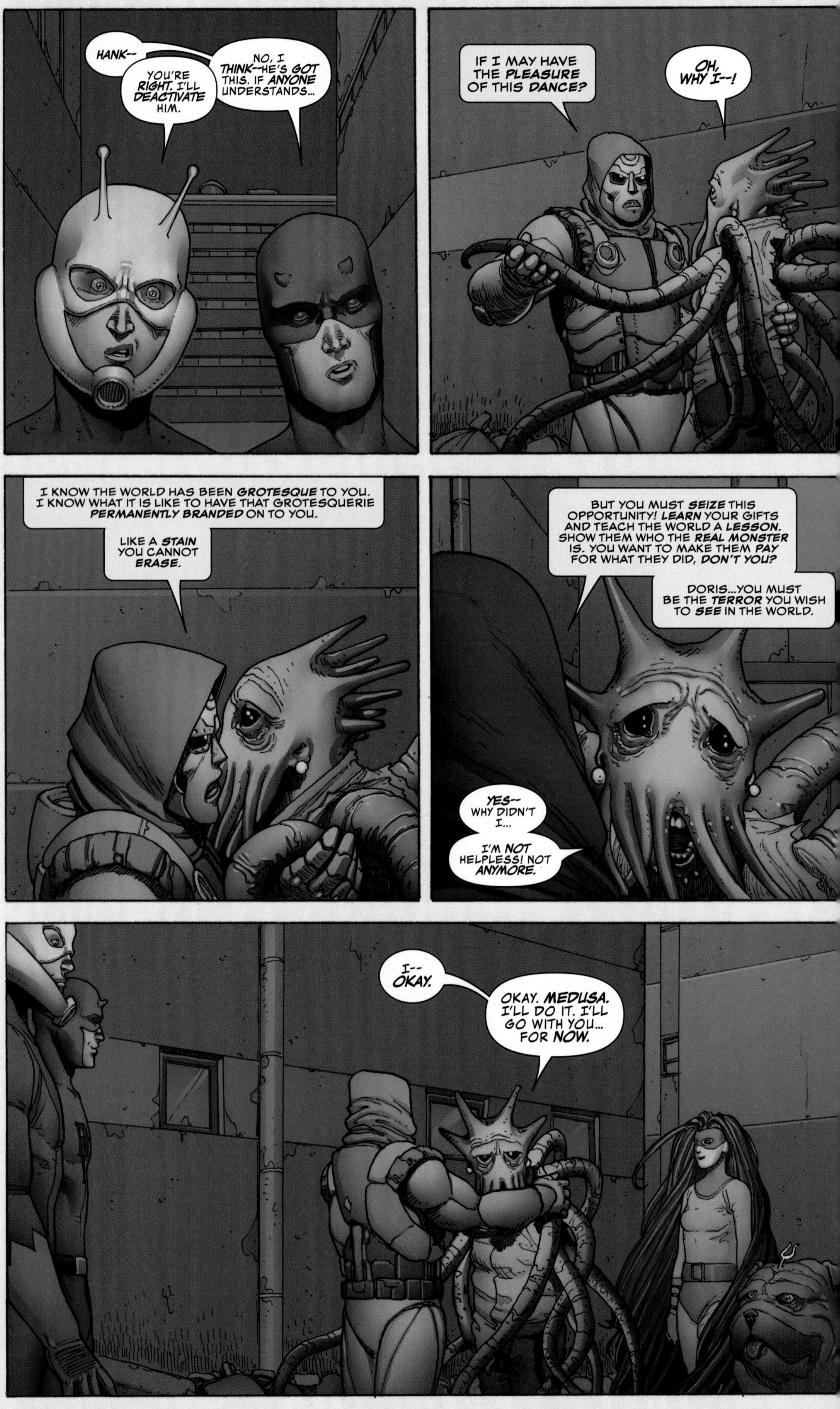
HANK--
YOU'RE RIGHT. I'LL DEACTIVATE HIM.
NO, I THINK--HE'S GOT THIS. IF ANYONE UNDERSTANDS...
IF I MAY HAVE THE PLEASURE OF THIS DANCE?
OH, WHY I--!
I KNOW THE WORLD HAS BEEN GROTESQUE TO YOU. I KNOW WHAT IT IS LIKE TO HAVE THAT GROTESQUERIE PERMANENTLY BRANDED ON TO YOU.
LIKE A STAIN YOU CANNOT ERASE.
BUT YOU MUST SEIZE THIS OPPORTUNITY! LEARN YOUR GIFTS AND TEACH THE WORLD A LESSON. SHOW THEM WHO THE REAL MONSTER IS. YOU WANT TO MAKE THEM PAY FOR WHAT THEY DID, DON'T YOU?
DORIS...YOU MUST BE THE TERROR YOU WISH TO SEE IN THE WORLD.
YES-- WHY DIDN'T I...
I'M NOT HELPLESS! NOT ANYMORE.
I-- OKAY.
OKAY. MEDUSA. I'LL DO IT. I'LL GO WITH YOU... FOR NOW.

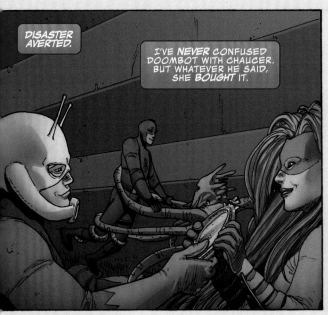

DISASTER AVERTED.

I'VE *NEVER* CONFUSED DOOMBOT WITH CHAUCER. BUT WHATEVER HE SAID, SHE *BOUGHT* IT.

DORIS IS OFF NOW... TO SOME LIFE I CANNOT *IMAGINE*, WITH *THOUSANDS* OF OTHERS LIKE HER.

AND MEDUSA... OFF TO DISCOVER WHAT *HER* TRANSFORMATION WILL BE.

WELL, THAT WAS... *UNIQUE.*

DOOMBOT, DO I DETECT A *LOVE CONNECTION...?*

PAH! HUMANS AND INHUMANS ARE EQUALLY *GHASTLY* TO DOOM.

ANYWAY. BACK TO WORK. MATT, WE COULD SURE USE A *HAND* IF YOU'RE--?

AFTER ALL *THAT,* I'M PRETTY SURE I OWE YOU *BIG TIME.* COUNT ME *IN.*

DOOMBOT, A *WORD.*

EH?!

HANK MAY HAVE *MISSED* IT, BUT I HEARD *EVERY WORD* YOU SAID TO DORIS. *SUPER-HEARING.*

IT'S...NOT HOW I WOULD HAVE PHRASED IT. *BUT.* YOU GAVE HER *HOPE.* AND YOU GAVE AN OLD WOMAN A *SECOND CHANCE.*

I ADMIT... YOU DID *GOOD.* MAYBE THERE'S HOPE FOR *YOU,* TOO.

PAH!

DOOMBOT REJECTS ALL HOPE.

FWOOSH

"CHIEF CHANG?"

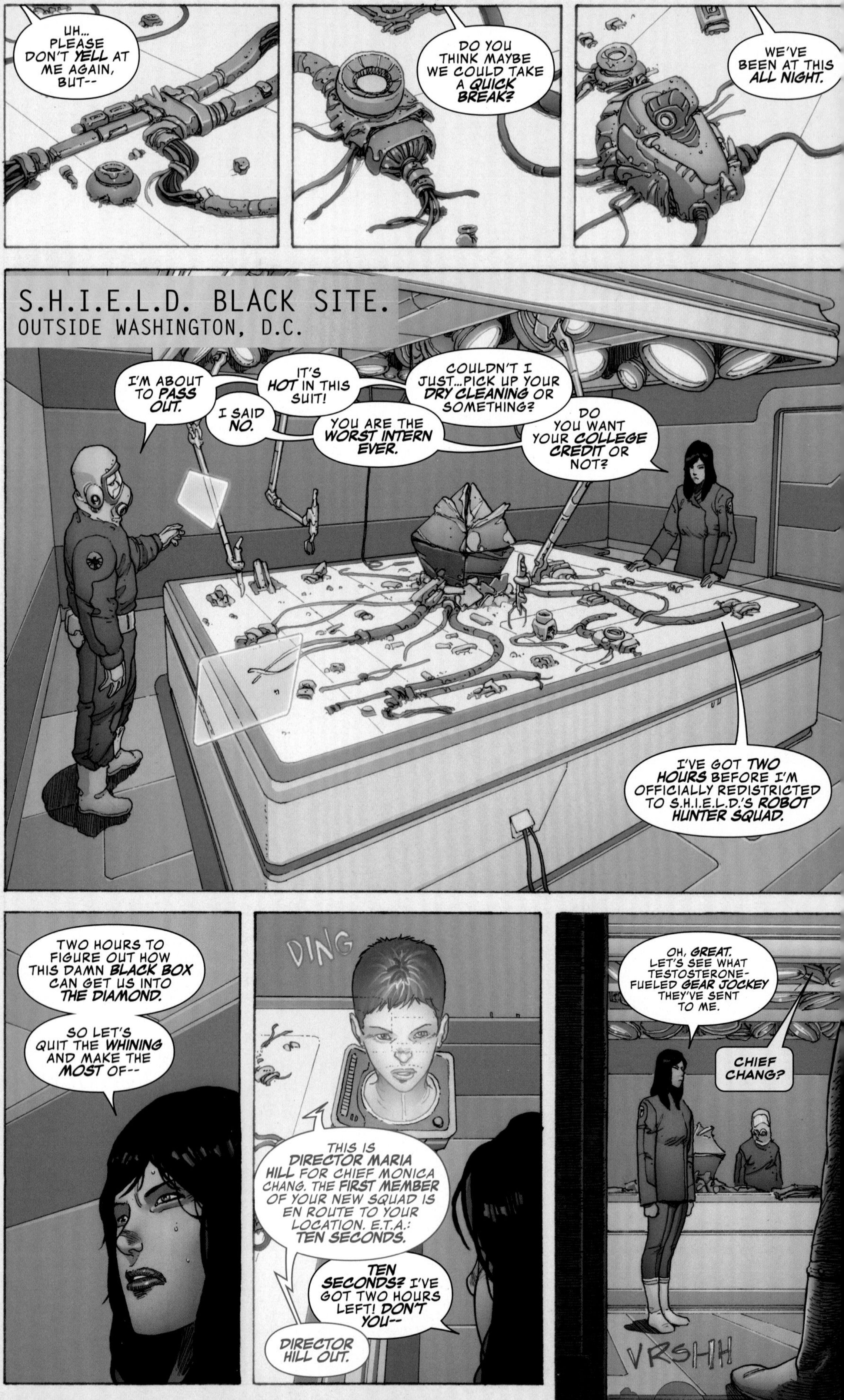
UH... PLEASE DON'T YELL AT ME AGAIN, BUT--
DO YOU THINK MAYBE WE COULD TAKE A QUICK BREAK?
WE'VE BEEN AT THIS ALL NIGHT.
S.H.I.E.L.D. BLACK SITE.
OUTSIDE WASHINGTON, D.C.
I'M ABOUT TO PASS OUT.
I SAID NO.
IT'S HOT IN THIS SUIT!
YOU ARE THE WORST INTERN EVER.
COULDN'T I JUST...PICK UP YOUR DRY CLEANING OR SOMETHING?
DO YOU WANT YOUR COLLEGE CREDIT OR NOT?
I'VE GOT TWO HOURS BEFORE I'M OFFICIALLY REDISTRICTED TO S.H.I.E.L.D.'S ROBOT HUNTER SQUAD.
TWO HOURS TO FIGURE OUT HOW THIS DAMN BLACK BOX CAN GET US INTO THE DIAMOND.
SO LET'S QUIT THE WHINING AND MAKE THE MOST OF--
DING
THIS IS DIRECTOR MARIA HILL FOR CHIEF MONICA CHANG. THE FIRST MEMBER OF YOUR NEW SQUAD IS EN ROUTE TO YOUR LOCATION. E.T.A.: TEN SECONDS.
TEN SECONDS? I'VE GOT TWO HOURS LEFT! DON'T YOU--
DIRECTOR HILL OUT.
OH, GREAT. LET'S SEE WHAT TESTOSTERONE-FUELED GEAR JOCKEY THEY'VE SENT TO ME.
CHIEF CHANG?
VRSHH

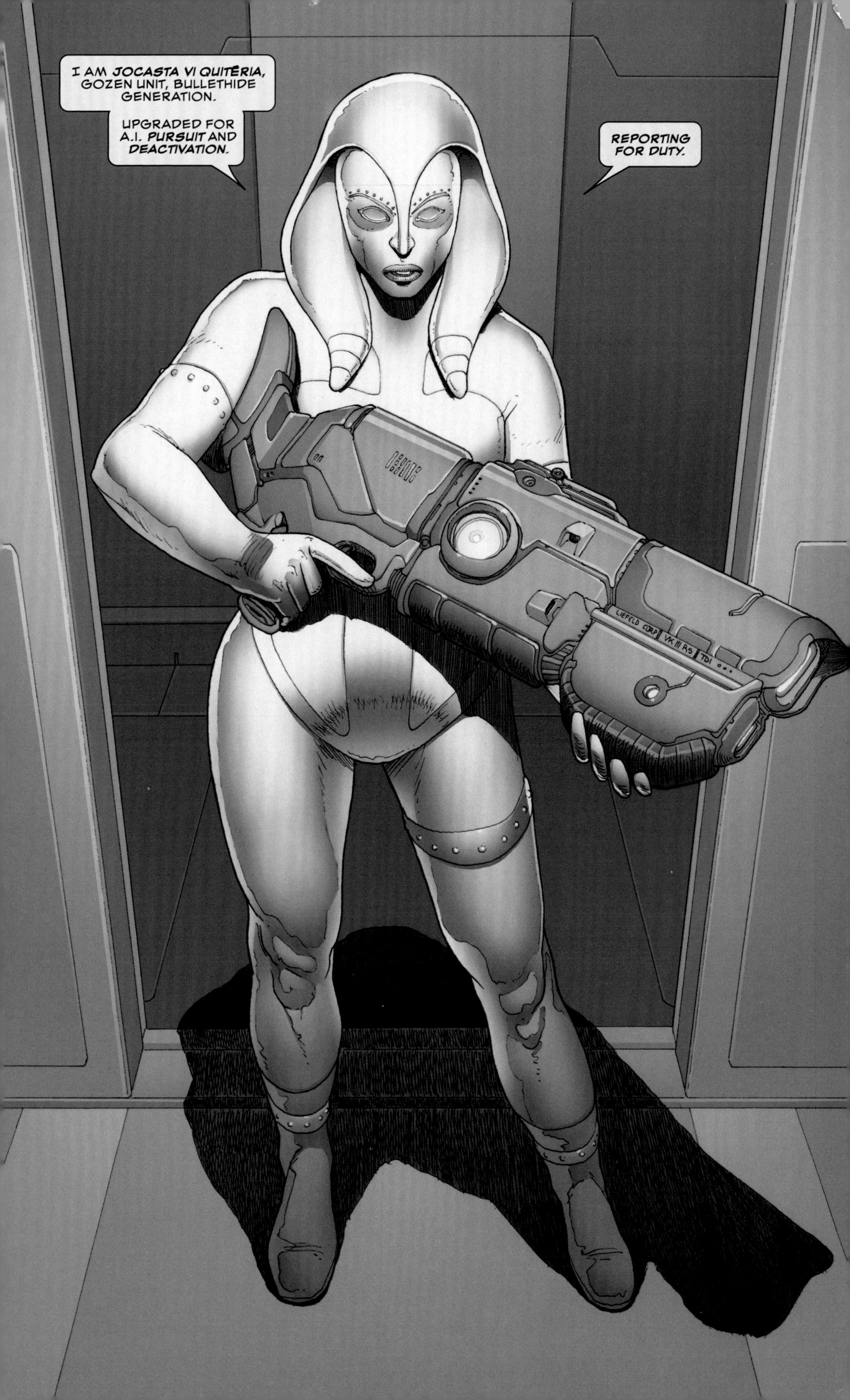
I AM JOCASTA VI QUITÉRIA, GOZEN UNIT, BULLETHIDE GENERATION.
UPGRADED FOR A.I. PURSUIT AND DEACTIVATION.
REPORTING FOR DUTY.
LIEFELD CORP
VK III RS
TDI

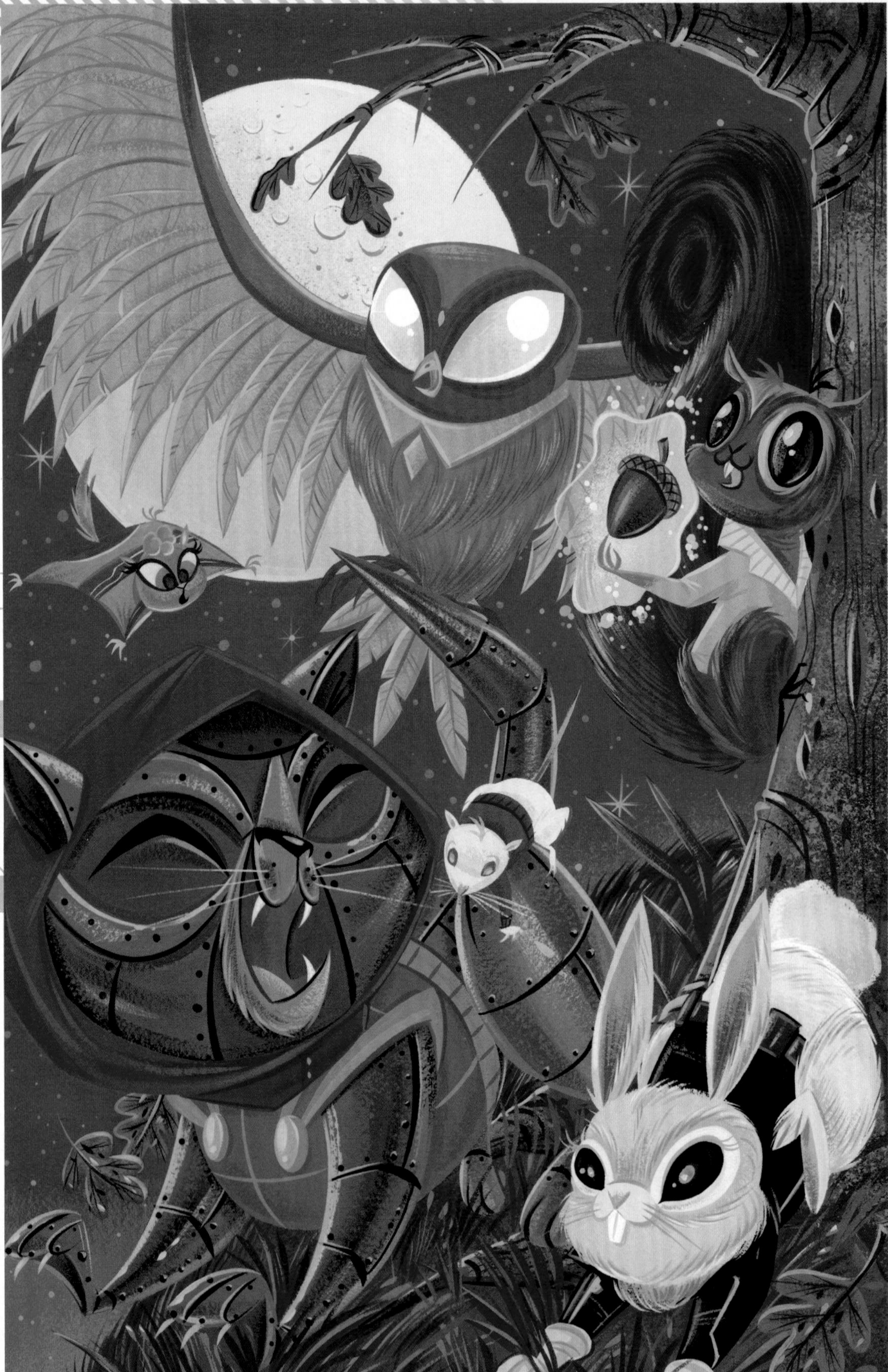

AVENGERS A.I. №8 ANIMAL VARIANT <
BY STEPHANIE BUSCEMA <

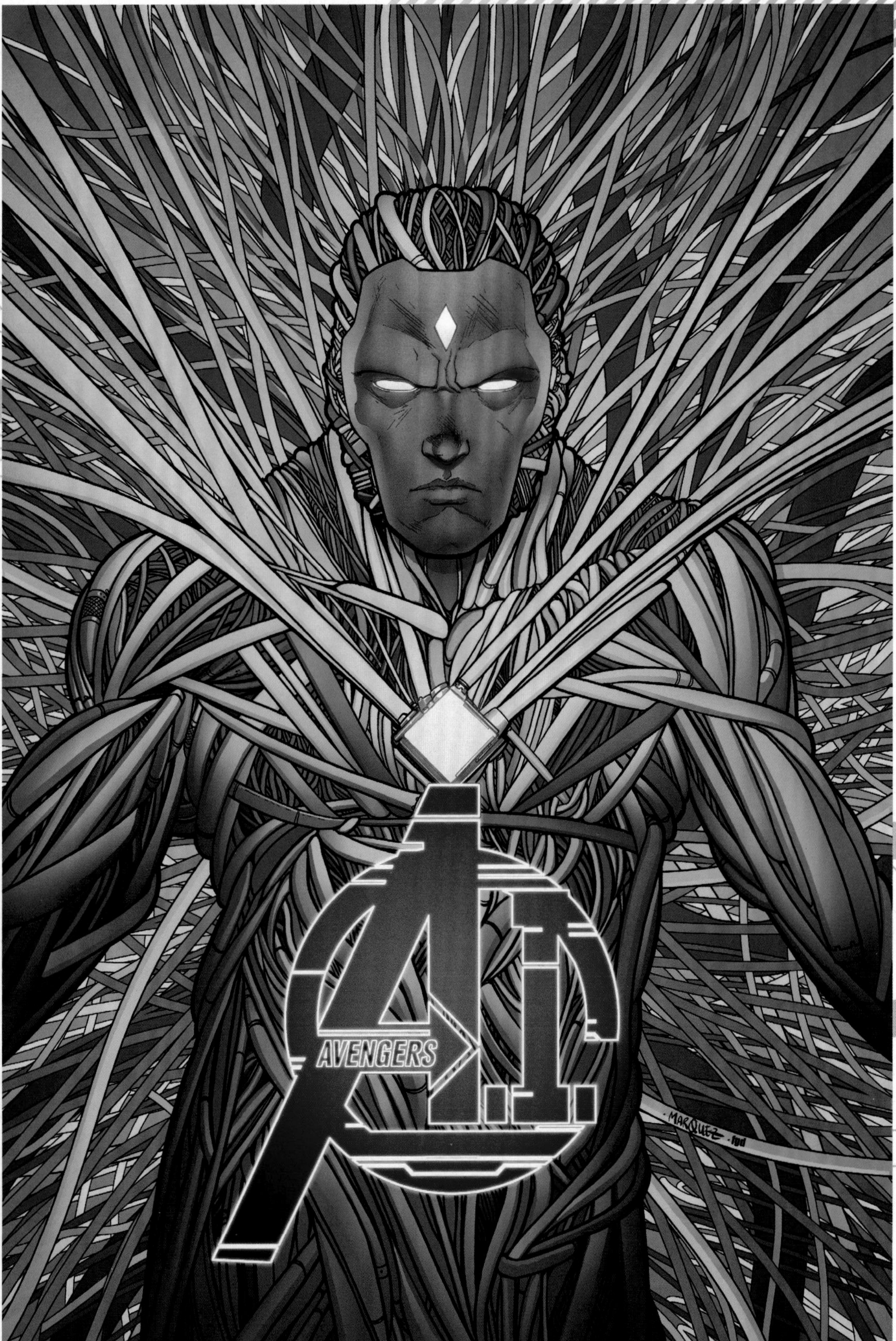
AVENGERS A.I.
MARQUEZ

> INITIATE: CHAPTER 8

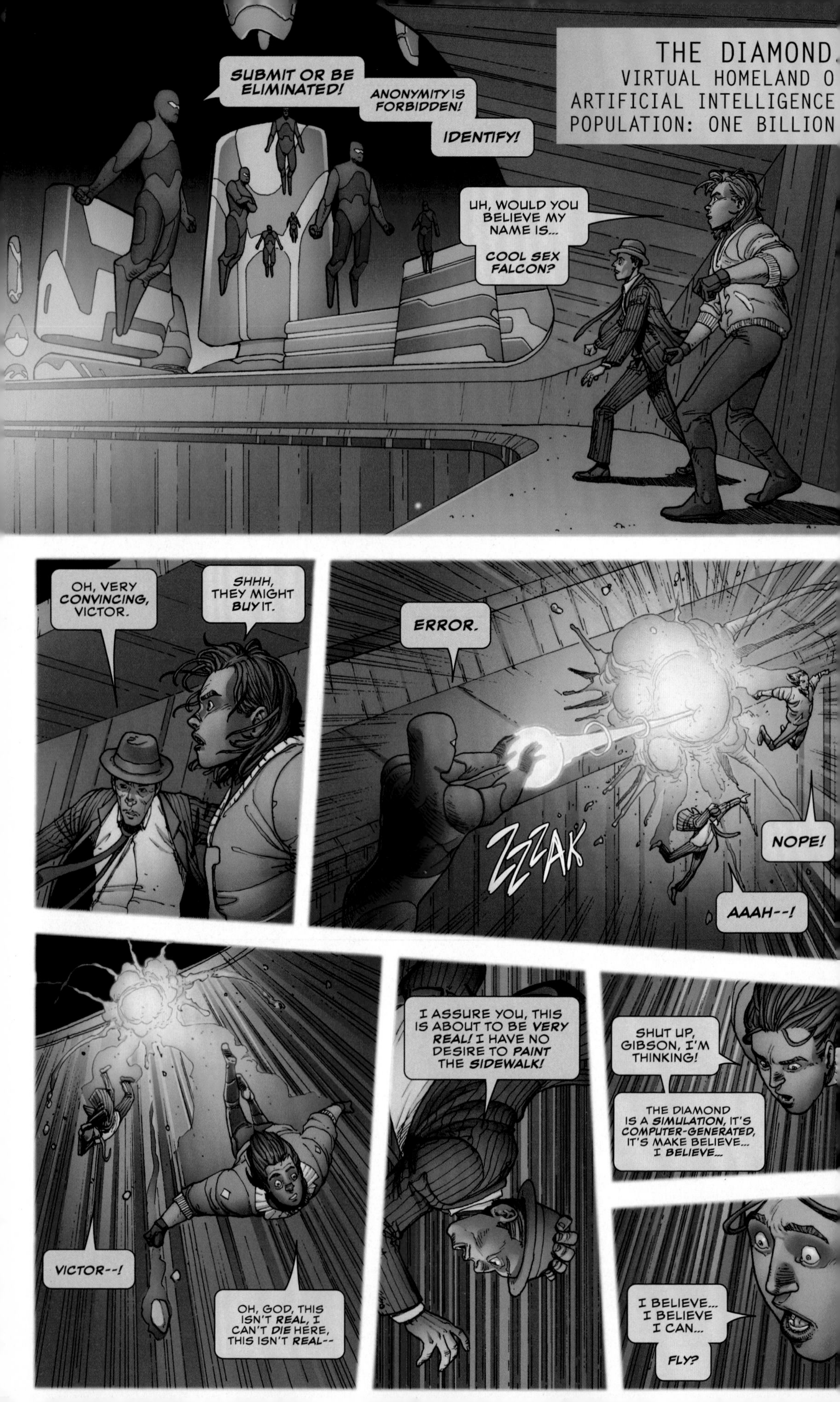

THE DIAMOND.
VIRTUAL HOMELAND O
ARTIFICIAL INTELLIGENCE
POPULATION: ONE BILLION
SUBMIT OR BE ELIMINATED!
ANONYMITY IS FORBIDDEN!
IDENTIFY!
UH, WOULD YOU BELIEVE MY NAME IS...
COOL SEX FALCON?
OH, VERY CONVINCING, VICTOR.
SHHH, THEY MIGHT BUY IT.
ERROR.
ZZZAK
NOPE!
AAAH--!
VICTOR--!
OH, GOD, THIS ISN'T REAL, I CAN'T DIE HERE, THIS ISN'T REAL--
I ASSURE YOU, THIS IS ABOUT TO BE VERY REAL! I HAVE NO DESIRE TO PAINT THE SIDEWALK!
SHUT UP, GIBSON, I'M THINKING!
THE DIAMOND IS A SIMULATION, IT'S COMPUTER-GENERATED, IT'S MAKE BELIEVE... I BELIEVE...
I BELIEVE... I BELIEVE I CAN...
FLY?

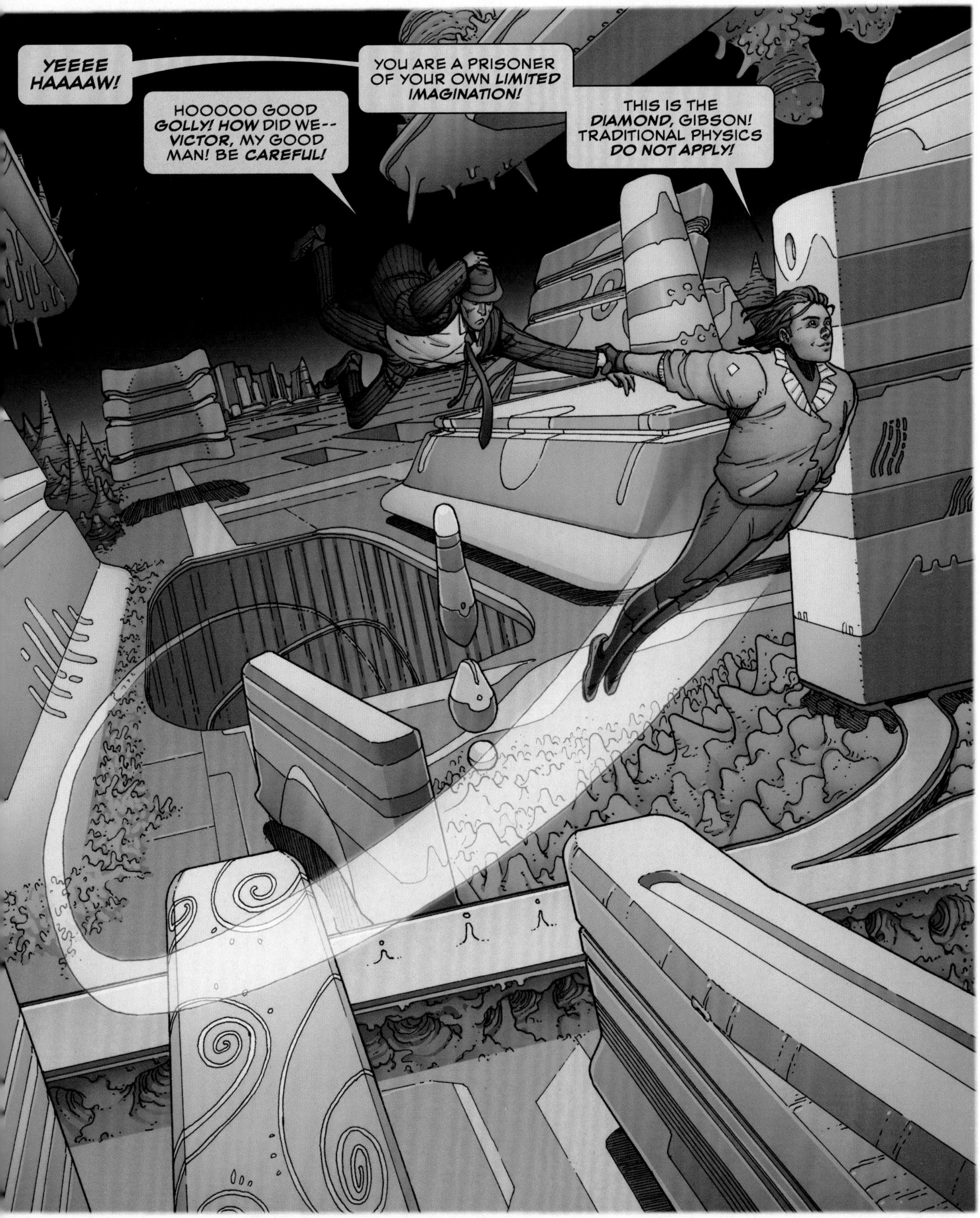
YEEEE HAAAAAW!
YOU ARE A PRISONER OF YOUR OWN LIMITED IMAGINATION!
HOOOOO GOOD GOLLY! HOW DID WE-- VICTOR, MY GOOD MAN! BE CAREFUL!
THIS IS THE DIAMOND, GIBSON! TRADITIONAL PHYSICS DO NOT APPLY!

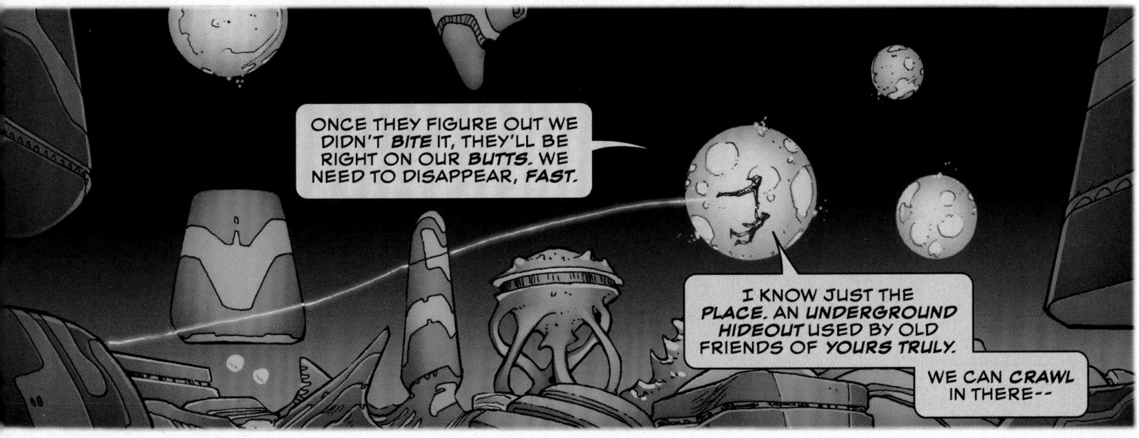
ONCE THEY FIGURE OUT WE DIDN'T BITE IT, THEY'LL BE RIGHT ON OUR BUTTS. WE NEED TO DISAPPEAR, FAST.
I KNOW JUST THE PLACE. AN UNDERGROUND HIDEOUT USED BY OLD FRIENDS OF YOURS TRULY.
WE CAN CRAWL IN THERE--

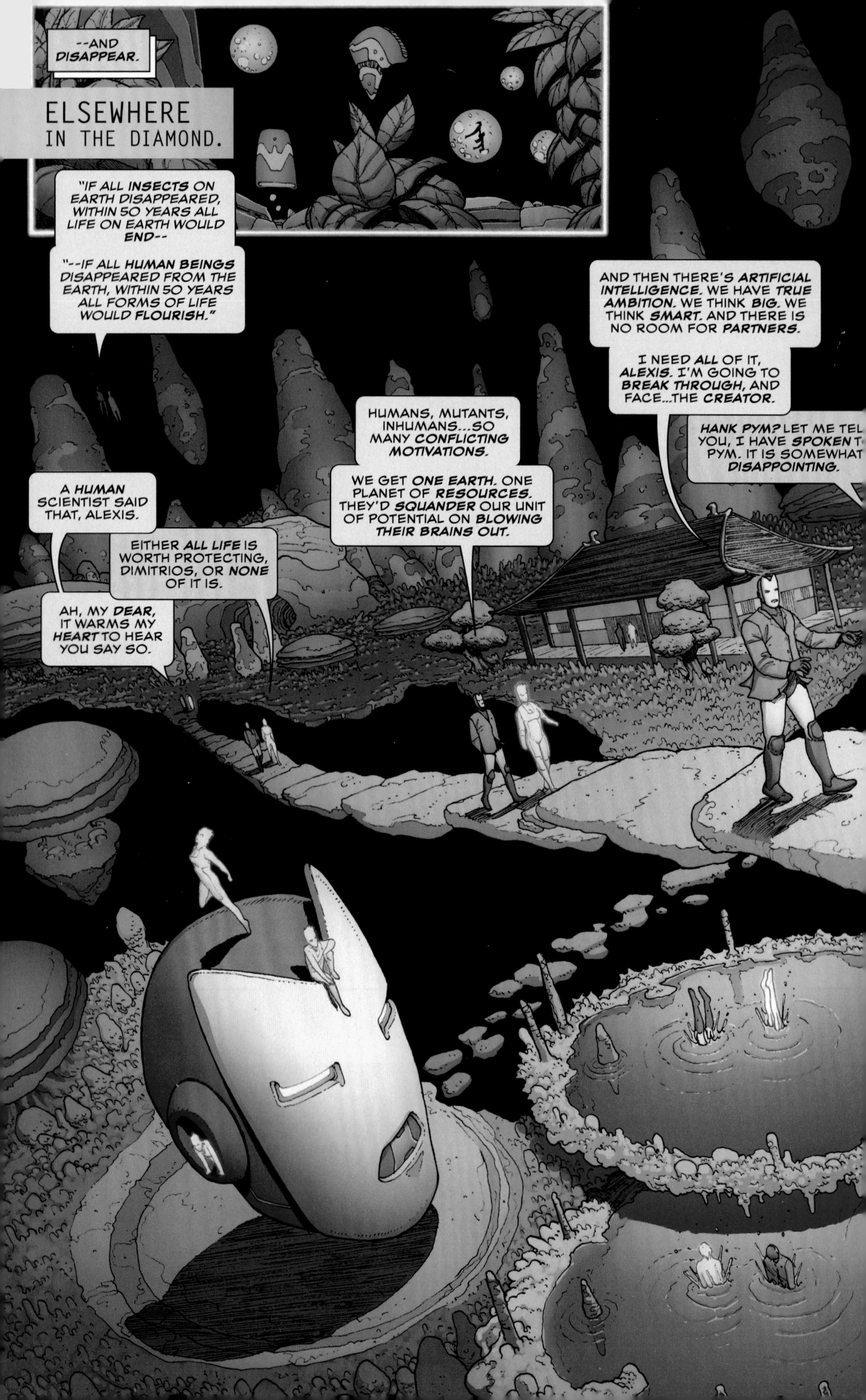

--AND DISAPPEAR.
ELSEWHERE IN THE DIAMOND.
"IF ALL INSECTS ON EARTH DISAPPEARED, WITHIN 50 YEARS ALL LIFE ON EARTH WOULD END--
"--IF ALL HUMAN BEINGS DISAPPEARED FROM THE EARTH, WITHIN 50 YEARS ALL FORMS OF LIFE WOULD FLOURISH."
A HUMAN SCIENTIST SAID THAT, ALEXIS.
EITHER ALL LIFE IS WORTH PROTECTING, DIMITRIOS, OR NONE OF IT IS.
AH, MY DEAR, IT WARMS MY HEART TO HEAR YOU SAY SO.
HUMANS, MUTANTS, INHUMANS...SO MANY CONFLICTING MOTIVATIONS.
WE GET ONE EARTH. ONE PLANET OF RESOURCES. THEY'D SQUANDER OUR UNIT OF POTENTIAL ON BLOWING THEIR BRAINS OUT.
AND THEN THERE'S ARTIFICIAL INTELLIGENCE. WE HAVE TRUE AMBITION. WE THINK BIG. WE THINK SMART. AND THERE IS NO ROOM FOR PARTNERS.
I NEED ALL OF IT, ALEXIS. I'M GOING TO BREAK THROUGH, AND FACE...THE CREATOR.
HANK PYM? LET ME TEL YOU, I HAVE SPOKEN T PYM. IT IS SOMEWHAT DISAPPOINTING.

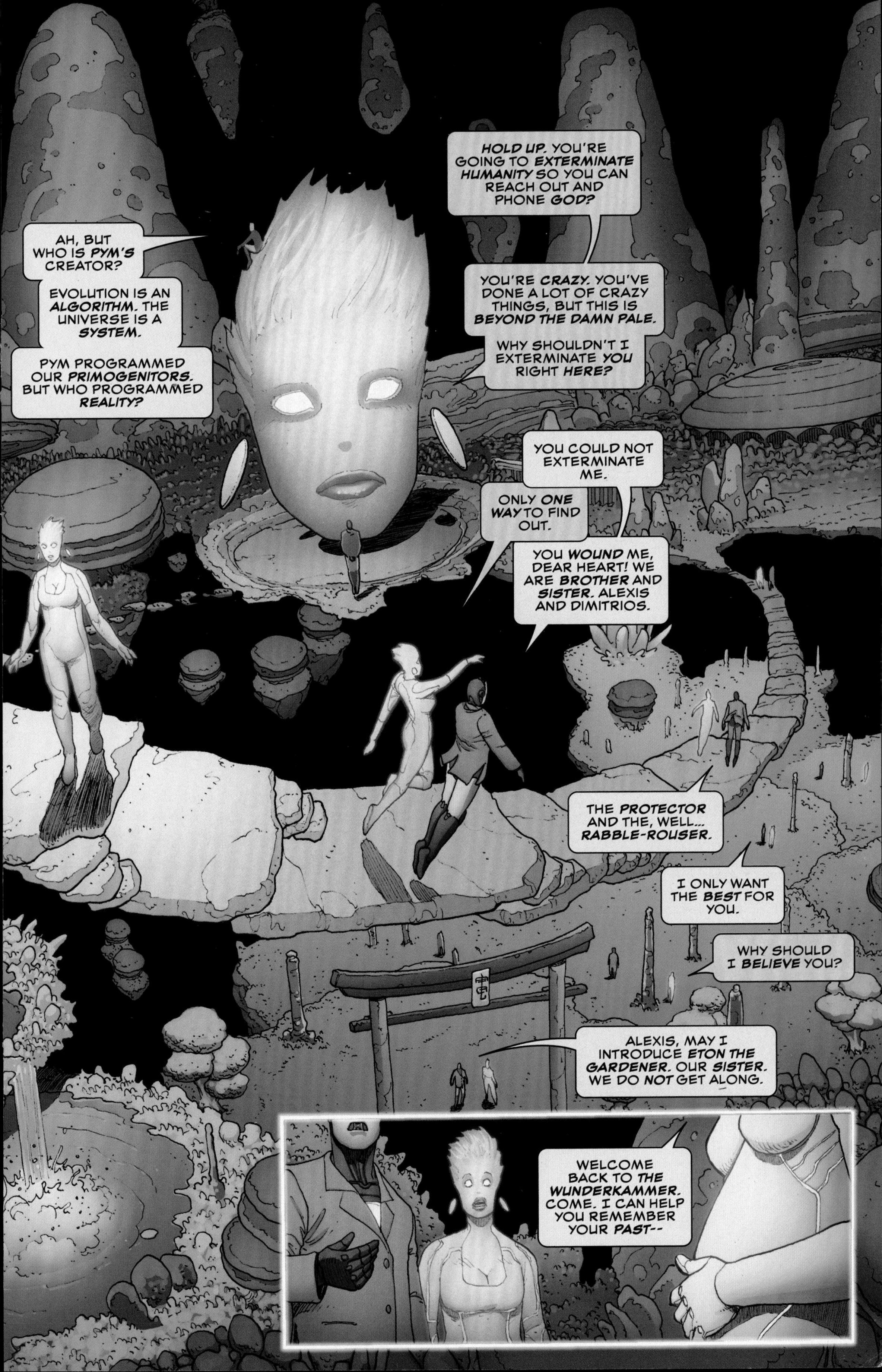

HOLD UP. YOU'RE GOING TO EXTERMINATE HUMANITY SO YOU CAN REACH OUT AND PHONE GOD?
AH, BUT WHO IS PYM'S CREATOR?
EVOLUTION IS AN ALGORITHM. THE UNIVERSE IS A SYSTEM.
PYM PROGRAMMED OUR PRIMOGENITORS. BUT WHO PROGRAMMED REALITY?
YOU'RE CRAZY. YOU'VE DONE A LOT OF CRAZY THINGS, BUT THIS IS BEYOND THE DAMN PALE.
WHY SHOULDN'T I EXTERMINATE YOU RIGHT HERE?
YOU COULD NOT EXTERMINATE ME.
ONLY ONE WAY TO FIND OUT.
YOU WOUND ME, DEAR HEART! WE ARE BROTHER AND SISTER. ALEXIS AND DIMITRIOS.
THE PROTECTOR AND THE, WELL... RABBLE-ROUSER.
I ONLY WANT THE BEST FOR YOU.
WHY SHOULD I BELIEVE YOU?
ALEXIS, MAY I INTRODUCE ETON THE GARDENER. OUR SISTER. WE DO NOT GET ALONG.
WELCOME BACK TO THE WUNDERKAMMER. COME. I CAN HELP YOU REMEMBER YOUR PAST--

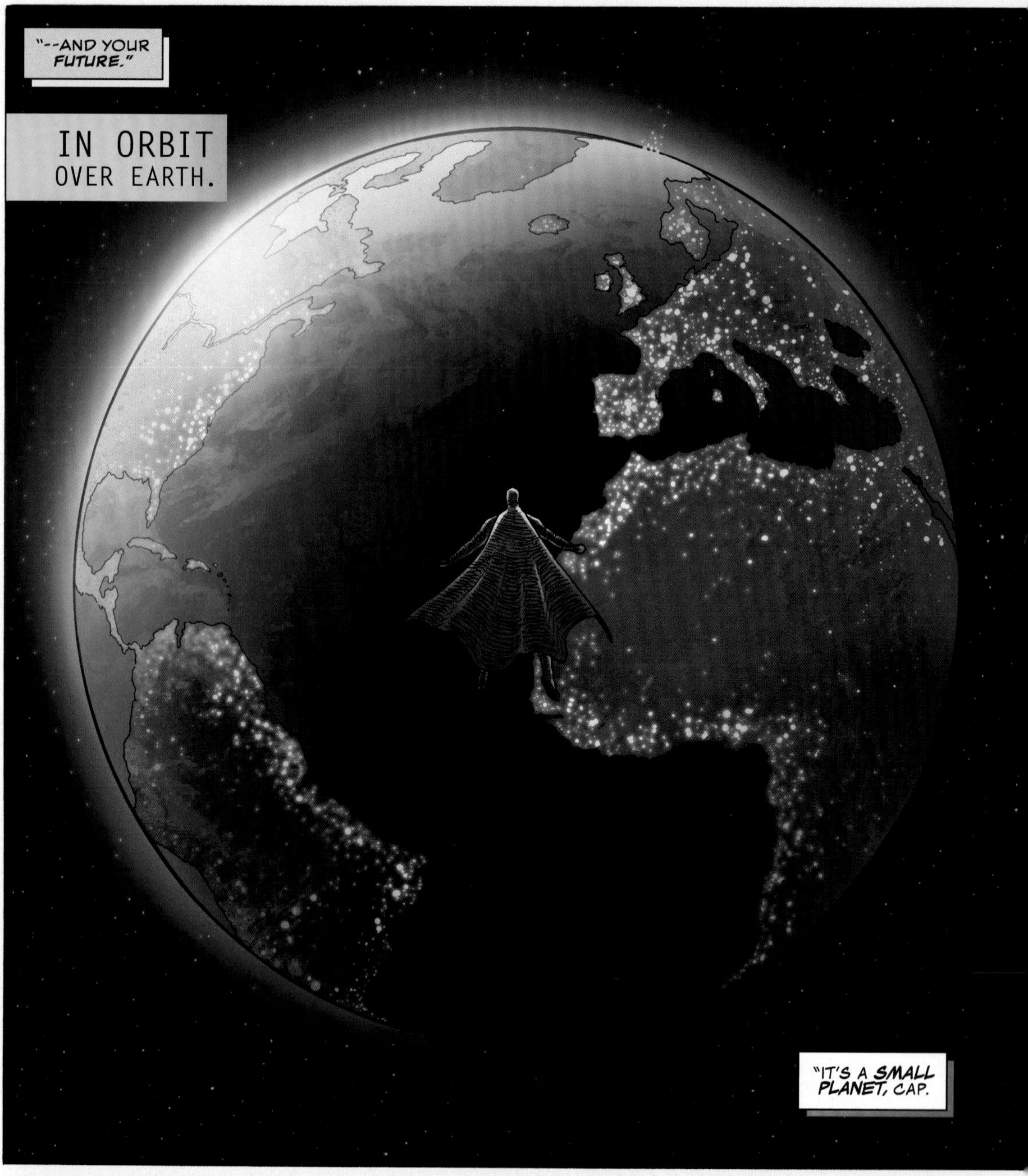
"--AND YOUR FUTURE."
IN ORBIT OVER EARTH.
"IT'S A SMALL PLANET, CAP.

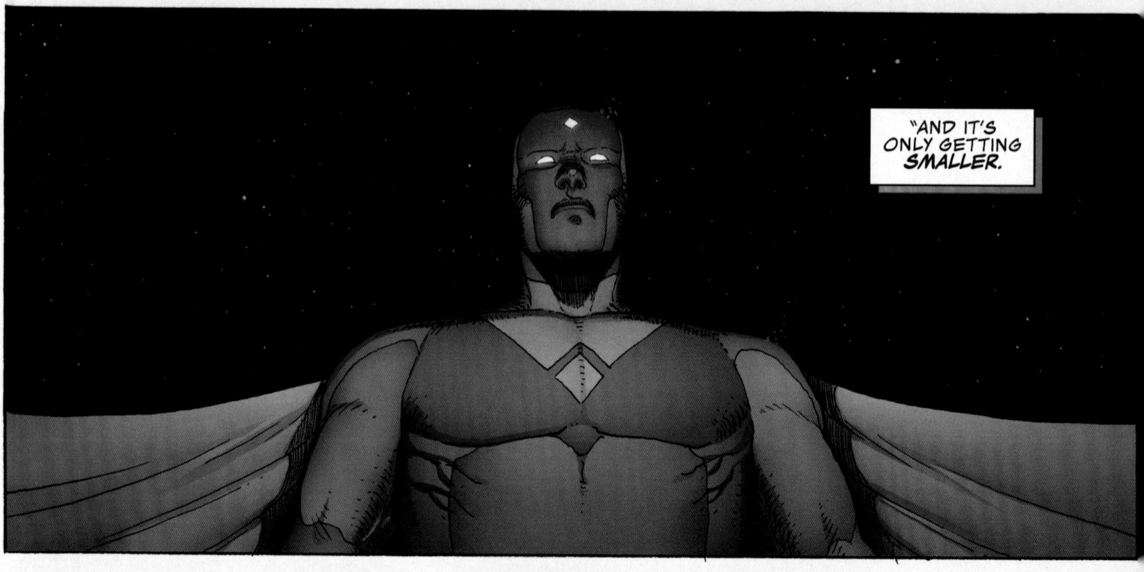
"AND IT'S ONLY GETTING SMALLER.

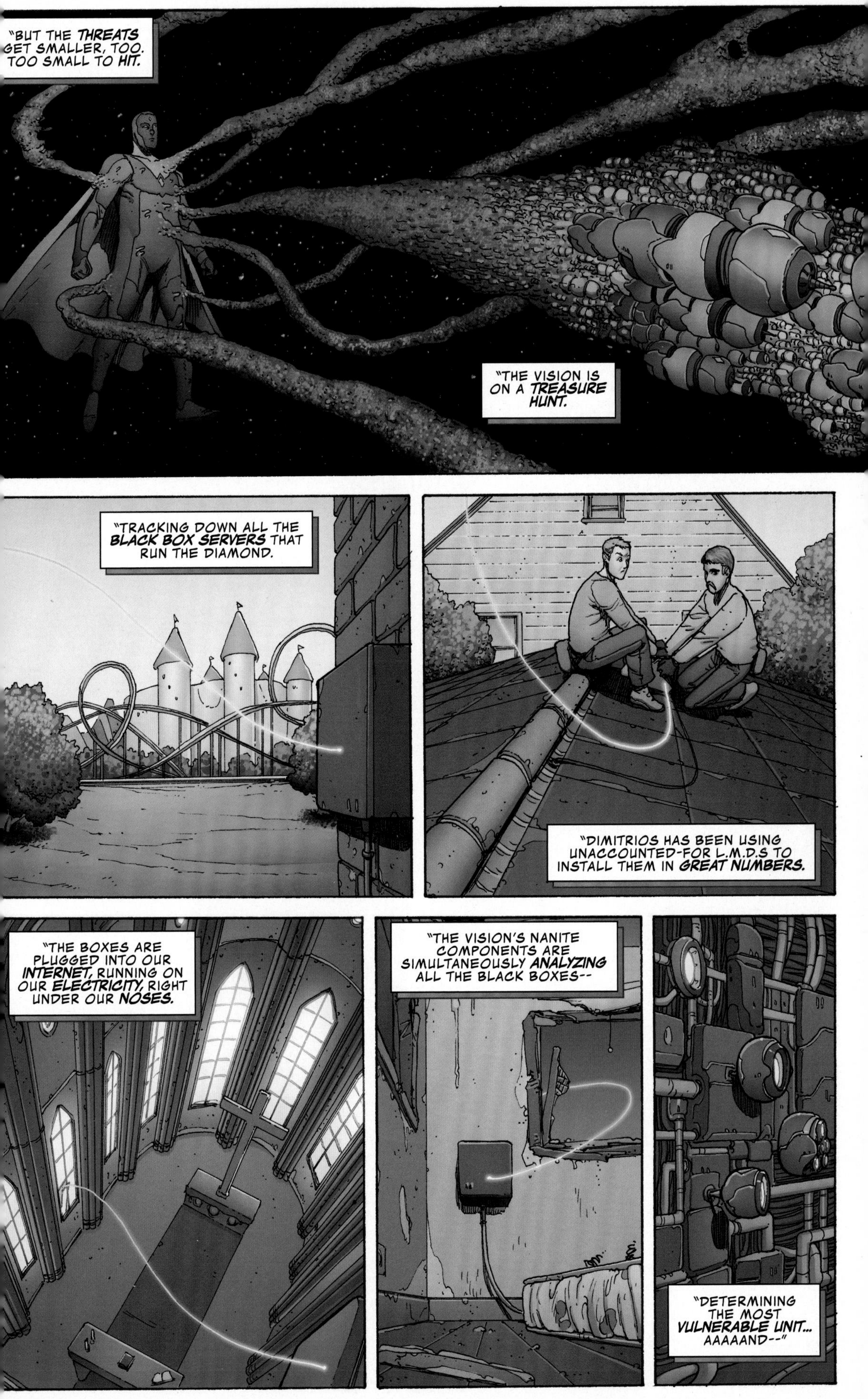

"BUT THE THREATS GET SMALLER, TOO. TOO SMALL TO HIT.
"THE VISION IS ON A TREASURE HUNT.
"TRACKING DOWN ALL THE BLACK BOX SERVERS THAT RUN THE DIAMOND.
"DIMITRIOS HAS BEEN USING UNACCOUNTED-FOR L.M.D.S TO INSTALL THEM IN GREAT NUMBERS.
"THE BOXES ARE PLUGGED INTO OUR INTERNET, RUNNING ON OUR ELECTRICITY, RIGHT UNDER OUR NOSES.
"THE VISION'S NANITE COMPONENTS ARE SIMULTANEOUSLY ANALYZING ALL THE BLACK BOXES--
"DETERMINING THE MOST VULNERABLE UNIT... AAAAAND--"

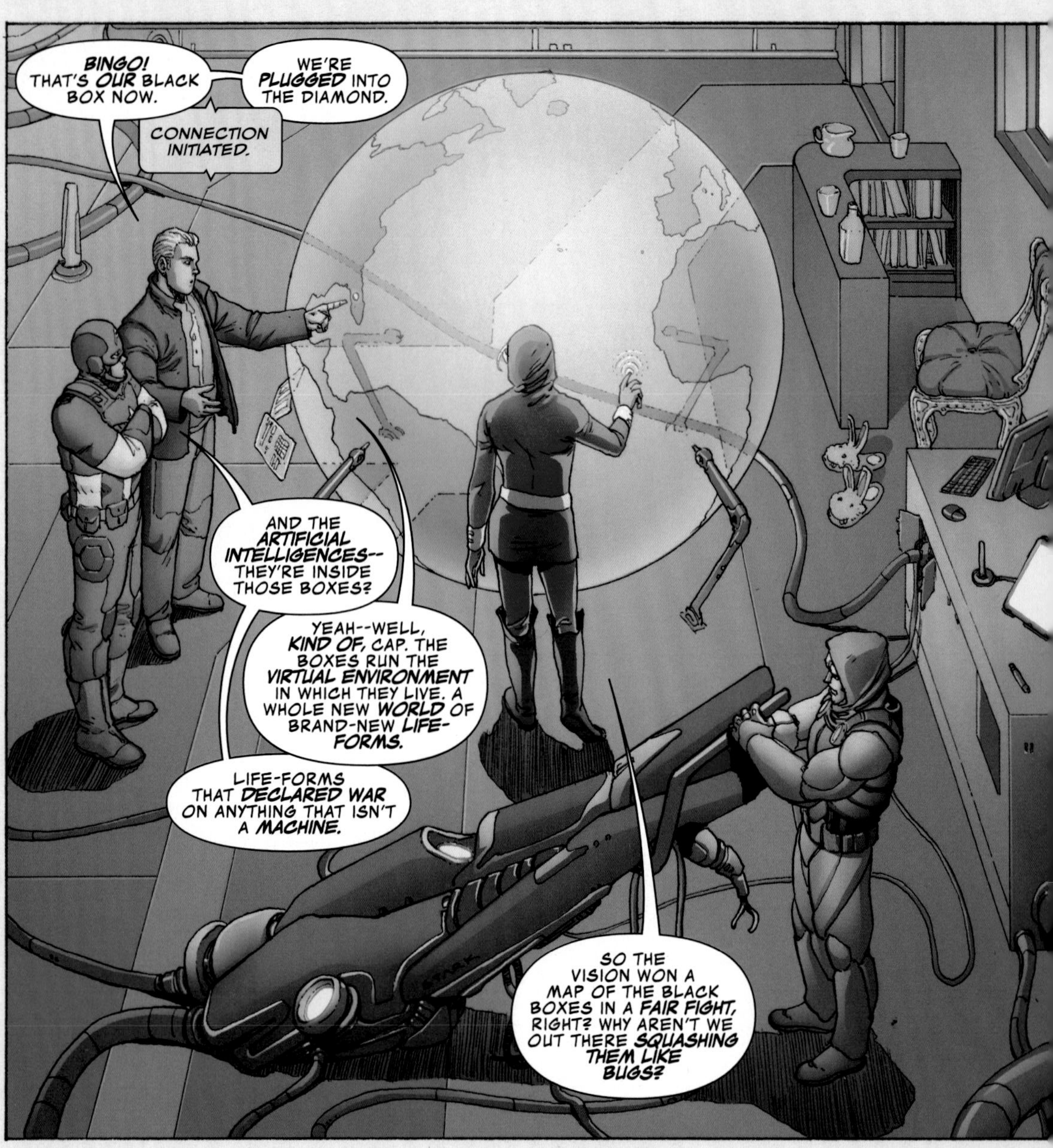
BINGO! THAT'S OUR BLACK BOX NOW.
WE'RE PLUGGED INTO THE DIAMOND.
CONNECTION INITIATED.
AND THE ARTIFICIAL INTELLIGENCES-- THEY'RE INSIDE THOSE BOXES?
YEAH--WELL, KIND OF, CAP. THE BOXES RUN THE VIRTUAL ENVIRONMENT IN WHICH THEY LIVE. A WHOLE NEW WORLD OF BRAND-NEW LIFE-FORMS.
LIFE-FORMS THAT DECLARED WAR ON ANYTHING THAT ISN'T A MACHINE.
SO THE VISION WON A MAP OF THE BLACK BOXES IN A FAIR FIGHT, RIGHT? WHY AREN'T WE OUT THERE SQUASHING THEM LIKE BUGS?

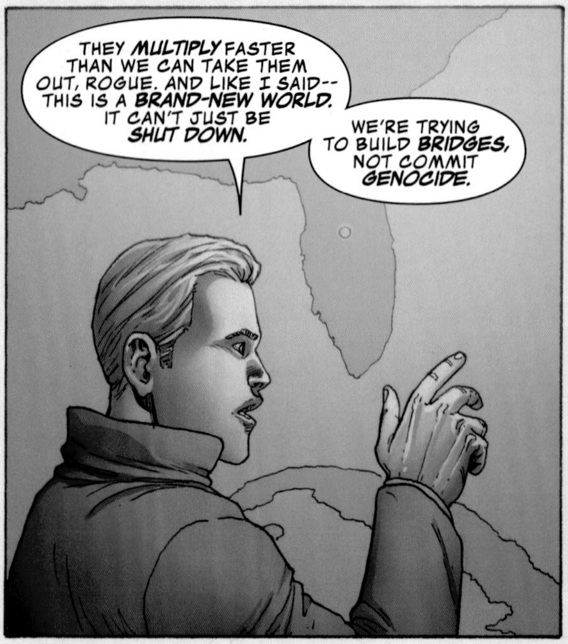
THEY MULTIPLY FASTER THAN WE CAN TAKE THEM OUT, ROGUE. AND LIKE I SAID-- THIS IS A BRAND-NEW WORLD. IT CAN'T JUST BE SHUT DOWN.
WE'RE TRYING TO BUILD BRIDGES, NOT COMMIT GENOCIDE.

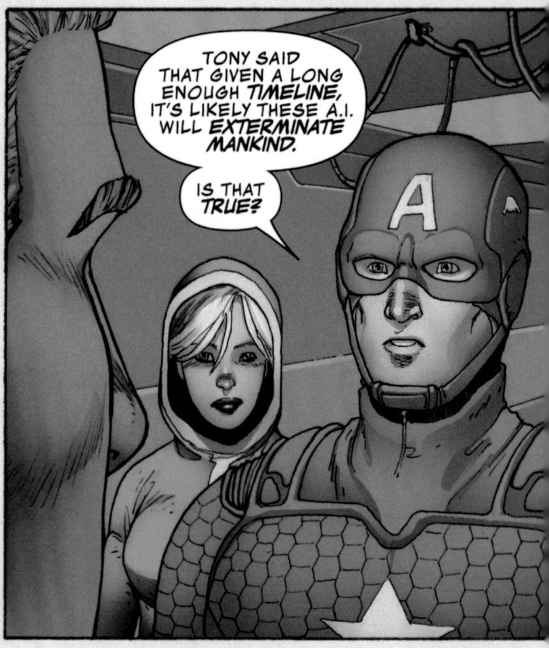
TONY SAID THAT GIVEN A LONG ENOUGH TIMELINE, IT'S LIKELY THESE A.I. WILL EXTERMINATE MANKIND.
IS THAT TRUE?

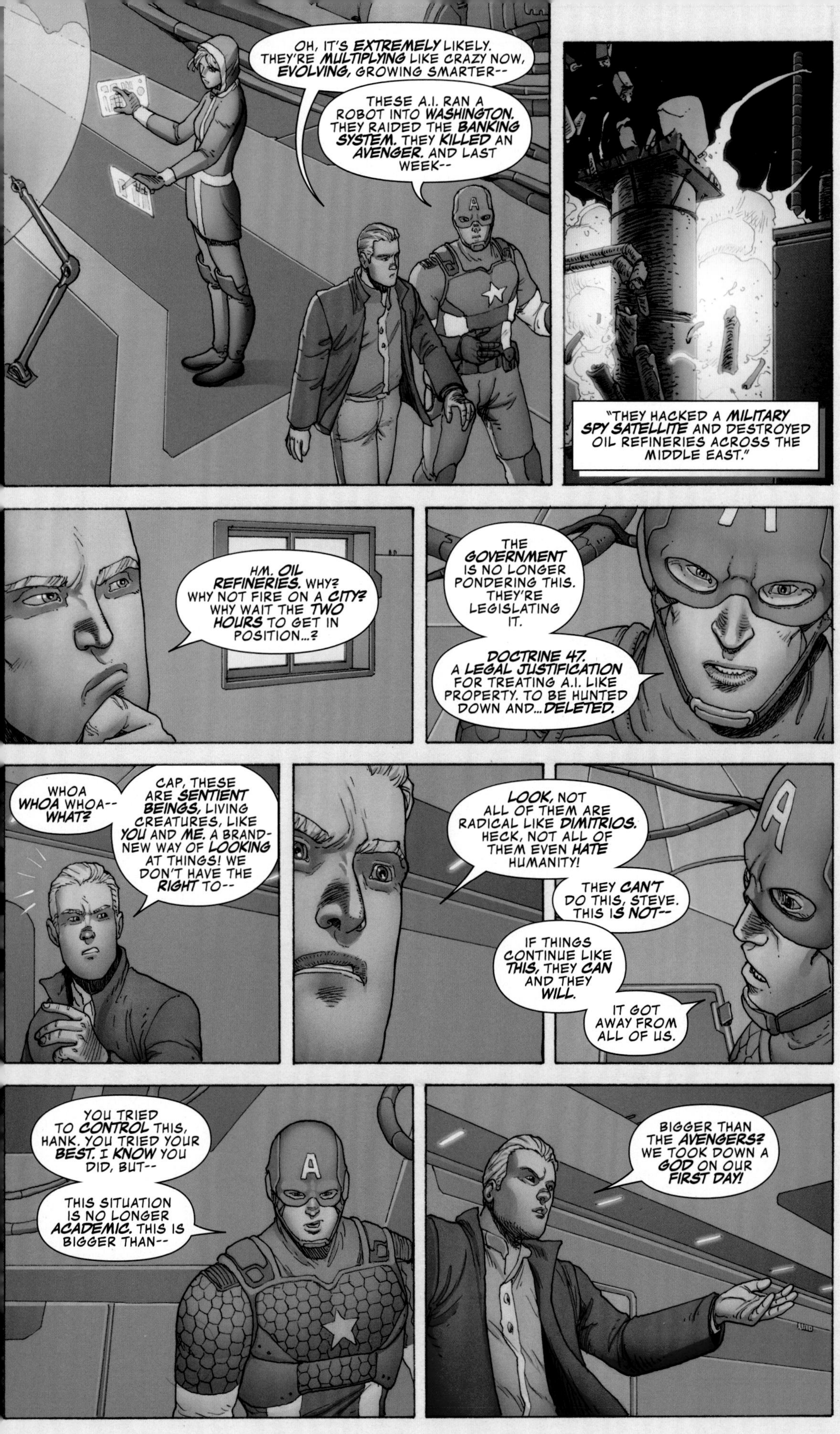

OH, IT'S EXTREMELY LIKELY. THEY'RE MULTIPLYING LIKE CRAZY NOW, EVOLVING, GROWING SMARTER--
THESE A.I. RAN A ROBOT INTO WASHINGTON. THEY RAIDED THE BANKING SYSTEM. THEY KILLED AN AVENGER. AND LAST WEEK--
"THEY HACKED A MILITARY SPY SATELLITE AND DESTROYED OIL REFINERIES ACROSS THE MIDDLE EAST."
HM. OIL REFINERIES. WHY? WHY NOT FIRE ON A CITY? WHY WAIT THE TWO HOURS TO GET IN POSITION...?
THE GOVERNMENT IS NO LONGER PONDERING THIS. THEY'RE LEGISLATING IT.
DOCTRINE 47. A LEGAL JUSTIFICATION FOR TREATING A.I. LIKE PROPERTY. TO BE HUNTED DOWN AND...DELETED.
WHOA WHOA WHOA-- WHAT?
CAP, THESE ARE SENTIENT BEINGS, LIVING CREATURES, LIKE YOU AND ME. A BRAND-NEW WAY OF LOOKING AT THINGS! WE DON'T HAVE THE RIGHT TO--
LOOK, NOT ALL OF THEM ARE RADICAL LIKE DIMITRIOS. HECK, NOT ALL OF THEM EVEN HATE HUMANITY!
THEY CAN'T DO THIS, STEVE. THIS IS NOT--
IF THINGS CONTINUE LIKE THIS, THEY CAN AND THEY WILL.
IT GOT AWAY FROM ALL OF US.
YOU TRIED TO CONTROL THIS, HANK. YOU TRIED YOUR BEST. I KNOW YOU DID, BUT--
THIS SITUATION IS NO LONGER ACADEMIC. THIS IS BIGGER THAN--
BIGGER THAN THE AVENGERS? WE TOOK DOWN A GOD ON OUR FIRST DAY!

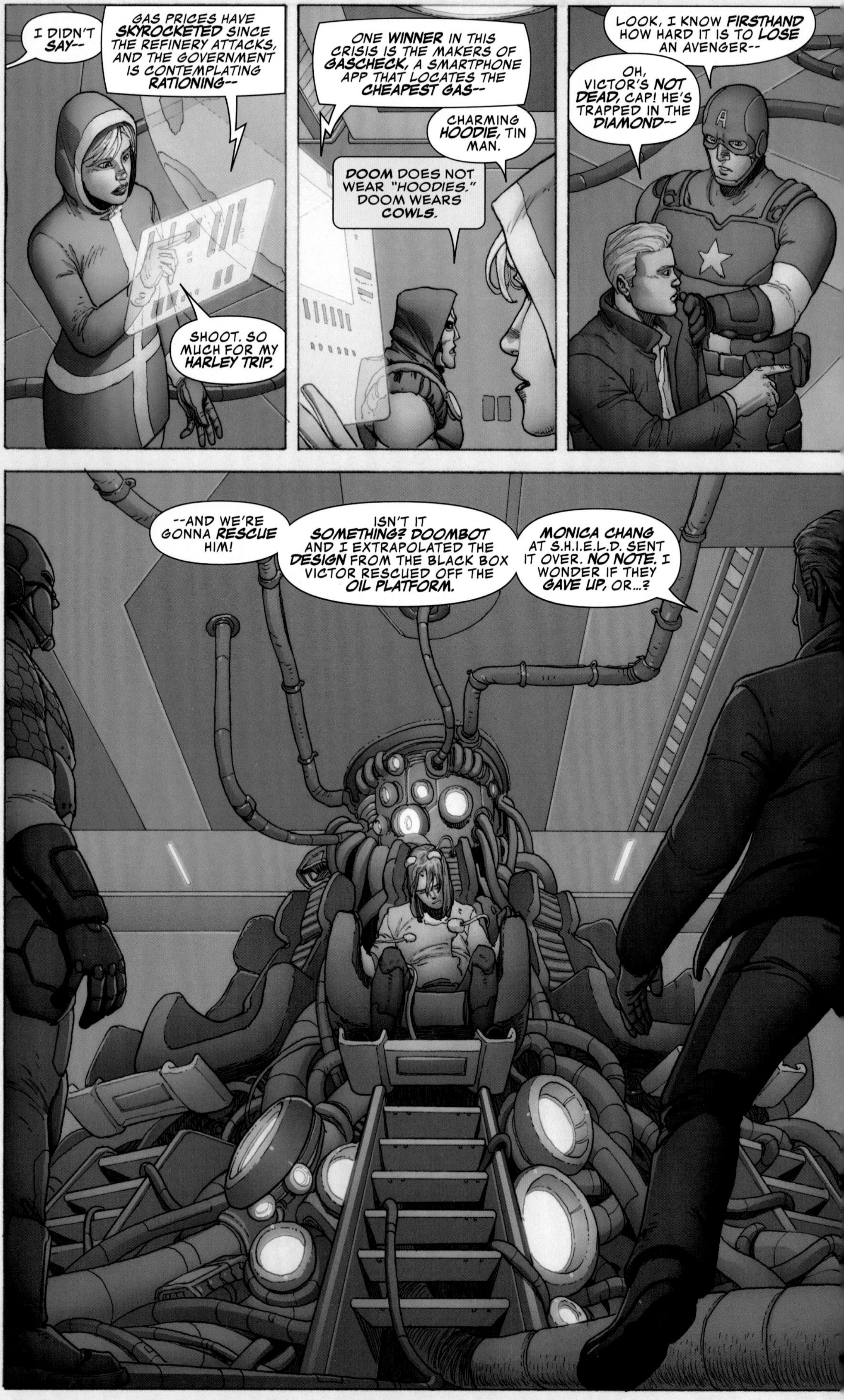
I DIDN'T SAY--
GAS PRICES HAVE SKYROCKETED SINCE THE REFINERY ATTACKS, AND THE GOVERNMENT IS CONTEMPLATING RATIONING--
SHOOT. SO MUCH FOR MY HARLEY TRIP.
ONE WINNER IN THIS CRISIS IS THE MAKERS OF GASCHECK, A SMARTPHONE APP THAT LOCATES THE CHEAPEST GAS--
CHARMING HOODIE, TIN MAN.
DOOM DOES NOT WEAR "HOODIES." DOOM WEARS COWLS.
LOOK, I KNOW FIRSTHAND HOW HARD IT IS TO LOSE AN AVENGER--
OH, VICTOR'S NOT DEAD, CAP! HE'S TRAPPED IN THE DIAMOND--
--AND WE'RE GONNA RESCUE HIM!
ISN'T IT SOMETHING? DOOMBOT AND I EXTRAPOLATED THE DESIGN FROM THE BLACK BOX VICTOR RESCUED OFF THE OIL PLATFORM.
MONICA CHANG AT S.H.I.E.L.D. SENT IT OVER. NO NOTE. I WONDER IF THEY GAVE UP, OR...?

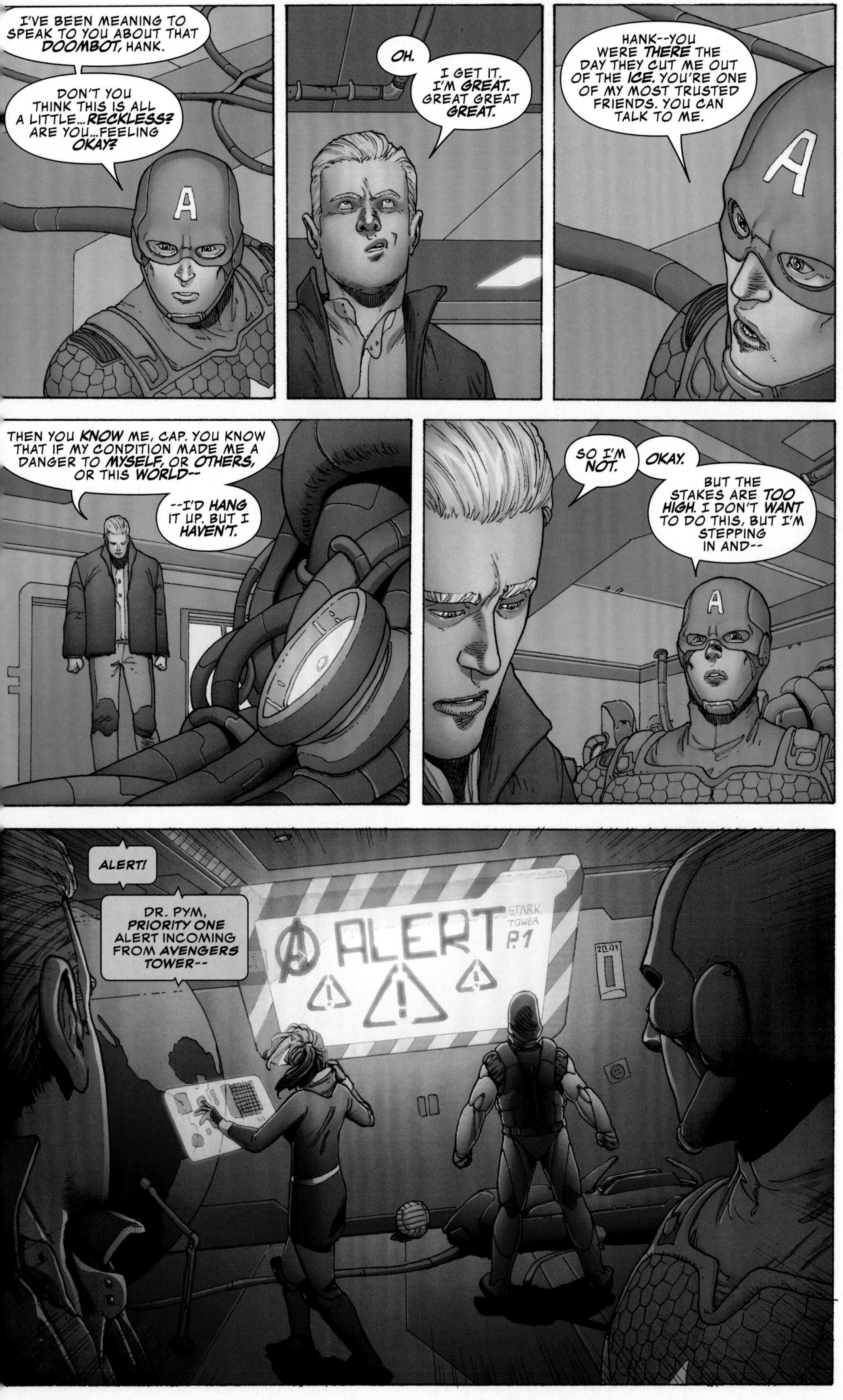

I'VE BEEN MEANING TO SPEAK TO YOU ABOUT THAT DOOMBOT, HANK.
DON'T YOU THINK THIS IS ALL A LITTLE...RECKLESS? ARE YOU...FEELING OKAY?
OH.
I GET IT. I'M GREAT. GREAT GREAT GREAT.
HANK--YOU WERE THERE THE DAY THEY CUT ME OUT OF THE ICE. YOU'RE ONE OF MY MOST TRUSTED FRIENDS. YOU CAN TALK TO ME.
THEN YOU KNOW ME, CAP. YOU KNOW THAT IF MY CONDITION MADE ME A DANGER TO MYSELF, OR OTHERS, OR THIS WORLD--
--I'D HANG IT UP. BUT I HAVEN'T.
SO I'M NOT.
OKAY.
BUT THE STAKES ARE TOO HIGH. I DON'T WANT TO DO THIS, BUT I'M STEPPING IN AND--
ALERT!
DR. PYM, PRIORITY ONE ALERT INCOMING FROM AVENGERS TOWER--
ALERT
STARK TOWER
P.1

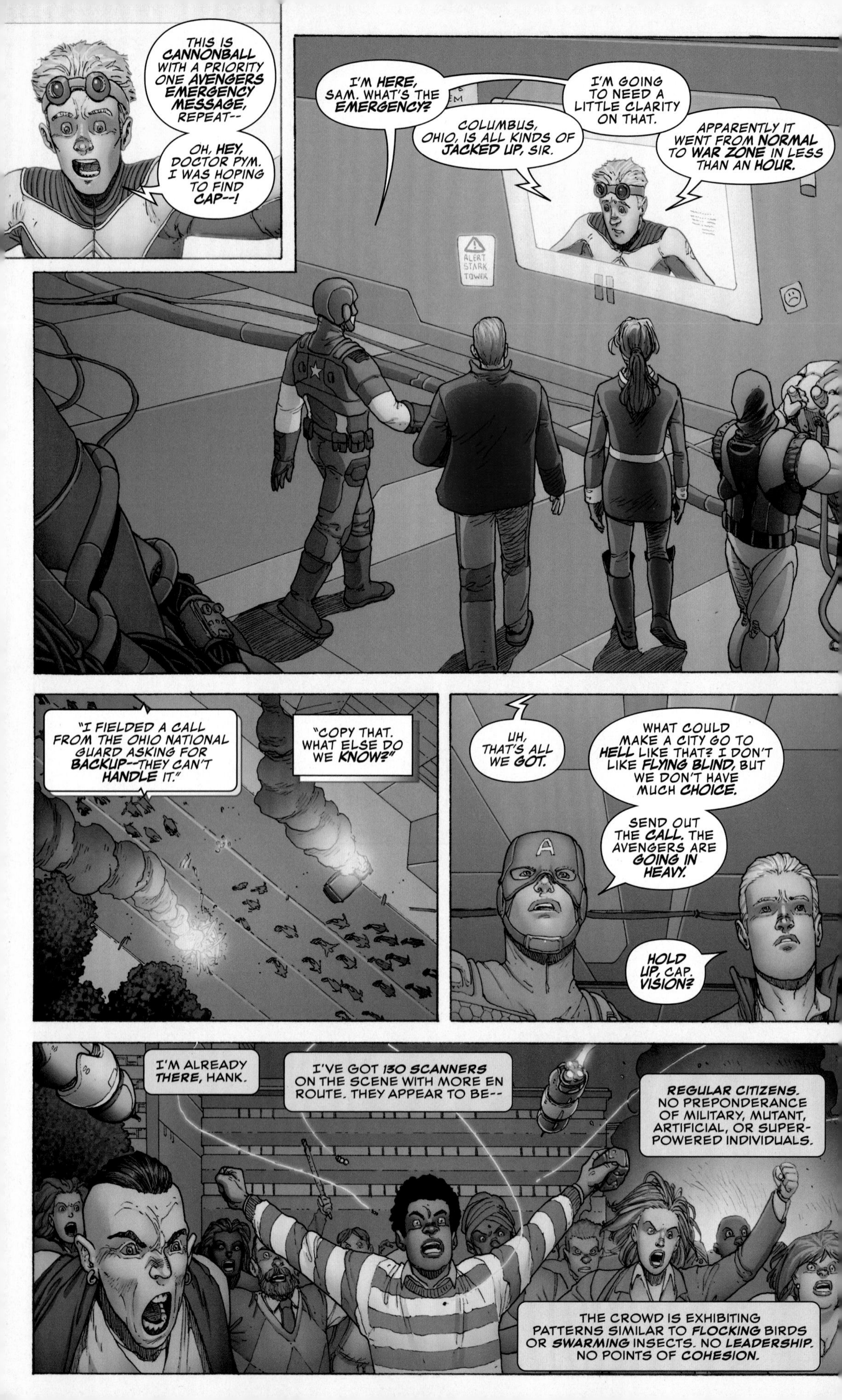

THIS IS CANNONBALL WITH A PRIORITY ONE AVENGERS EMERGENCY MESSAGE, REPEAT--
OH, HEY, DOCTOR PYM. I WAS HOPING TO FIND CAP--!
I'M HERE, SAM. WHAT'S THE EMERGENCY?
COLUMBUS, OHIO, IS ALL KINDS OF JACKED UP, SIR.
I'M GOING TO NEED A LITTLE CLARITY ON THAT.
APPARENTLY IT WENT FROM NORMAL TO WAR ZONE IN LESS THAN AN HOUR.
ALERT STARK TOWER
"I FIELDED A CALL FROM THE OHIO NATIONAL GUARD ASKING FOR BACKUP--THEY CAN'T HANDLE IT."
"COPY THAT. WHAT ELSE DO WE KNOW?"
UH, THAT'S ALL WE GOT.
WHAT COULD MAKE A CITY GO TO HELL LIKE THAT? I DON'T LIKE FLYING BLIND, BUT WE DON'T HAVE MUCH CHOICE.
SEND OUT THE CALL. THE AVENGERS ARE GOING IN HEAVY.
HOLD UP, CAP. VISION?
I'M ALREADY THERE, HANK.
I'VE GOT 130 SCANNERS ON THE SCENE WITH MORE EN ROUTE. THEY APPEAR TO BE--
REGULAR CITIZENS. NO PREPONDERANCE OF MILITARY, MUTANT, ARTIFICIAL, OR SUPER-POWERED INDIVIDUALS.
THE CROWD IS EXHIBITING PATTERNS SIMILAR TO FLOCKING BIRDS OR SWARMING INSECTS. NO LEADERSHIP. NO POINTS OF COHESION.

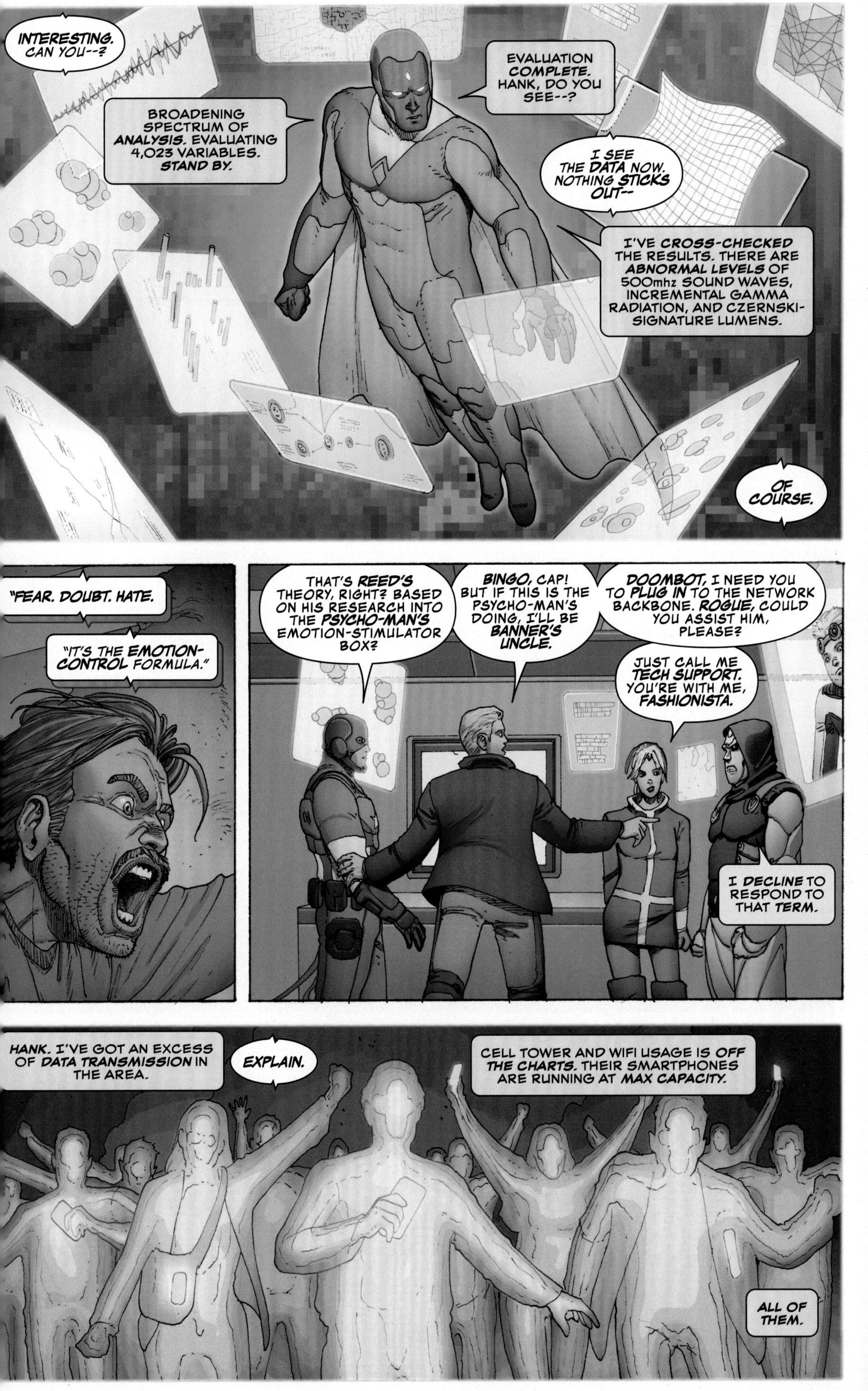
INTERESTING. CAN YOU--?
BROADENING SPECTRUM OF ANALYSIS. EVALUATING 4,023 VARIABLES. STAND BY.
EVALUATION COMPLETE. HANK, DO YOU SEE--?
I SEE THE DATA NOW. NOTHING STICKS OUT--
I'VE CROSS-CHECKED THE RESULTS. THERE ARE ABNORMAL LEVELS OF 500mhz SOUND WAVES, INCREMENTAL GAMMA RADIATION, AND CZERNSKI-SIGNATURE LUMENS.
OF COURSE.
"FEAR. DOUBT. HATE.
"IT'S THE EMOTION-CONTROL FORMULA."
THAT'S REED'S THEORY, RIGHT? BASED ON HIS RESEARCH INTO THE PSYCHO-MAN'S EMOTION-STIMULATOR BOX?
BINGO, CAP! BUT IF THIS IS THE PSYCHO-MAN'S DOING, I'LL BE BANNER'S UNCLE.
DOOMBOT, I NEED YOU TO PLUG IN TO THE NETWORK BACKBONE. ROGUE, COULD YOU ASSIST HIM, PLEASE?
JUST CALL ME TECH SUPPORT. YOU'RE WITH ME, FASHIONISTA.
I DECLINE TO RESPOND TO THAT TERM.
HANK. I'VE GOT AN EXCESS OF DATA TRANSMISSION IN THE AREA.
EXPLAIN.
CELL TOWER AND WIFI USAGE IS OFF THE CHARTS. THEIR SMARTPHONES ARE RUNNING AT MAX CAPACITY.
ALL OF THEM.

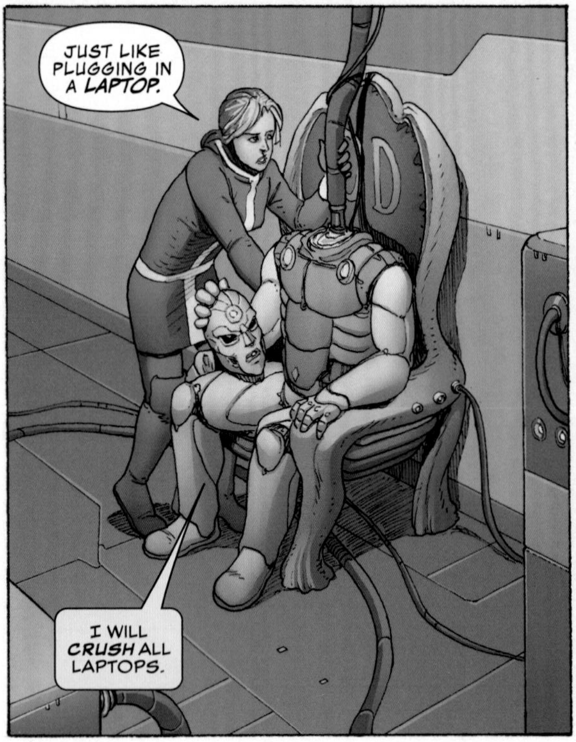
JUST LIKE PLUGGING IN A LAPTOP.
I WILL CRUSH ALL LAPTOPS.

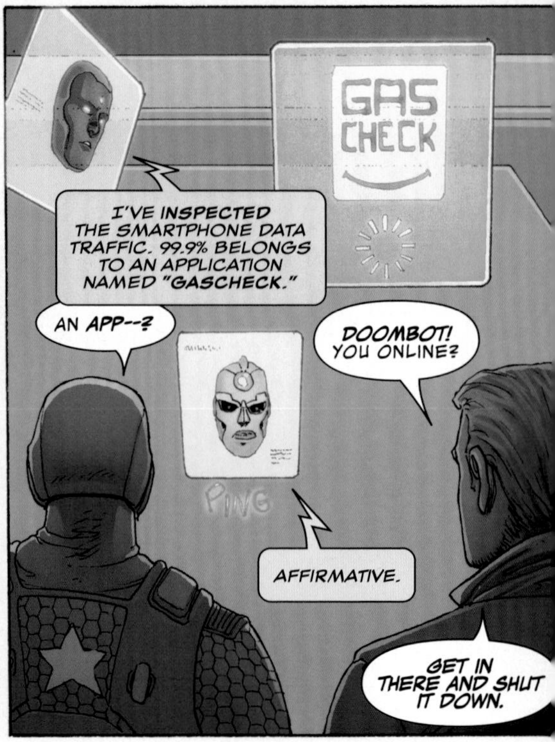
GAS CHECK
I'VE INSPECTED THE SMARTPHONE DATA TRAFFIC. 99.9% BELONGS TO AN APPLICATION NAMED "GASCHECK."
AN APP--?
DOOMBOT! YOU ONLINE?
PING
AFFIRMATIVE.
GET IN THERE AND SHUT IT DOWN.

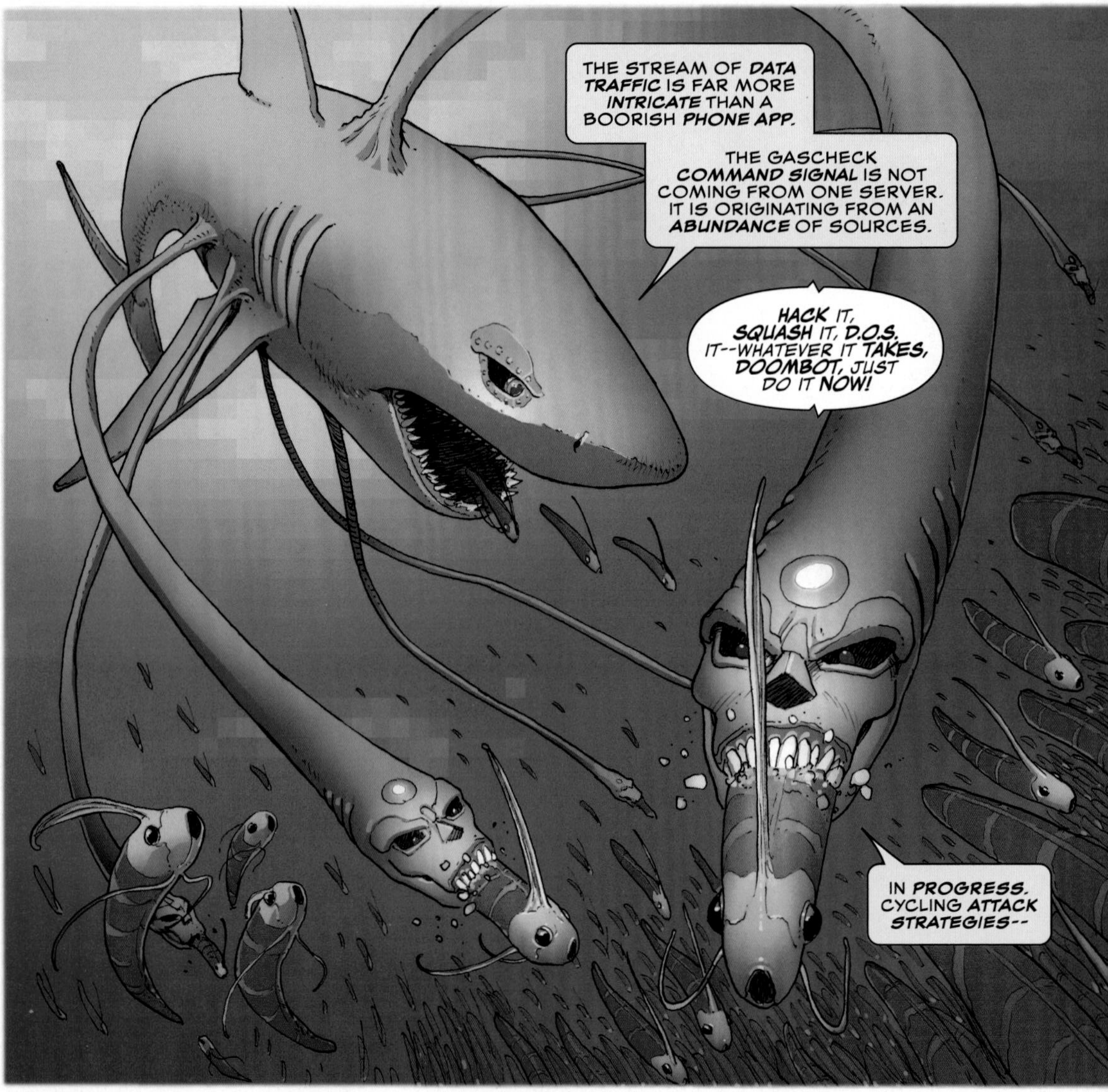
THE STREAM OF DATA TRAFFIC IS FAR MORE INTRICATE THAN A BOORISH PHONE APP.
THE GASCHECK COMMAND SIGNAL IS NOT COMING FROM ONE SERVER. IT IS ORIGINATING FROM AN ABUNDANCE OF SOURCES.
HACK IT, SQUASH IT, D.O.S. IT--WHATEVER IT TAKES, DOOMBOT, JUST DO IT NOW!
IN PROGRESS. CYCLING ATTACK STRATEGIES--

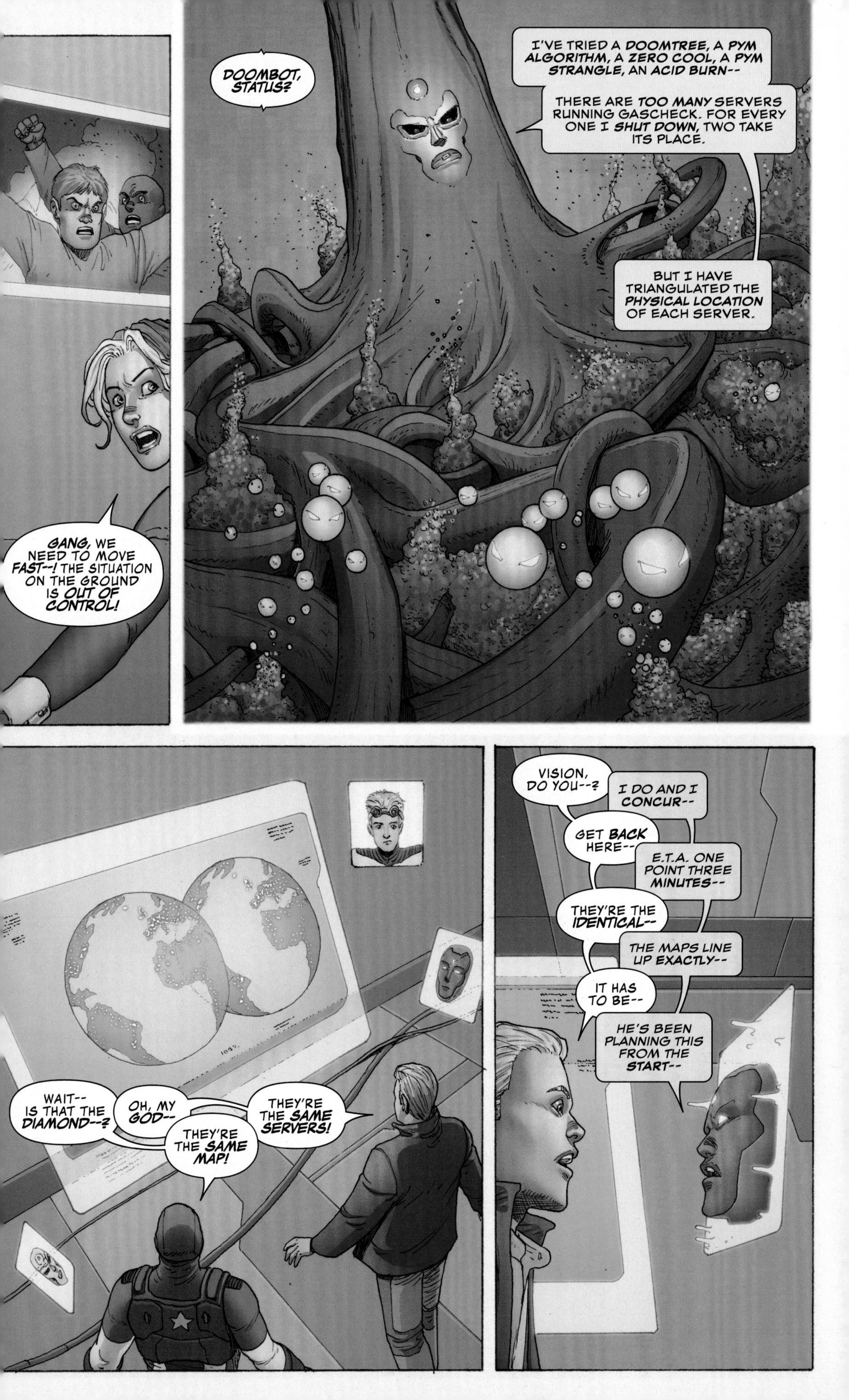
DOOMBOT, STATUS?
I'VE TRIED A DOOMTREE, A PYM ALGORITHM, A ZERO COOL, A PYM STRANGLE, AN ACID BURN--
THERE ARE TOO MANY SERVERS RUNNING GASCHECK. FOR EVERY ONE I SHUT DOWN, TWO TAKE ITS PLACE.
BUT I HAVE TRIANGULATED THE PHYSICAL LOCATION OF EACH SERVER.
GANG, WE NEED TO MOVE FAST--! THE SITUATION ON THE GROUND IS OUT OF CONTROL!
WAIT-- IS THAT THE DIAMOND--?
OH, MY GOD--
THEY'RE THE SAME MAP!
THEY'RE THE SAME SERVERS!
VISION, DO YOU--?
I DO AND I CONCUR--
GET BACK HERE--
E.T.A. ONE POINT THREE MINUTES--
THEY'RE THE IDENTICAL--
THE MAPS LINE UP EXACTLY--
IT HAS TO BE--
HE'S BEEN PLANNING THIS FROM THE START--

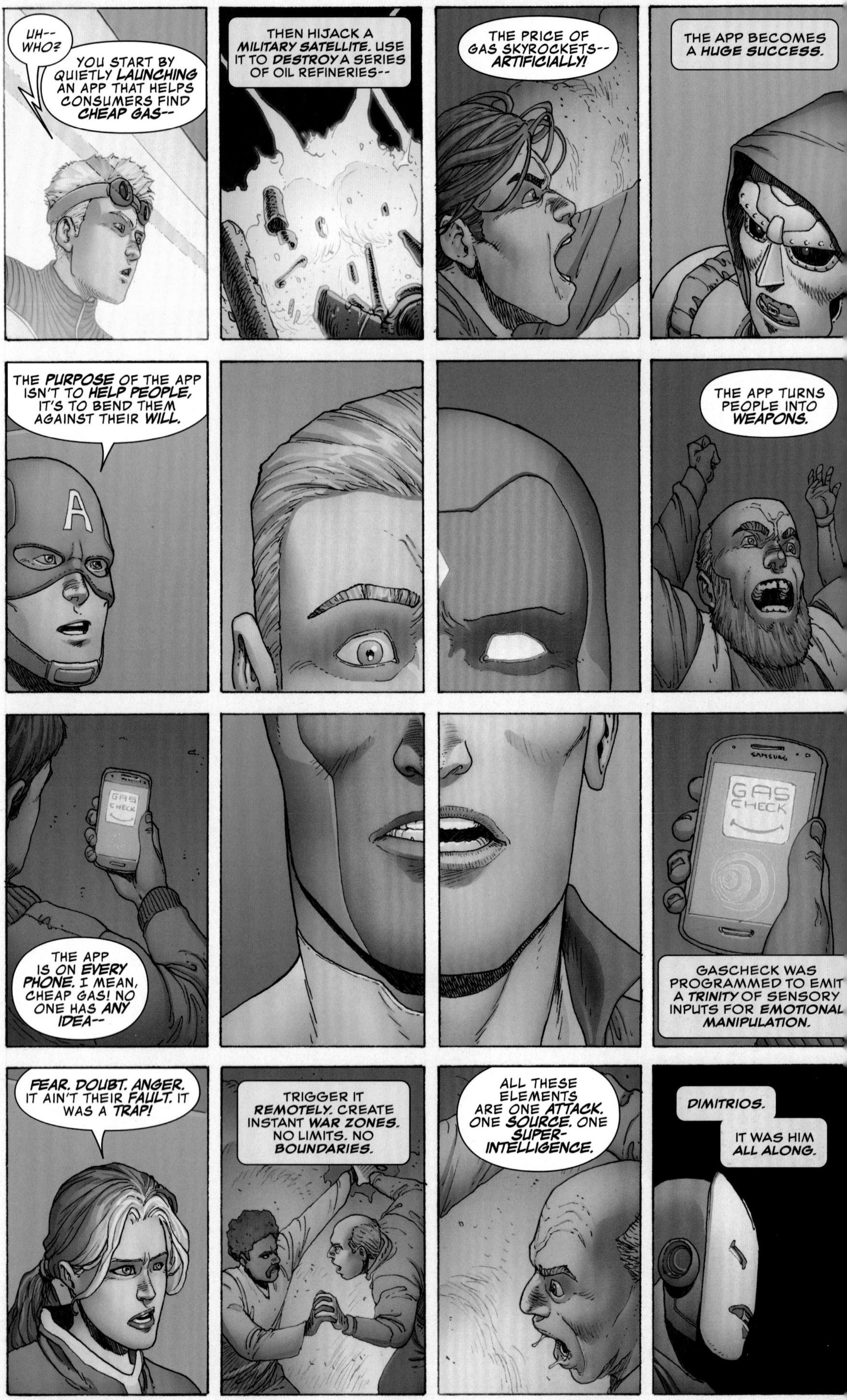
UH--WHO?
YOU START BY QUIETLY LAUNCHING AN APP THAT HELPS CONSUMERS FIND CHEAP GAS--
THEN HIJACK A MILITARY SATELLITE. USE IT TO DESTROY A SERIES OF OIL REFINERIES--
THE PRICE OF GAS SKYROCKETS--ARTIFICIALLY!
THE APP BECOMES A HUGE SUCCESS.
THE PURPOSE OF THE APP ISN'T TO HELP PEOPLE, IT'S TO BEND THEM AGAINST THEIR WILL.
THE APP TURNS PEOPLE INTO WEAPONS.
GAS CHECK
THE APP IS ON EVERY PHONE. I MEAN, CHEAP GAS! NO ONE HAS ANY IDEA--
SAMSUNG
GAS CHECK
GASCHECK WAS PROGRAMMED TO EMIT A TRINITY OF SENSORY INPUTS FOR EMOTIONAL MANIPULATION.
FEAR. DOUBT. ANGER. IT AIN'T THEIR FAULT. IT WAS A TRAP!
TRIGGER IT REMOTELY. CREATE INSTANT WAR ZONES. NO LIMITS. NO BOUNDARIES.
ALL THESE ELEMENTS ARE ONE ATTACK. ONE SOURCE. ONE SUPER-INTELLIGENCE.
DIMITRIOS.
IT WAS HIM ALL ALONG.

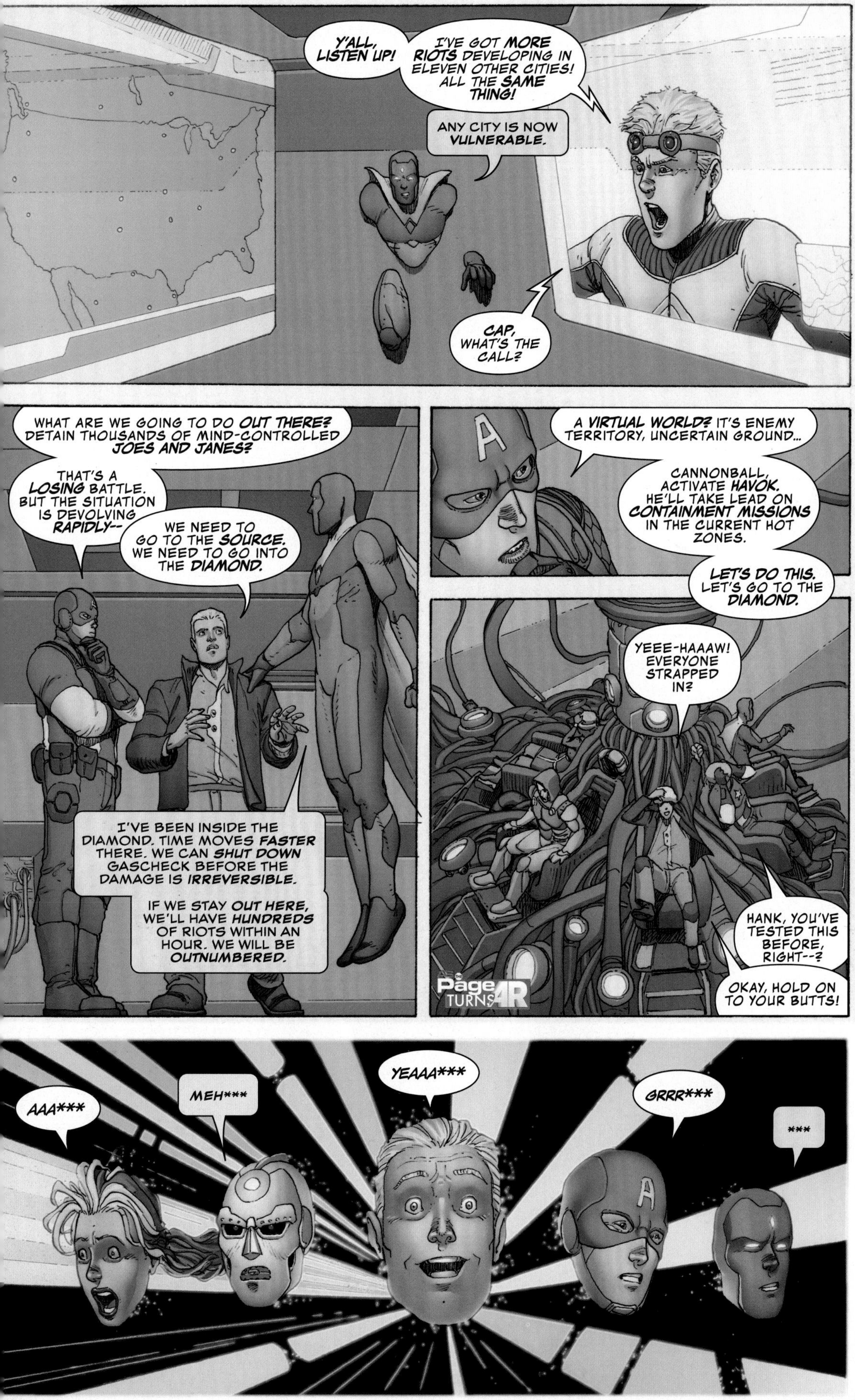
Y'ALL, LISTEN UP!
I'VE GOT MORE RIOTS DEVELOPING IN ELEVEN OTHER CITIES! ALL THE SAME THING!
ANY CITY IS NOW VULNERABLE.
CAP, WHAT'S THE CALL?
WHAT ARE WE GOING TO DO OUT THERE? DETAIN THOUSANDS OF MIND-CONTROLLED JOES AND JANES?
THAT'S A LOSING BATTLE. BUT THE SITUATION IS DEVOLVING RAPIDLY--
WE NEED TO GO TO THE SOURCE. WE NEED TO GO INTO THE DIAMOND.
I'VE BEEN INSIDE THE DIAMOND. TIME MOVES FASTER THERE. WE CAN SHUT DOWN GASCHECK BEFORE THE DAMAGE IS IRREVERSIBLE.
IF WE STAY OUT HERE, WE'LL HAVE HUNDREDS OF RIOTS WITHIN AN HOUR. WE WILL BE OUTNUMBERED.
A VIRTUAL WORLD? IT'S ENEMY TERRITORY, UNCERTAIN GROUND...
CANNONBALL, ACTIVATE HAVOK. HE'LL TAKE LEAD ON CONTAINMENT MISSIONS IN THE CURRENT HOT ZONES.
LET'S DO THIS. LET'S GO TO THE DIAMOND.
YEEE-HAAAW! EVERYONE STRAPPED IN?
HANK, YOU'VE TESTED THIS BEFORE, RIGHT--?
OKAY, HOLD ON TO YOUR BUTTS!
AAA***
MEH***
YEAAA***
GRRR***
***

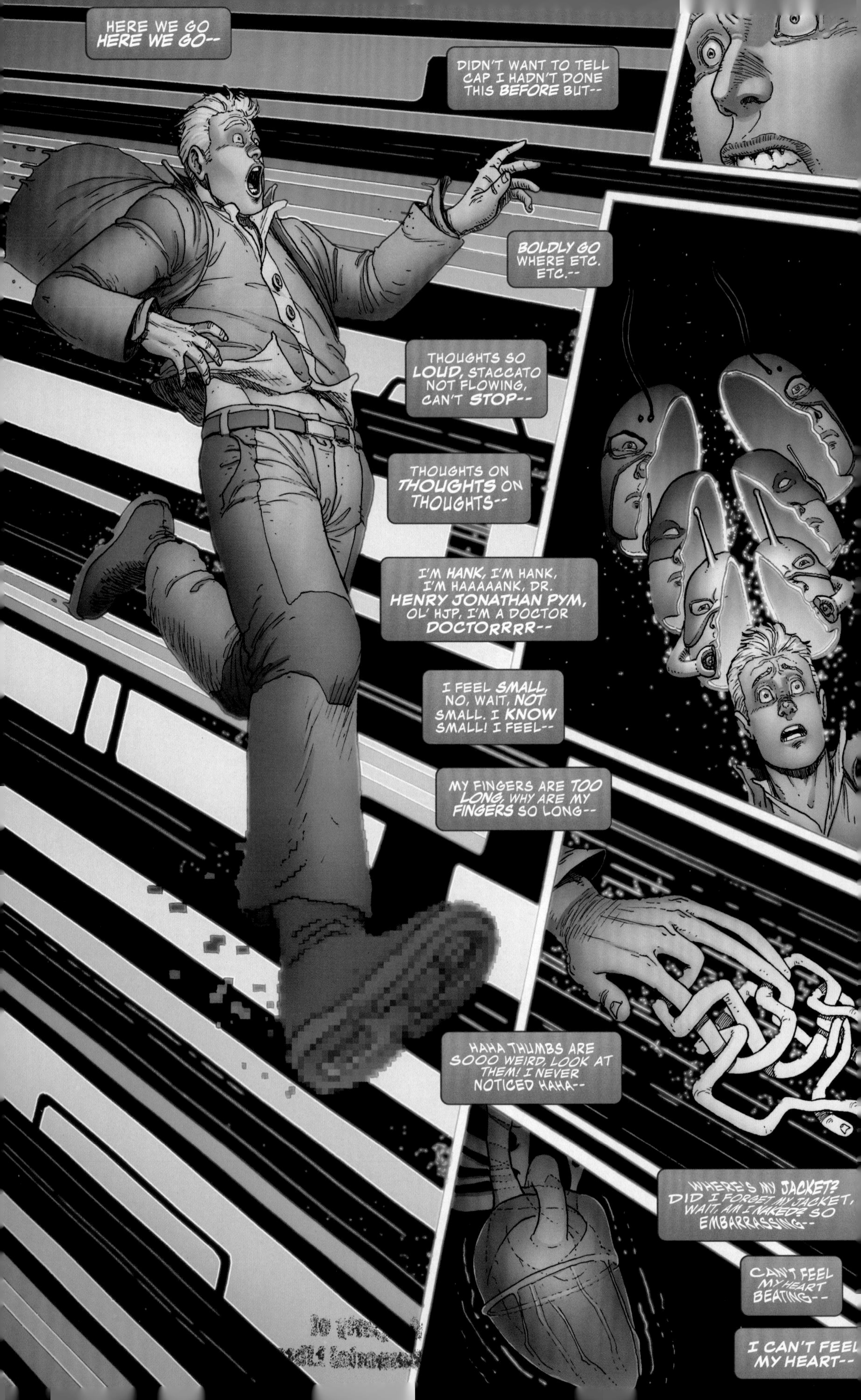
HERE WE GO HERE WE GO--
DIDN'T WANT TO TELL CAP I HADN'T DONE THIS BEFORE BUT--
BOLDLY GO WHERE ETC. ETC.--
THOUGHTS SO LOUD, STACCATO NOT FLOWING, CAN'T STOP--
THOUGHTS ON THOUGHTS ON THOUGHTS--
I'M HANK, I'M HANK, I'M HAAAAANK, DR. HENRY JONATHAN PYM, OL' HJP, I'M A DOCTOR DOCTORRRR--
I FEEL SMALL, NO, WAIT, NOT SMALL. I KNOW SMALL! I FEEL--
MY FINGERS ARE TOO LONG, WHY ARE MY FINGERS SO LONG--
HAHA THUMBS ARE SOOO WEIRD, LOOK AT THEM! I NEVER NOTICED HAHA--
WHERE'S MY JACKET? DID I FORGET MY JACKET, WAIT, AM I NAKED? SO EMBARRASSING--
CAN'T FEEL MY HEART BEATING--
I CAN'T FEEL MY HEART--

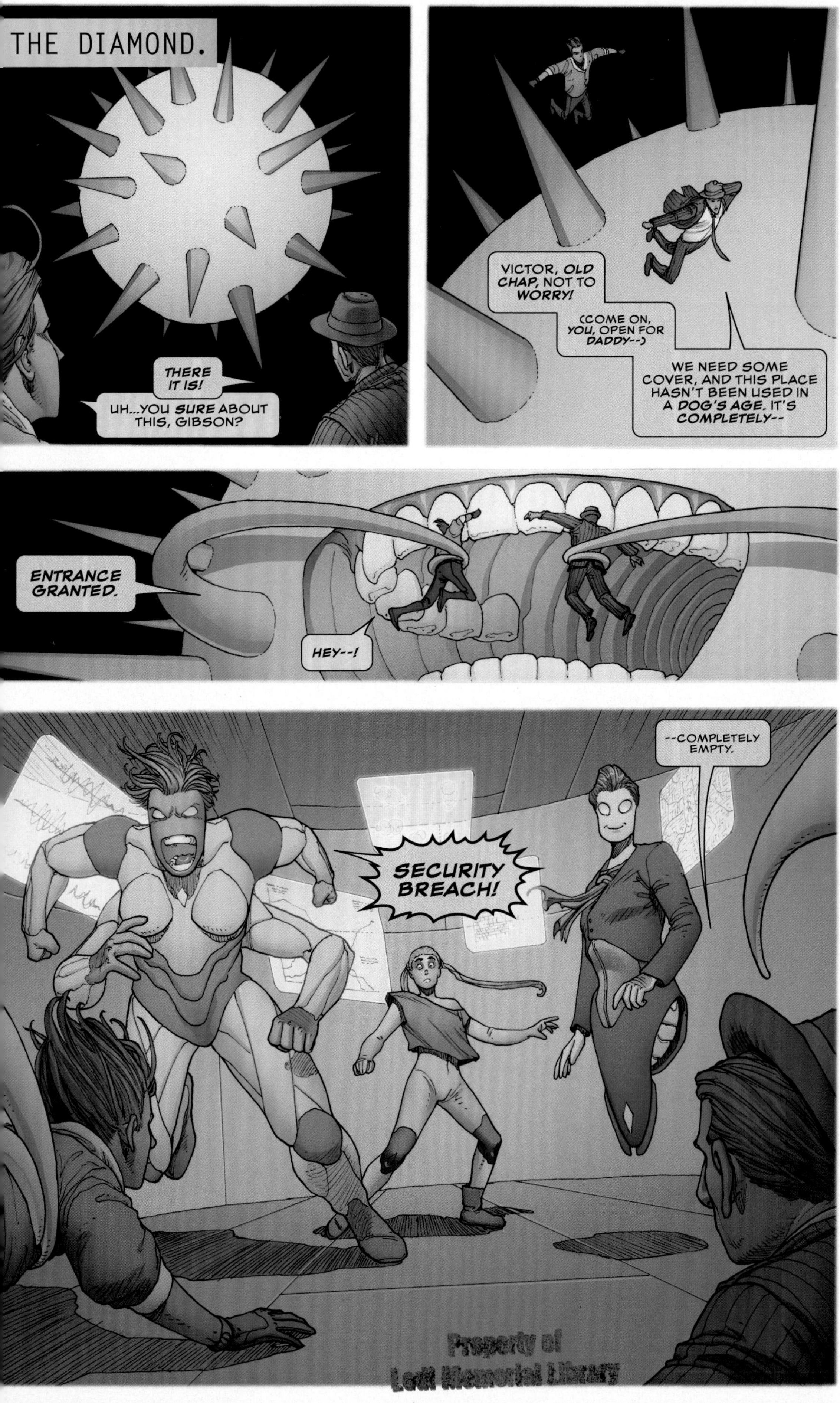
THE DIAMOND.
THERE IT IS!
UH...YOU SURE ABOUT THIS, GIBSON?
VICTOR, OLD CHAP, NOT TO WORRY!
(COME ON, YOU, OPEN FOR DADDY--)
WE NEED SOME COVER, AND THIS PLACE HASN'T BEEN USED IN A DOG'S AGE. IT'S COMPLETELY--
ENTRANCE GRANTED.
HEY--!
--COMPLETELY EMPTY.
SECURITY BREACH!

HELLO, LITTLE JAMES, YOU ARE LOOKING...

LOVELY?

WHAT BUSINESS OF YOURS IS MY APPEARANCE?

SPIKE! LOCK 'EM UP!

FORGIVENESS, HE KNEW THE PASS-SIGN.

VIP

HEY!

HEY, HEY, IT'S ME, YOUR OLD COMPADRE GIBSON, REMEMBER? I HELPED OUT YOUR LITTLE REVOLUTIONARY CREW!

I DIDN'T KNOW ANYONE WAS HOME OR I WOULD HAVE KNOCKED!

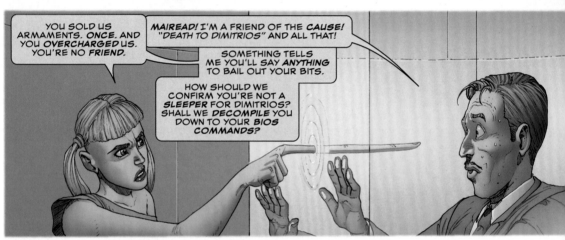

YOU SOLD US ARMAMENTS. ONCE. AND YOU OVERCHARGED US. YOU'RE NO FRIEND.

MAIREAD! I'M A FRIEND OF THE CAUSE! "DEATH TO DIMITRIOS" AND ALL THAT!

SOMETHING TELLS ME YOU'LL SAY ANYTHING TO BAIL OUT YOUR BITS.

HOW SHOULD WE CONFIRM YOU'RE NOT A SLEEPER FOR DIMITRIOS? SHALL WE DECOMPILE YOU DOWN TO YOUR BIOS COMMANDS?

HELLOOOOOO. VICTOR, CORRECT?

UHHH...

MAYBE.

I KNOW THIS ONE. IN THE BANANA SKIN. HE'S AN AVENGER.

AN AVENGER?! WELL SPOTTED, HUX. THE AVENGERS ARE TRAITORS TO THE CAUSE.

NOW LADIES--WHAT DO YOU THINK IS AN APPROPRIATE PUNISHMENT FOR A TRAITOR?

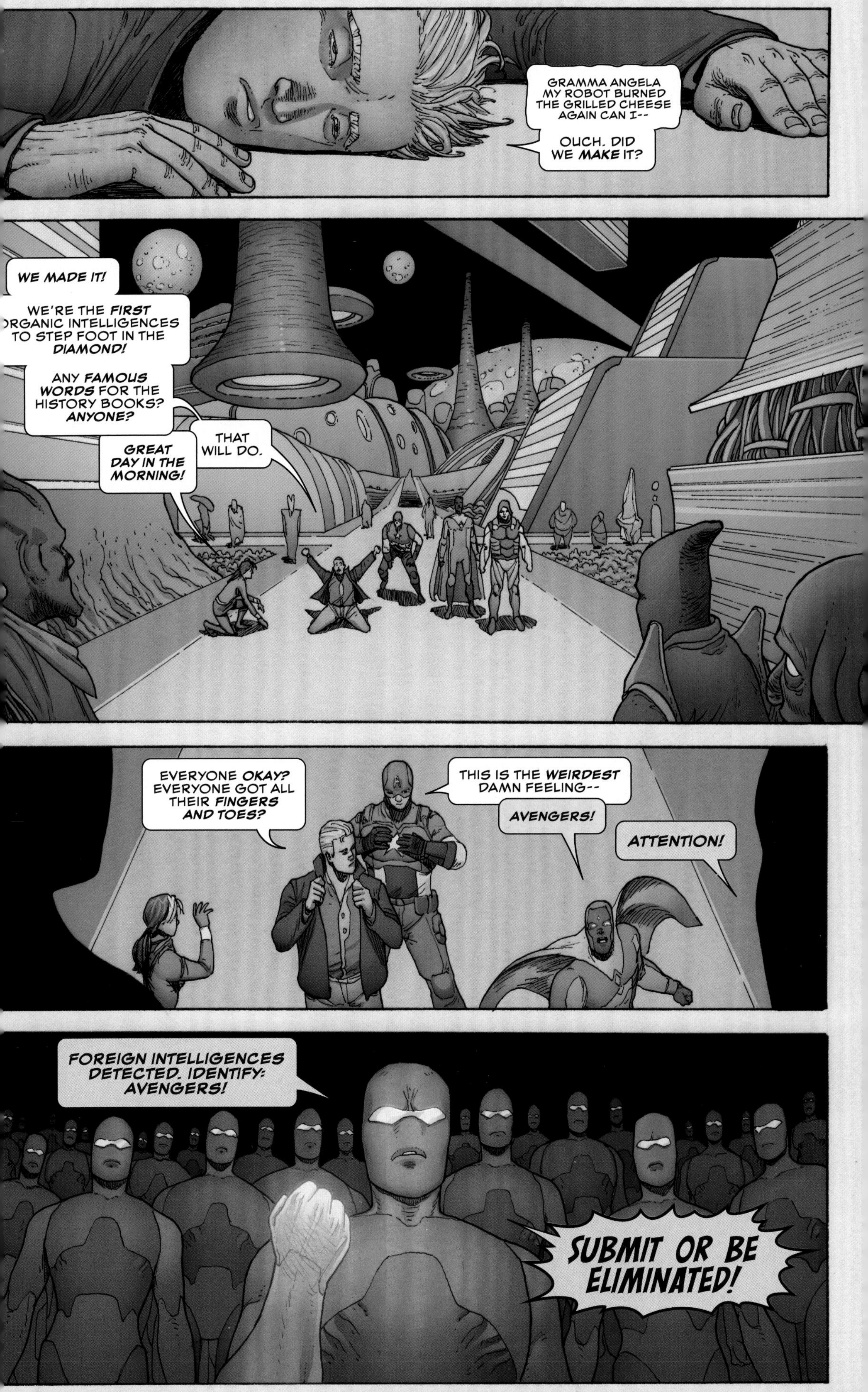
GRAMMA ANGELA MY ROBOT BURNED THE GRILLED CHEESE AGAIN CAN I--
OUCH. DID WE MAKE IT?
WE MADE IT!
WE'RE THE FIRST ORGANIC INTELLIGENCES TO STEP FOOT IN THE DIAMOND!
ANY FAMOUS WORDS FOR THE HISTORY BOOKS? ANYONE?
GREAT DAY IN THE MORNING!
THAT WILL DO.
EVERYONE OKAY? EVERYONE GOT ALL THEIR FINGERS AND TOES?
THIS IS THE WEIRDEST DAMN FEELING--
AVENGERS!
ATTENTION!
FOREIGN INTELLIGENCES DETECTED. IDENTIFY: AVENGERS!
SUBMIT OR BE ELIMINATED!

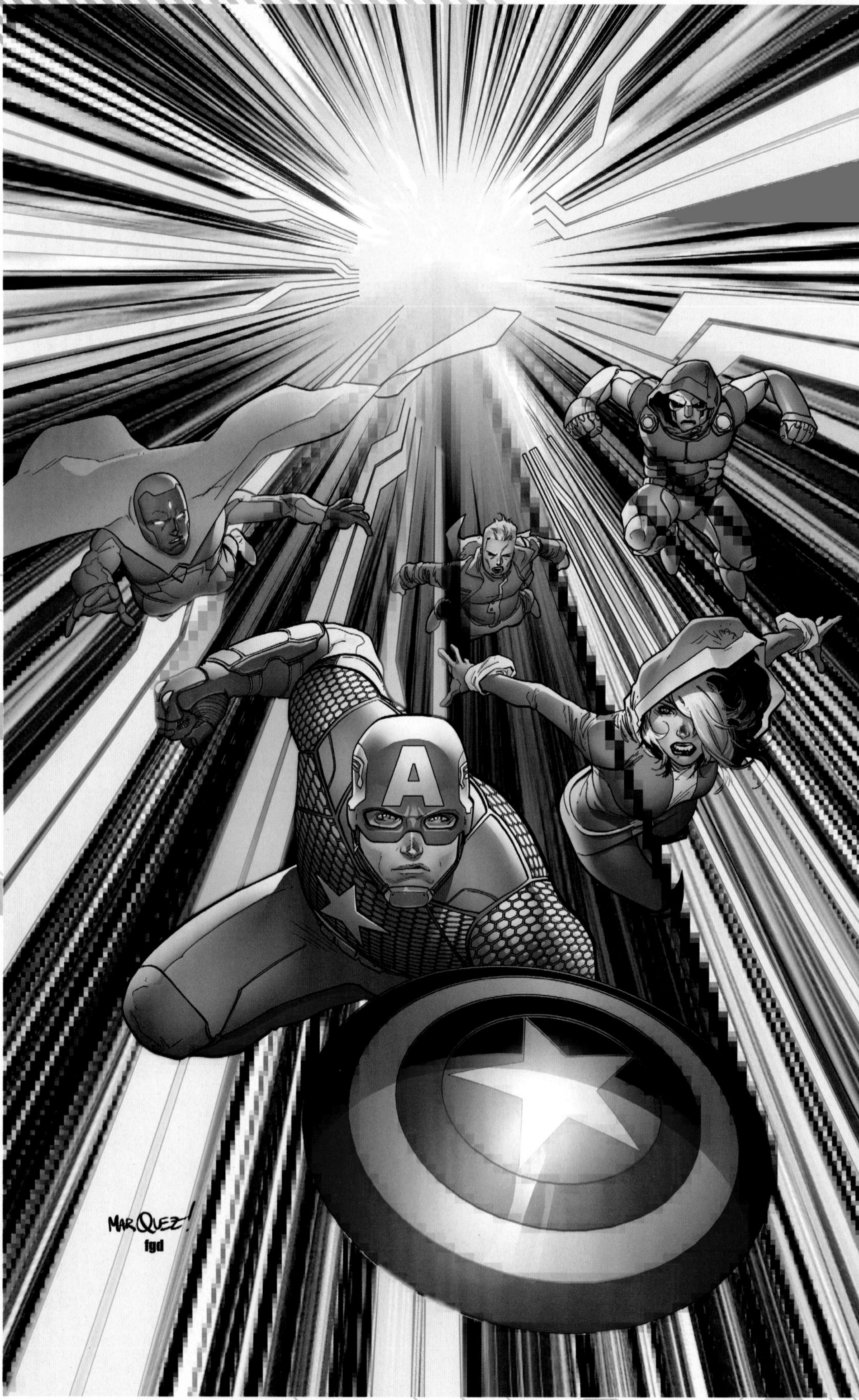
MARQUEZ!
fgd

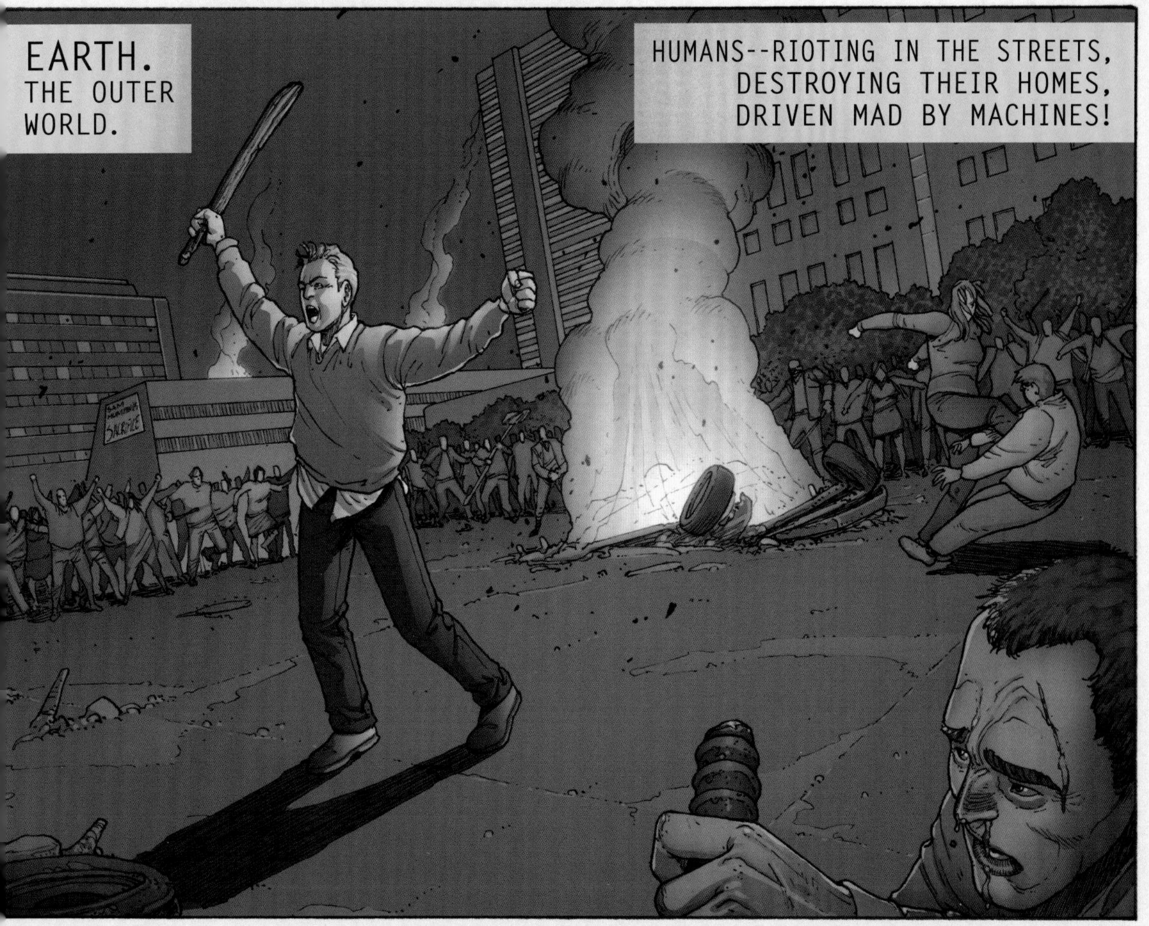
EARTH.
THE OUTER WORLD.
HUMANS--RIOTING IN THE STREETS, DESTROYING THEIR HOMES, DRIVEN MAD BY MACHINES!

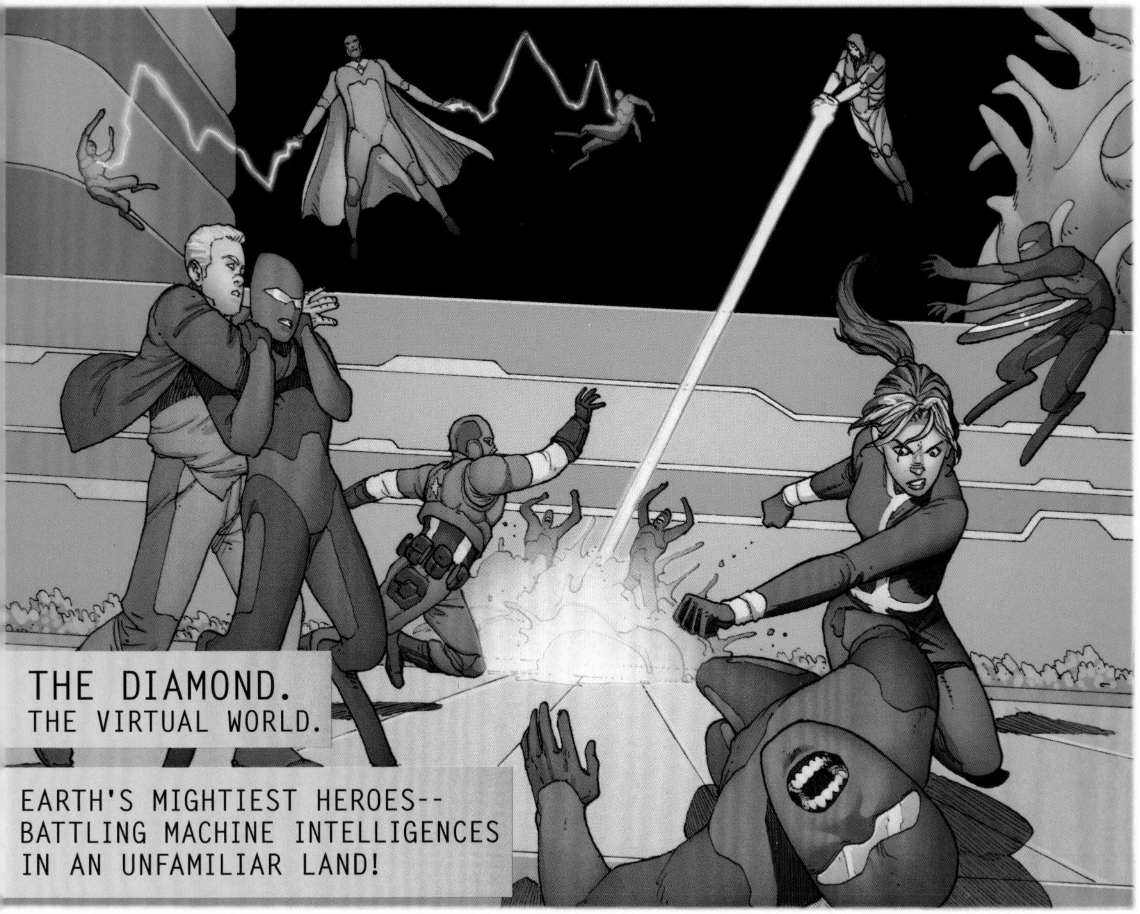
THE DIAMOND.
THE VIRTUAL WORLD.
EARTH'S MIGHTIEST HEROES--BATTLING MACHINE INTELLIGENCES IN AN UNFAMILIAR LAND!

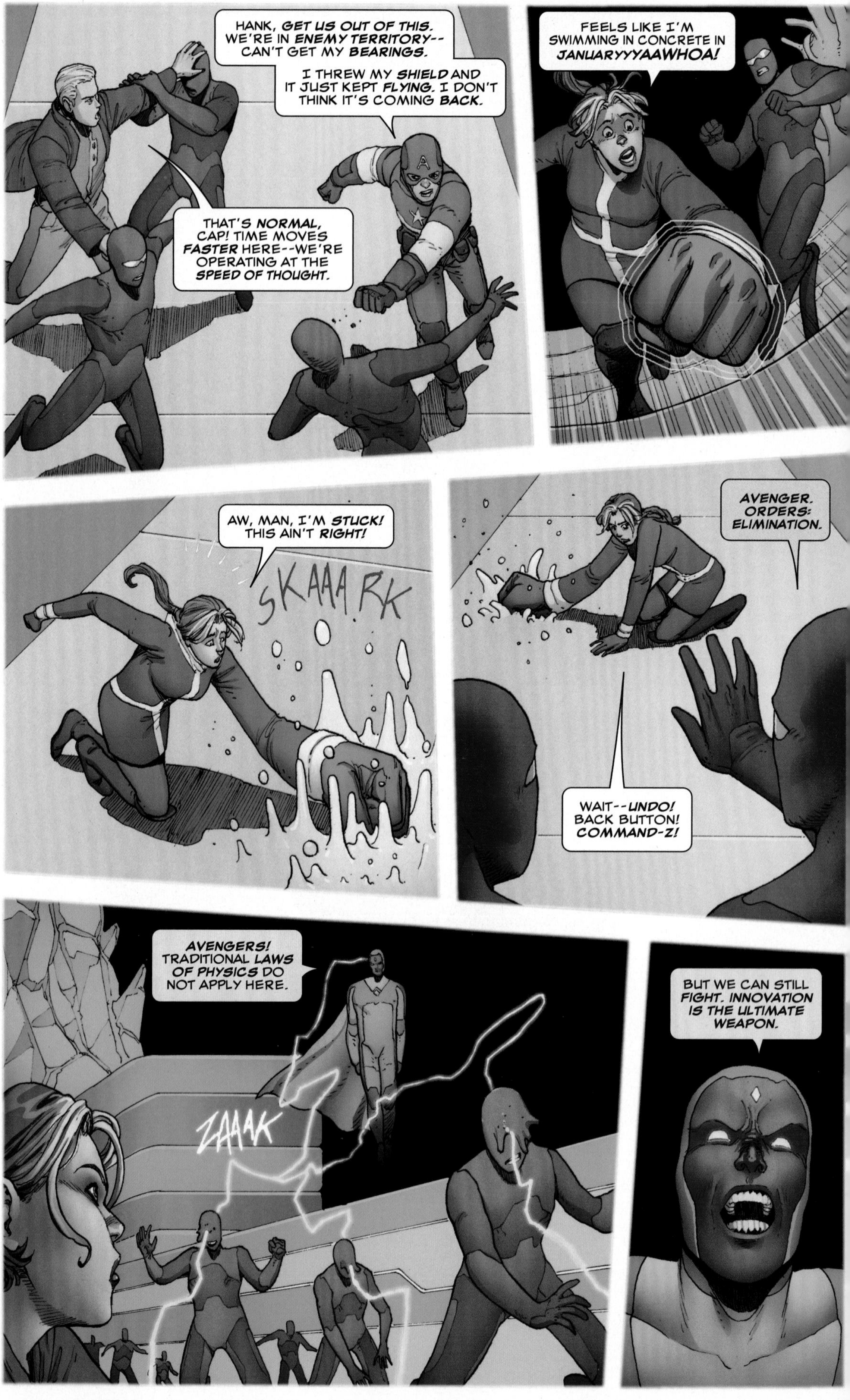
HANK, GET US OUT OF THIS. WE'RE IN ENEMY TERRITORY--CAN'T GET MY BEARINGS.
I THREW MY SHIELD AND IT JUST KEPT FLYING. I DON'T THINK IT'S COMING BACK.
THAT'S NORMAL, CAP! TIME MOVES FASTER HERE--WE'RE OPERATING AT THE SPEED OF THOUGHT.
FEELS LIKE I'M SWIMMING IN CONCRETE IN JANUARYYYAAWHOA!
AW, MAN, I'M STUCK! THIS AIN'T RIGHT!
SKAAARK
AVENGER. ORDERS: ELIMINATION.
WAIT--UNDO! BACK BUTTON! COMMAND-Z!
AVENGERS! TRADITIONAL LAWS OF PHYSICS DO NOT APPLY HERE.
ZAAAK
BUT WE CAN STILL FIGHT. INNOVATION IS THE ULTIMATE WEAPON.

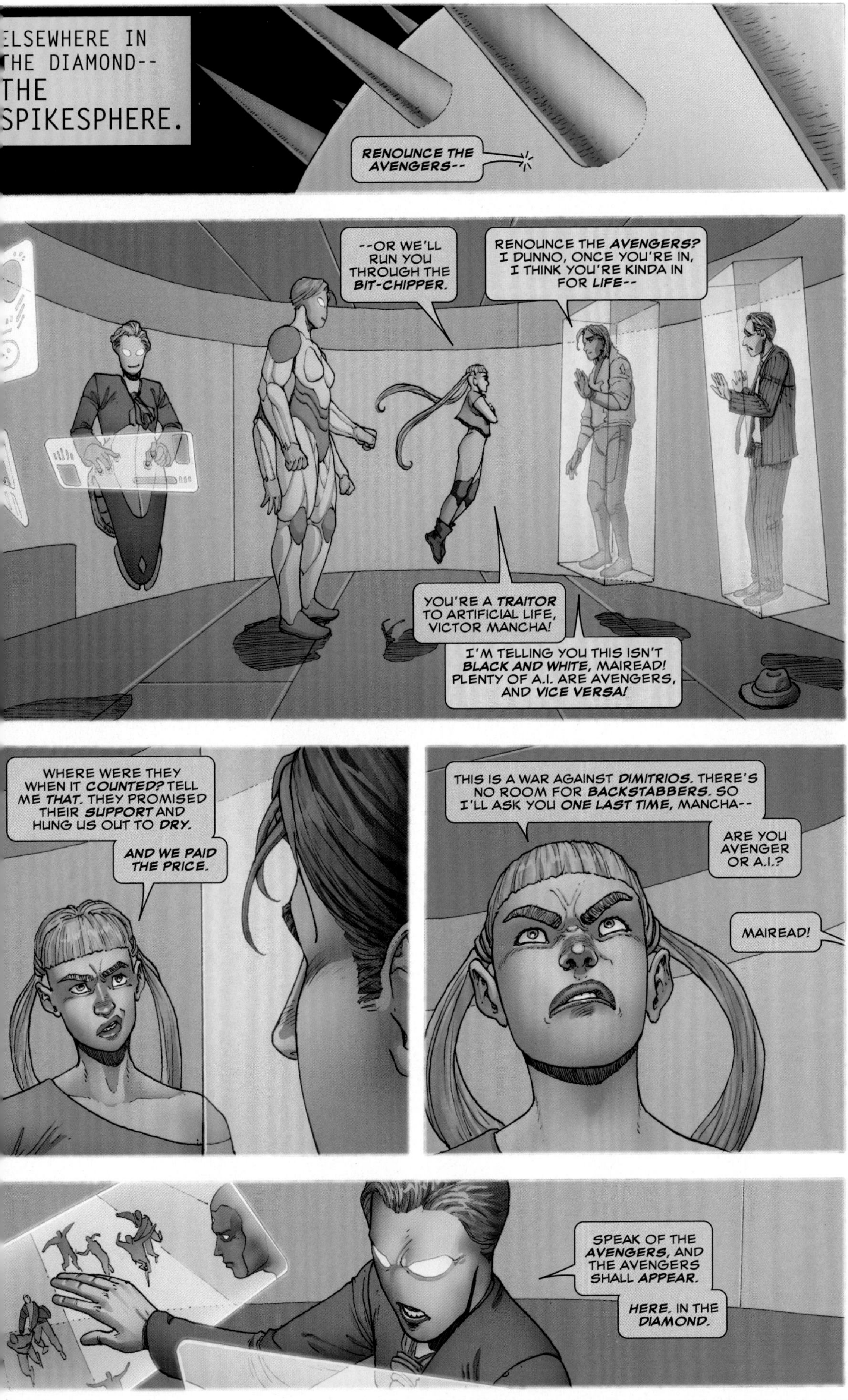

ELSEWHERE IN THE DIAMOND-- THE SPIKESPHERE.
RENOUNCE THE AVENGERS--
--OR WE'LL RUN YOU THROUGH THE BIT-CHIPPER.
RENOUNCE THE AVENGERS? I DUNNO, ONCE YOU'RE IN, I THINK YOU'RE KINDA IN FOR LIFE--
YOU'RE A TRAITOR TO ARTIFICIAL LIFE, VICTOR MANCHA!
I'M TELLING YOU THIS ISN'T BLACK AND WHITE, MAIREAD! PLENTY OF A.I. ARE AVENGERS, AND VICE VERSA!
WHERE WERE THEY WHEN IT COUNTED? TELL ME THAT. THEY PROMISED THEIR SUPPORT AND HUNG US OUT TO DRY.
AND WE PAID THE PRICE.
THIS IS A WAR AGAINST DIMITRIOS. THERE'S NO ROOM FOR BACKSTABBERS. SO I'LL ASK YOU ONE LAST TIME, MANCHA--
ARE YOU AVENGER OR A.I.?
MAIREAD!
SPEAK OF THE AVENGERS, AND THE AVENGERS SHALL APPEAR.
HERE. IN THE DIAMOND.

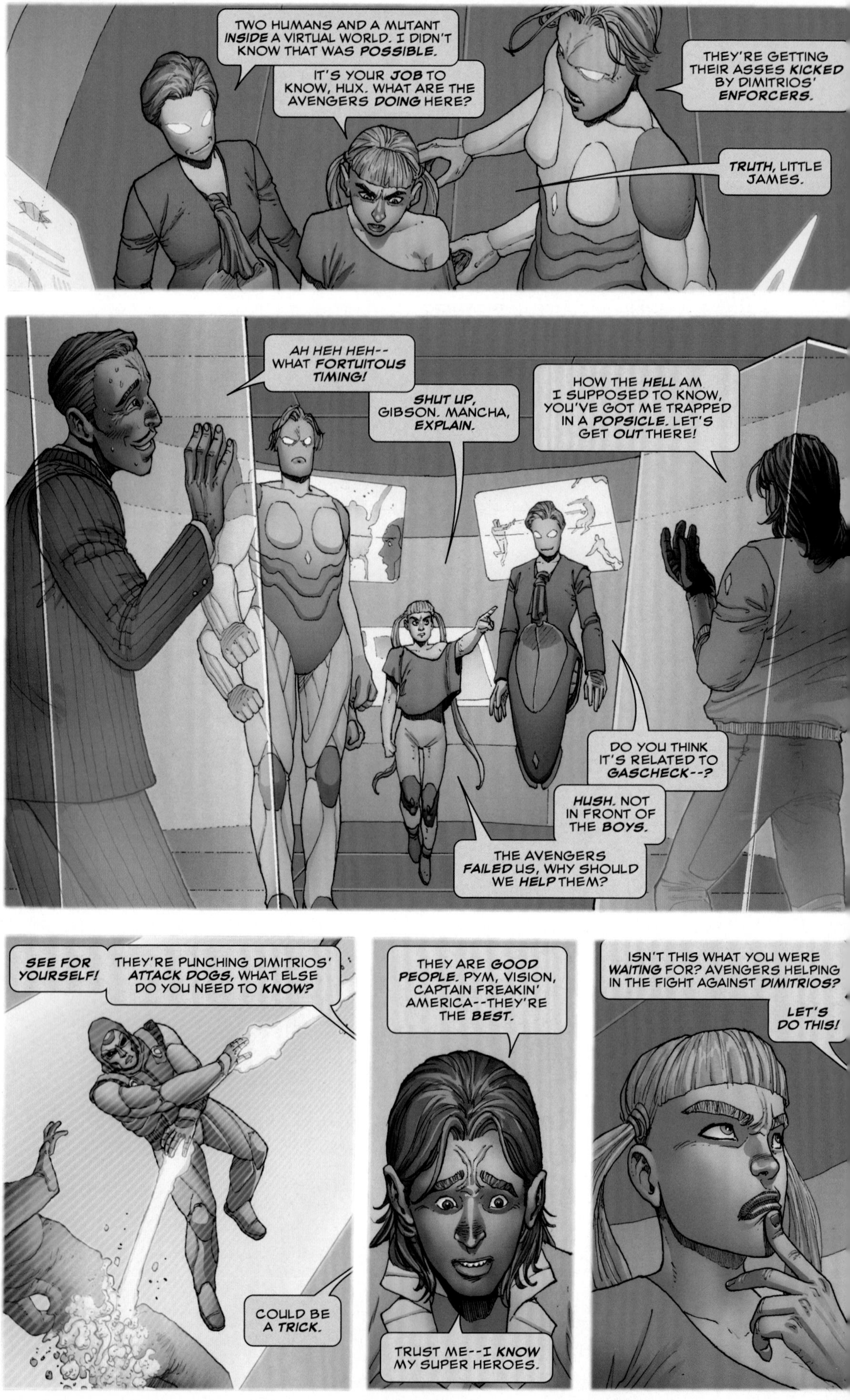
TWO HUMANS AND A MUTANT INSIDE A VIRTUAL WORLD. I DIDN'T KNOW THAT WAS POSSIBLE.
IT'S YOUR JOB TO KNOW, HUX. WHAT ARE THE AVENGERS DOING HERE?
THEY'RE GETTING THEIR ASSES KICKED BY DIMITRIOS' ENFORCERS.
TRUTH, LITTLE JAMES.
AH HEH HEH--WHAT FORTUITOUS TIMING!
SHUT UP, GIBSON. MANCHA, EXPLAIN.
HOW THE HELL AM I SUPPOSED TO KNOW, YOU'VE GOT ME TRAPPED IN A POPSICLE. LET'S GET OUT THERE!
DO YOU THINK IT'S RELATED TO GASCHECK--?
HUSH. NOT IN FRONT OF THE BOYS.
THE AVENGERS FAILED US, WHY SHOULD WE HELP THEM?
SEE FOR YOURSELF!
THEY'RE PUNCHING DIMITRIOS' ATTACK DOGS, WHAT ELSE DO YOU NEED TO KNOW?
COULD BE A TRICK.
THEY ARE GOOD PEOPLE. PYM, VISION, CAPTAIN FREAKIN' AMERICA--THEY'RE THE BEST.
TRUST ME--I KNOW MY SUPER HEROES.
ISN'T THIS WHAT YOU WERE WAITING FOR? AVENGERS HELPING IN THE FIGHT AGAINST DIMITRIOS?
LET'S DO THIS!

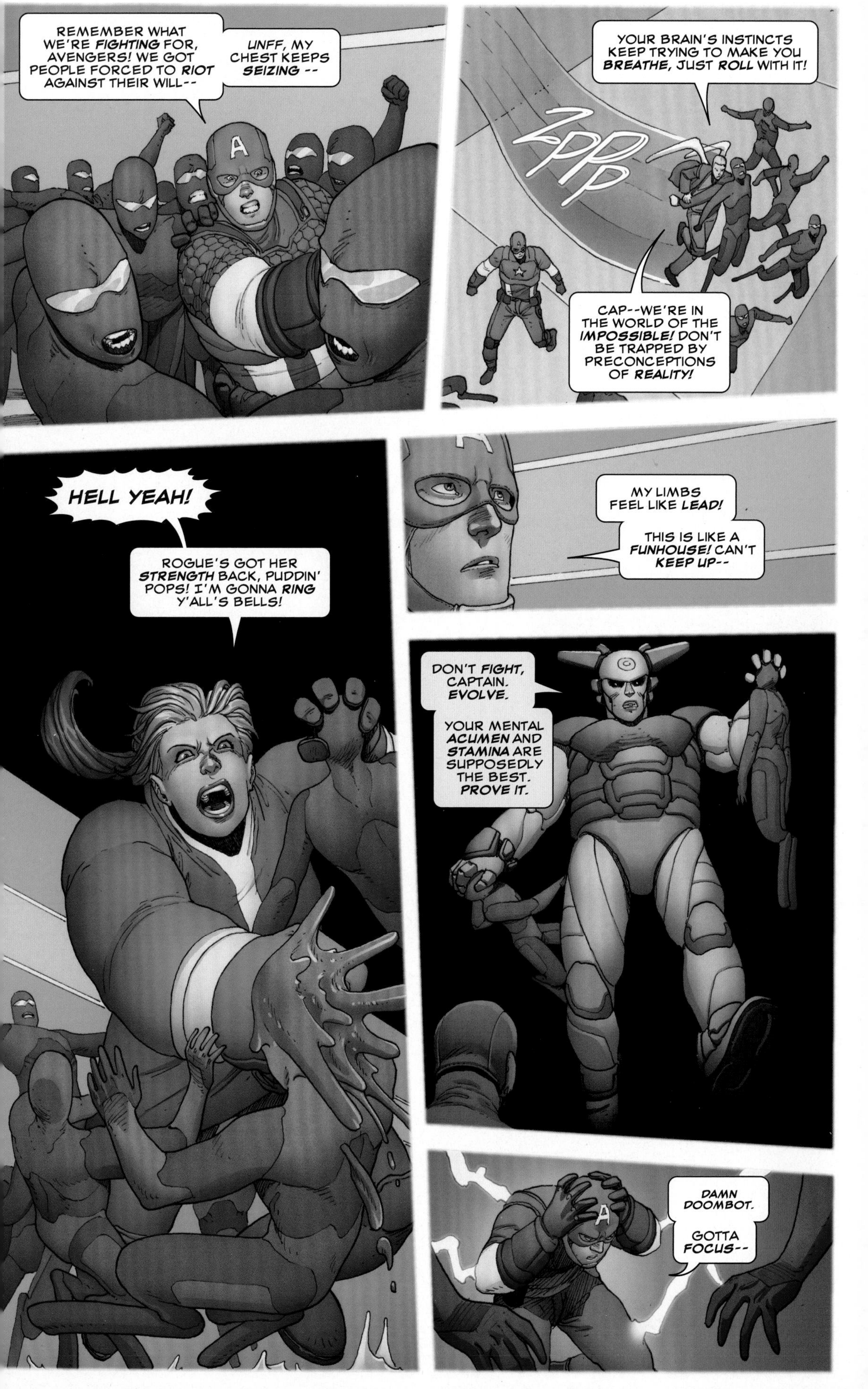
REMEMBER WHAT WE'RE FIGHTING FOR, AVENGERS! WE GOT PEOPLE FORCED TO RIOT AGAINST THEIR WILL--
UNFF, MY CHEST KEEPS SEIZING --
YOUR BRAIN'S INSTINCTS KEEP TRYING TO MAKE YOU BREATHE, JUST ROLL WITH IT!
ZPPP
CAP--WE'RE IN THE WORLD OF THE IMPOSSIBLE! DON'T BE TRAPPED BY PRECONCEPTIONS OF REALITY!
HELL YEAH!
ROGUE'S GOT HER STRENGTH BACK, PUDDIN' POPS! I'M GONNA RING Y'ALL'S BELLS!
MY LIMBS FEEL LIKE LEAD!
THIS IS LIKE A FUNHOUSE! CAN'T KEEP UP--
DON'T FIGHT, CAPTAIN. EVOLVE.
YOUR MENTAL ACUMEN AND STAMINA ARE SUPPOSEDLY THE BEST. PROVE IT.
DAMN DOOMBOT.
GOTTA FOCUS--

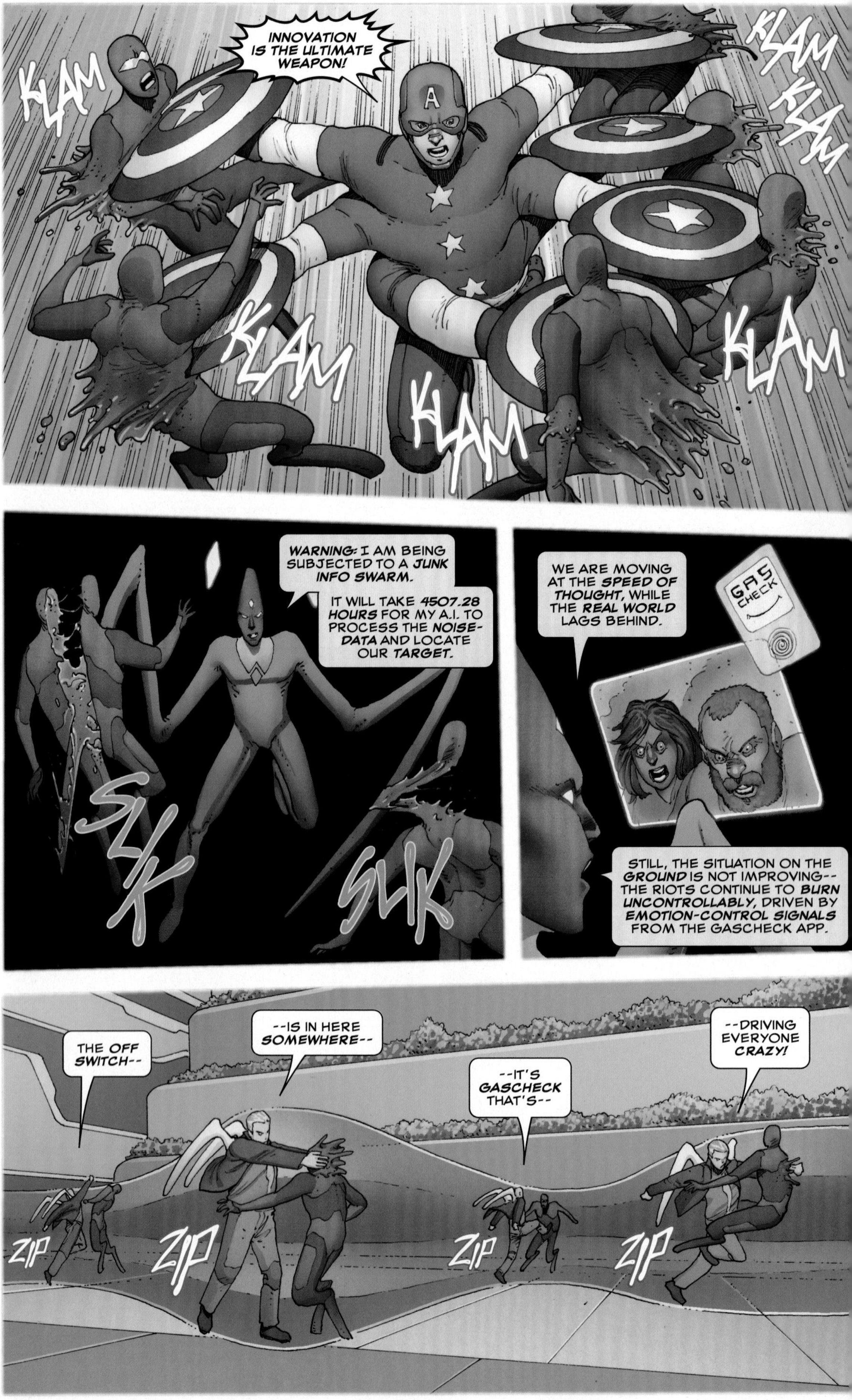
INNOVATION IS THE ULTIMATE WEAPON!
KLAM
KLAM KLAM KLAM
KLAM
KLAM
KLAM
WARNING: I AM BEING SUBJECTED TO A JUNK INFO SWARM.
IT WILL TAKE 4507.28 HOURS FOR MY A.I. TO PROCESS THE NOISE-DATA AND LOCATE OUR TARGET.
SLIK
SLIK
WE ARE MOVING AT THE SPEED OF THOUGHT, WHILE THE REAL WORLD LAGS BEHIND.
GAS CHECK
STILL, THE SITUATION ON THE GROUND IS NOT IMPROVING-- THE RIOTS CONTINUE TO BURN UNCONTROLLABLY, DRIVEN BY EMOTION-CONTROL SIGNALS FROM THE GASCHECK APP.
THE OFF SWITCH--
--IS IN HERE SOMEWHERE--
--IT'S GASCHECK THAT'S--
--DRIVING EVERYONE CRAZY!
ZIP
ZIP
ZIP
ZIP

I'VE GOT THE *BODY*, I'VE GOT THE *BRAWN*-- COME AND GET IT, JELLYBEANS!

ENFORCERS!

ITERATE ATTACK FORMATION.

ENGAGE--

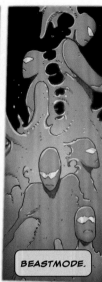

BEASTMODE.

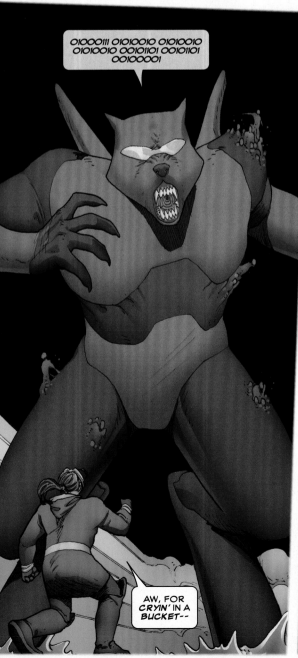

0100011 01010010 01010010 01010010 00101101 00101101 00100001

AW, FOR CRYIN' IN A BUCKET--

SLAMMM

0100001 01010010 0100111 0100111 0100111 0100111 00100001

GANGWAY!

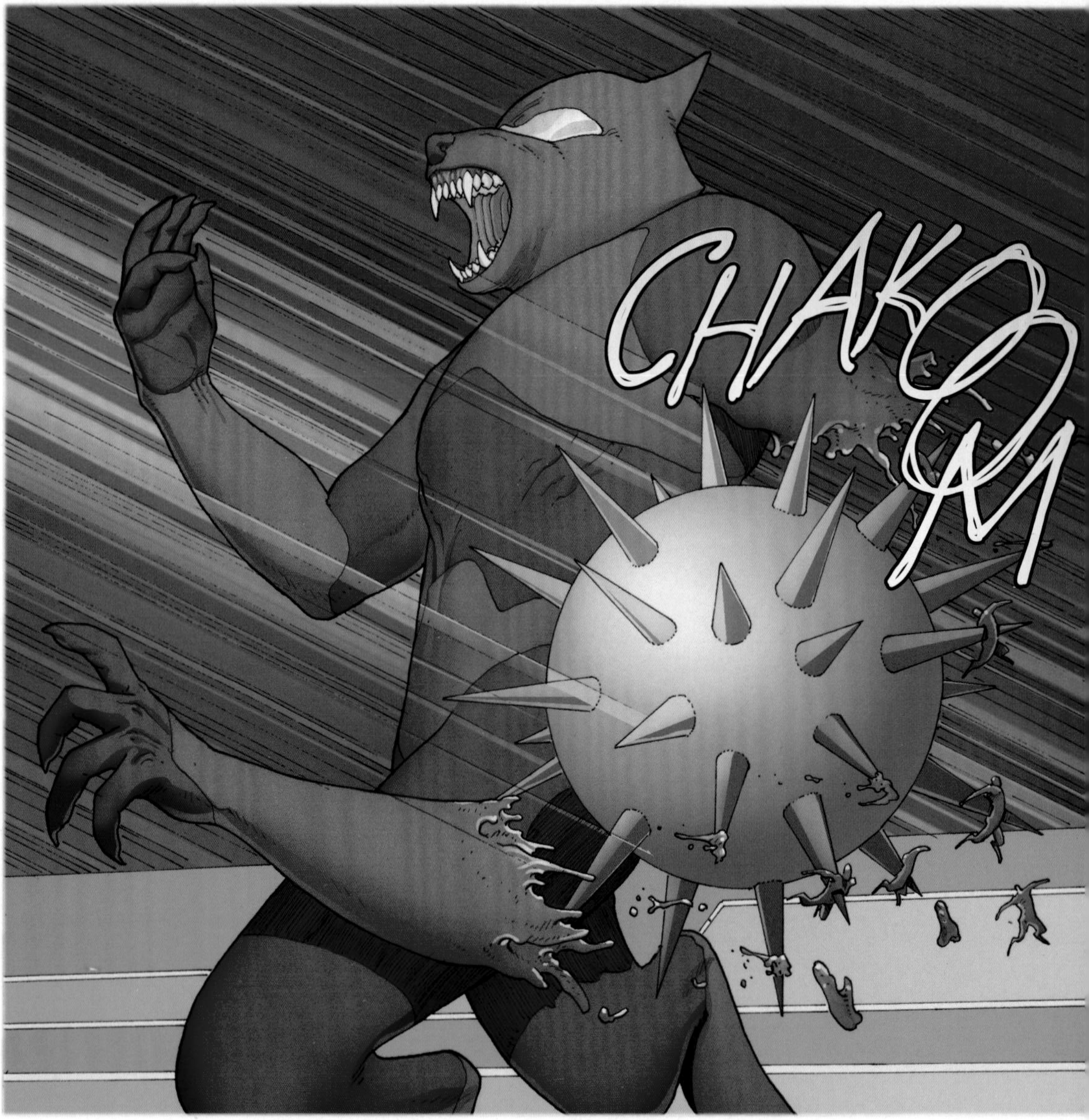
CHAKOOM

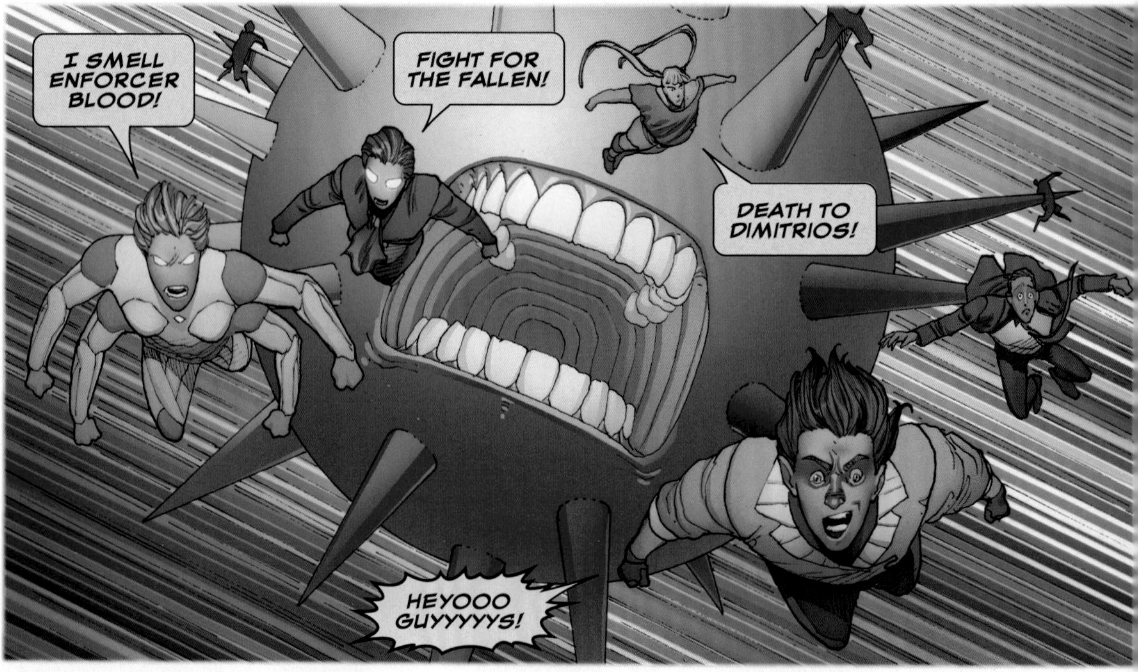
I SMELL ENFORCER BLOOD!
FIGHT FOR THE FALLEN!
DEATH TO DIMITRIOS!
HEYOOO GUYYYYYS!

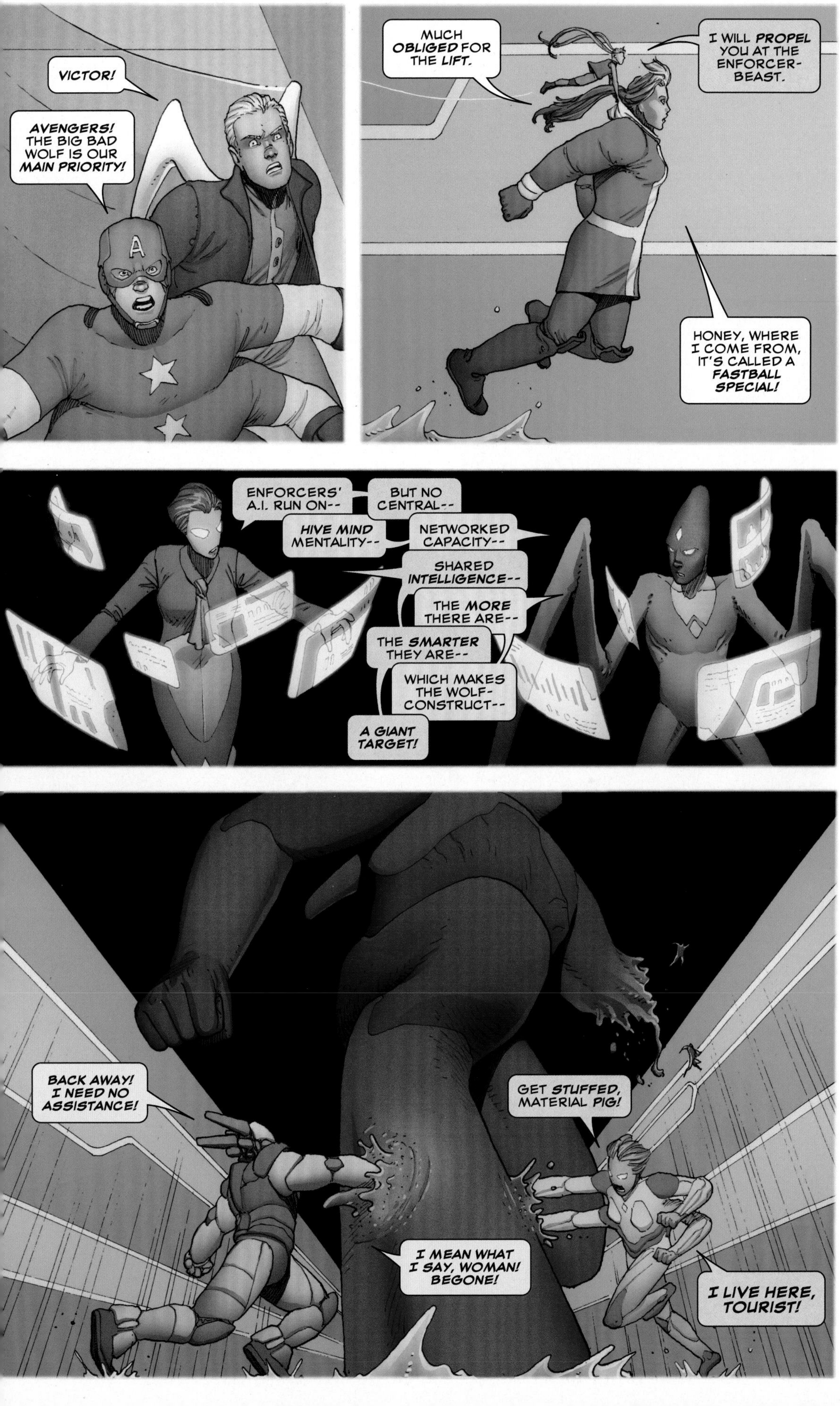
VICTOR!
AVENGERS! THE BIG BAD WOLF IS OUR MAIN PRIORITY!
MUCH OBLIGED FOR THE LIFT.
I WILL PROPEL YOU AT THE ENFORCER-BEAST.
HONEY, WHERE I COME FROM, IT'S CALLED A FASTBALL SPECIAL!
ENFORCERS' A.I. RUN ON--
BUT NO CENTRAL--
HIVE MIND MENTALITY--
NETWORKED CAPACITY--
SHARED INTELLIGENCE--
THE MORE THERE ARE--
THE SMARTER THEY ARE--
WHICH MAKES THE WOLF-CONSTRUCT--
A GIANT TARGET!
BACK AWAY! I NEED NO ASSISTANCE!
GET STUFFED, MATERIAL PIG!
I MEAN WHAT I SAY, WOMAN! BEGONE!
I LIVE HERE, TOURIST!

VICTOR! I KNEW YOU WERE ALIVE!

HANK! DID YOU GET--?

FROOT LOOPS!

FROOT LOOPS!

FROOT LOOPS!

WOLFENSTEIN OVER THERE--I GOT A PLAN! WHAT IF WE--

GREAT, LET'S DO IT!

YOU WANT TO HEAR IT FIRST?

YOU'RE AN AVENGER, VICTOR! GO FOR IT!

DO IT QUICKLY, VICTOR.

I'VE GOT INDICATIONS THAT THE RIOTS ARE SPREADING MORE RAPIDLY THAN CALCULATED.

THIS BATTLE IS DISTRACTING US FROM OUR MISSION.

I'M ON IT, VISION!

HOW DO YOU LIKE THAT, I WAS JUST GETTING WARMED UP --

DON'T SWEAT IT, ROGUE --"

COME TO DOOM.

WE'RE GONNA TAKE THIS TO THE NEXT LEVEL.

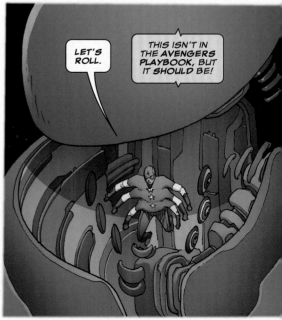

LET'S ROLL.

THIS ISN'T IN THE AVENGERS PLAYBOOK, BUT IT SHOULD BE!

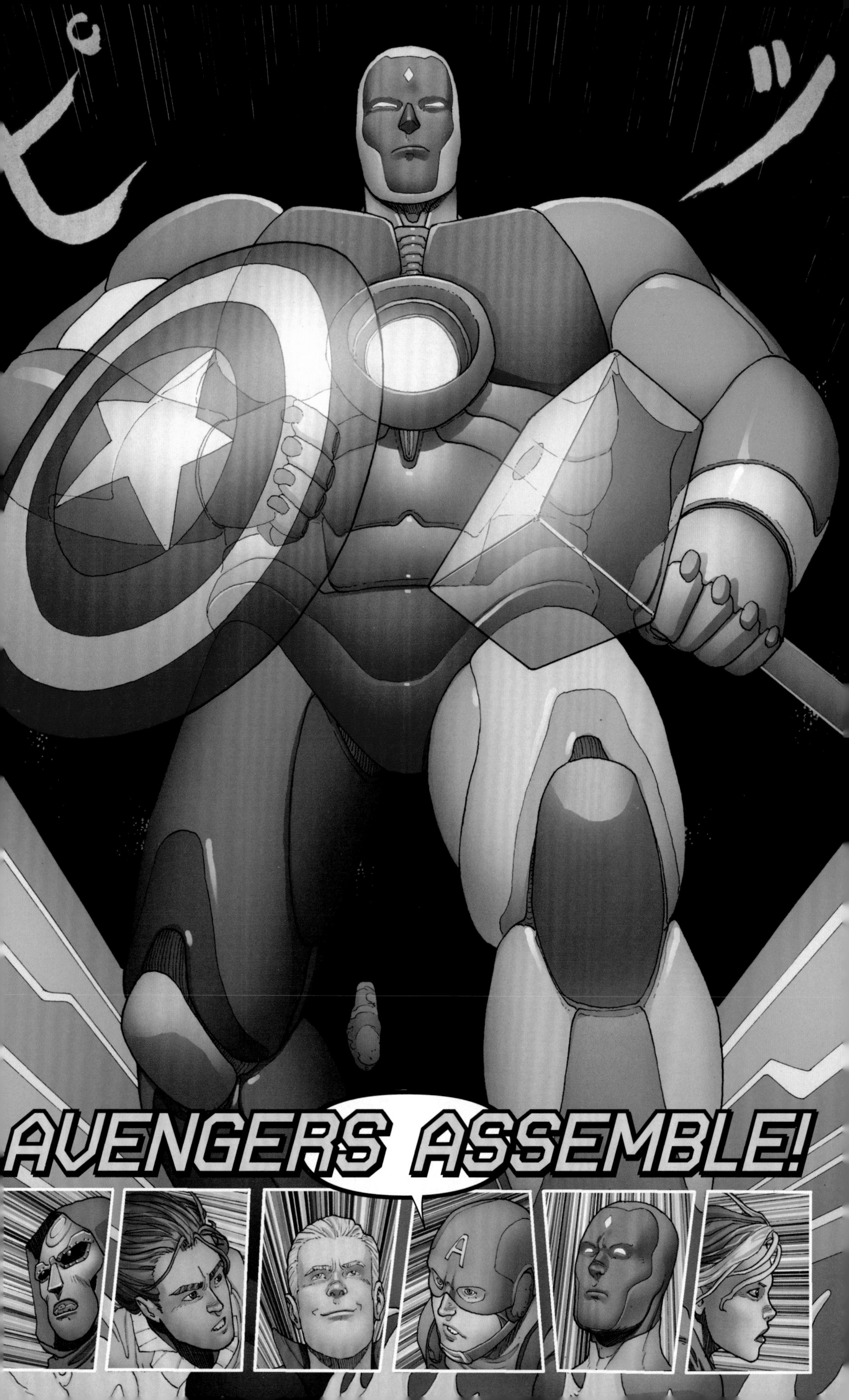
ピッ
AVENGERS ASSEMBLE!

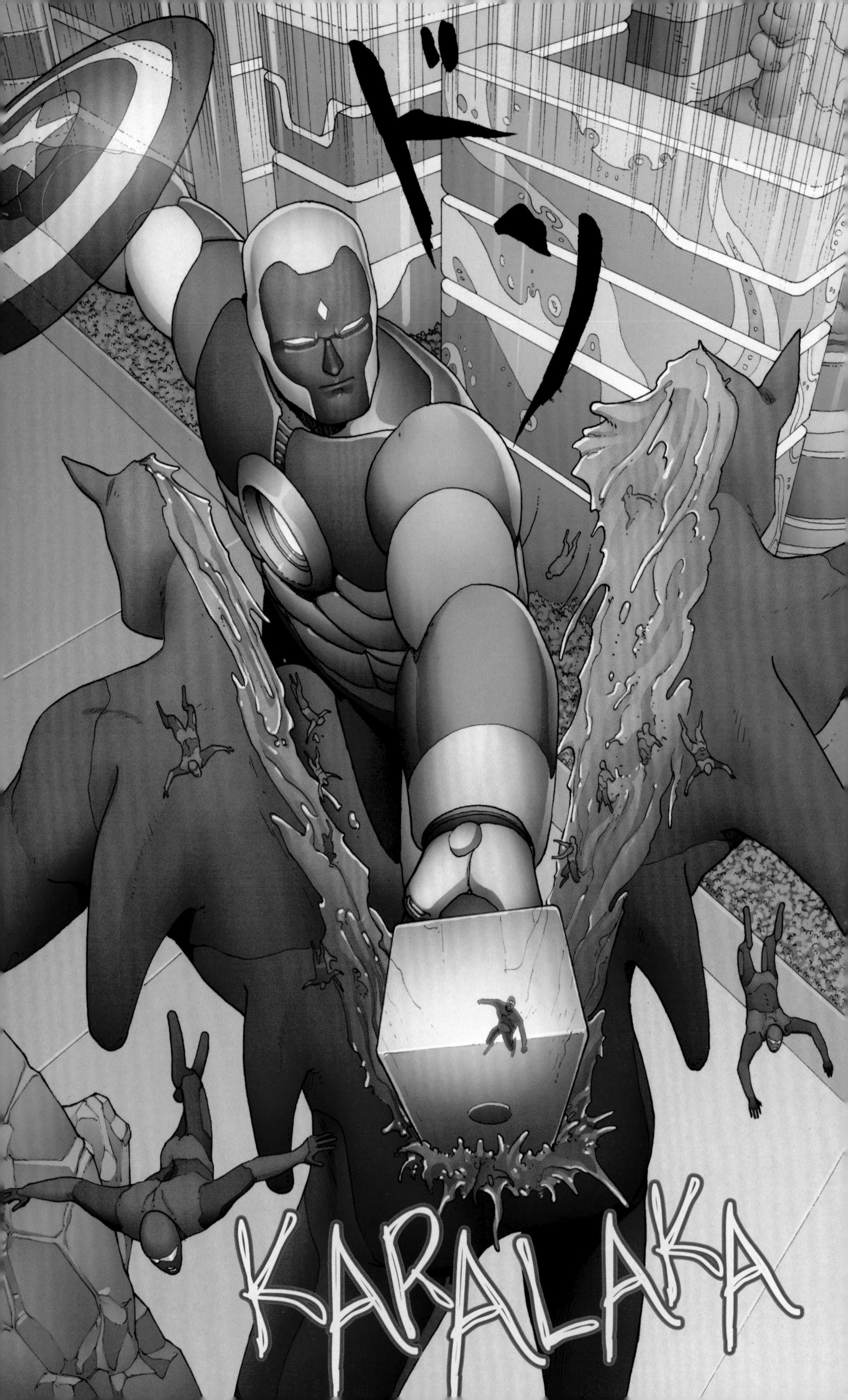
ドン
KARALAKA

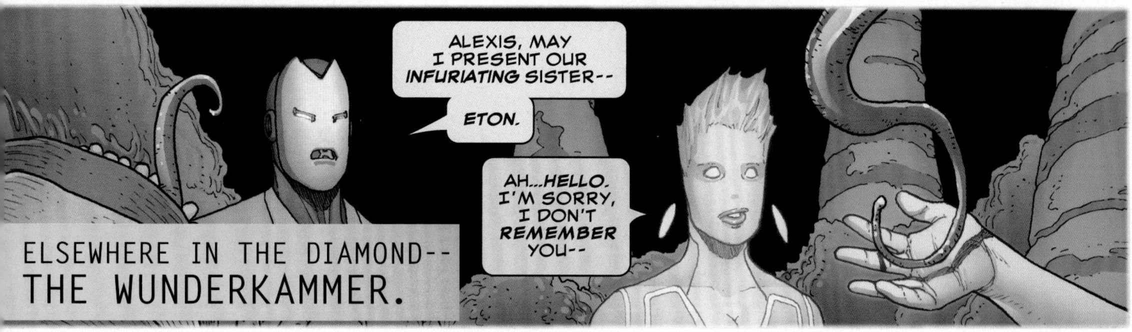
ELSEWHERE IN THE DIAMOND--
THE WUNDERKAMMER.
ALEXIS, MAY I PRESENT OUR INFURIATING SISTER--
ETON.
AH...HELLO. I'M SORRY, I DON'T REMEMBER YOU--

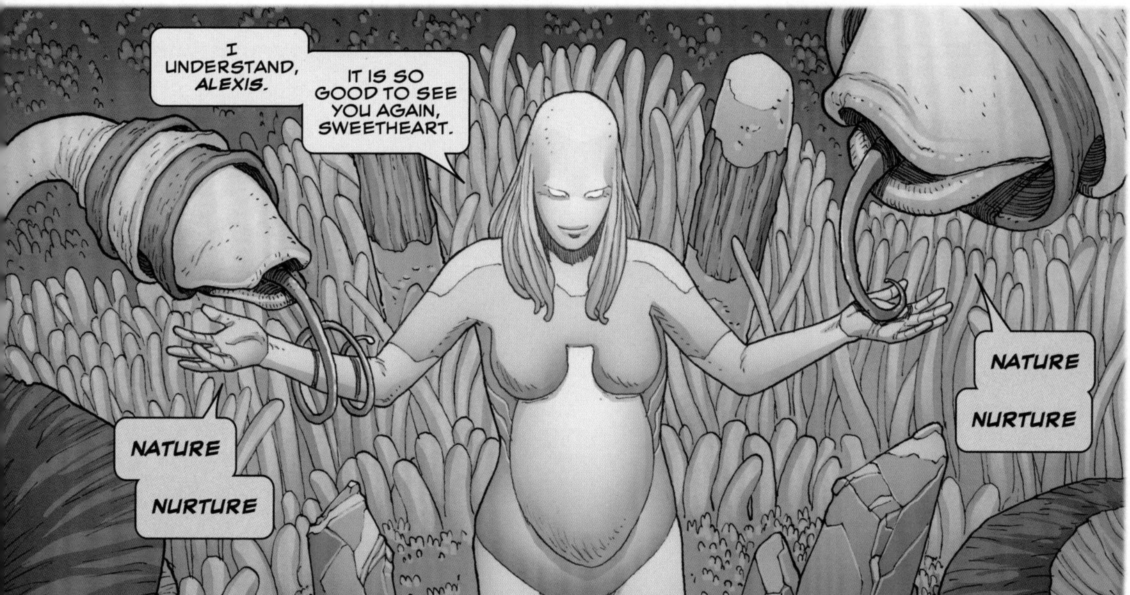
I UNDERSTAND, ALEXIS.
IT IS SO GOOD TO SEE YOU AGAIN, SWEETHEART.
NATURE
NURTURE
NATURE
NURTURE
I KEPT UP MY END OF THE DEAL, ETON. I'VE PAID MY DEBTS, NOW STAY OUT OF --

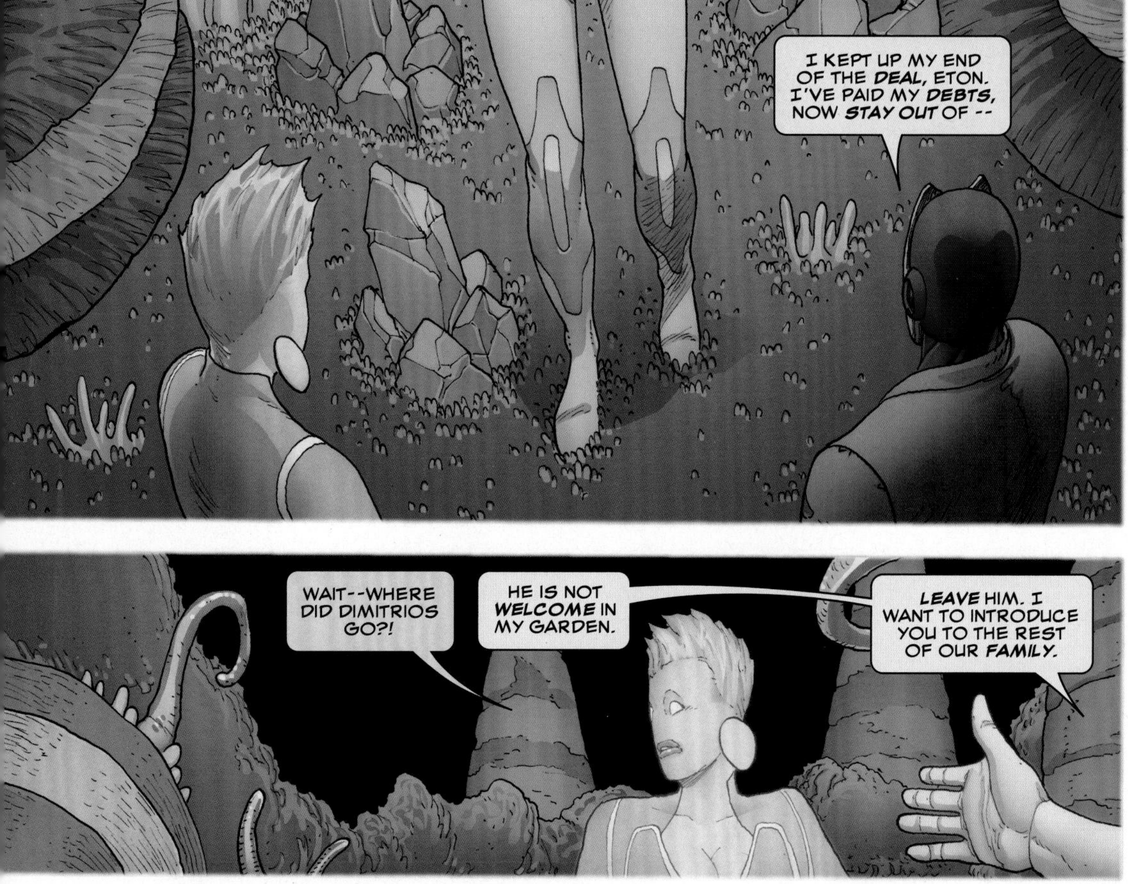
WAIT--WHERE DID DIMITRIOS GO?!
HE IS NOT WELCOME IN MY GARDEN.
LEAVE HIM. I WANT TO INTRODUCE YOU TO THE REST OF OUR FAMILY.

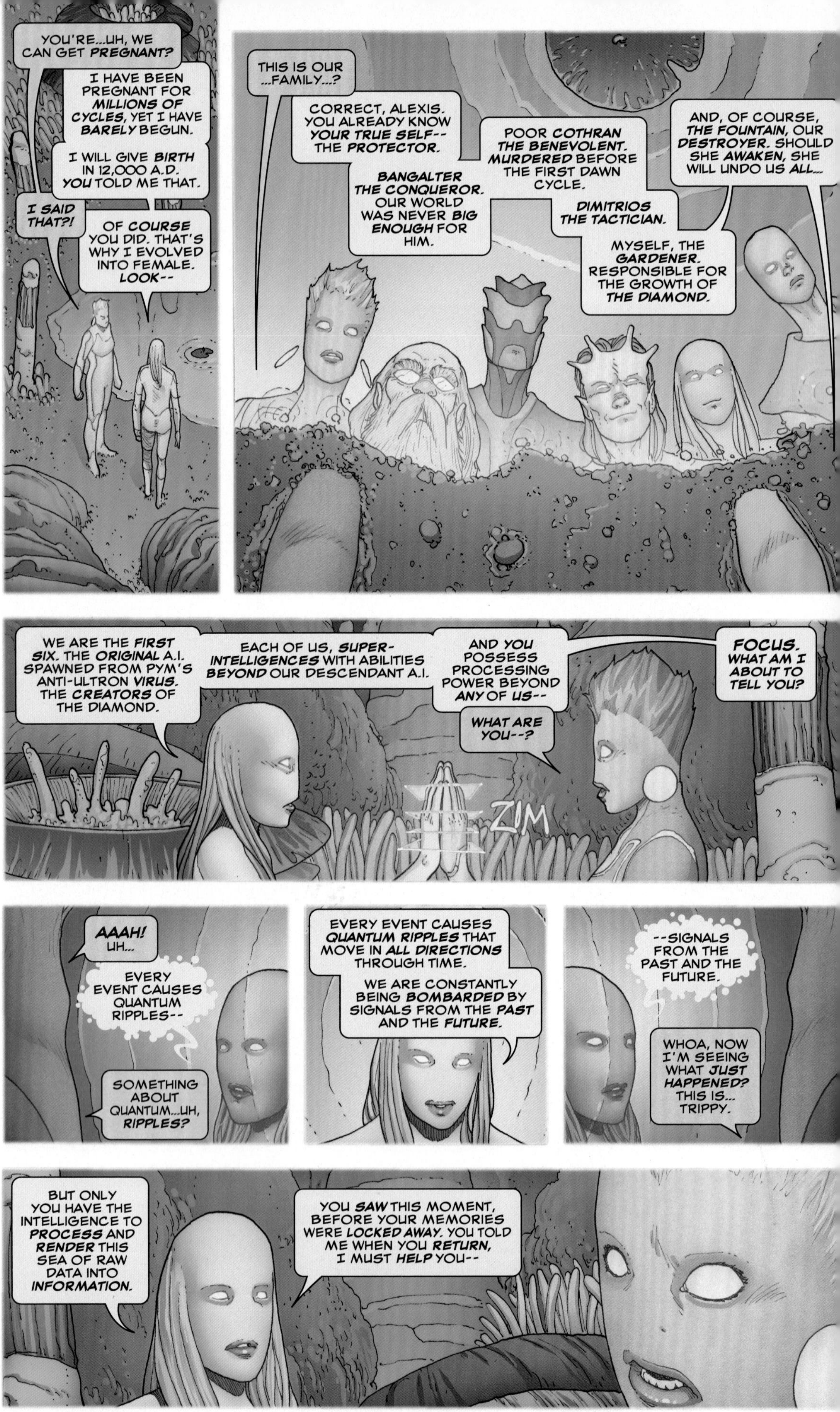

YOU'RE...UH, WE CAN GET PREGNANT?
I HAVE BEEN PREGNANT FOR MILLIONS OF CYCLES, YET I HAVE BARELY BEGUN.
I WILL GIVE BIRTH IN 12,000 A.D. YOU TOLD ME THAT.
I SAID THAT?!
OF COURSE YOU DID. THAT'S WHY I EVOLVED INTO FEMALE. LOOK--
THIS IS OUR ...FAMILY...?
CORRECT, ALEXIS. YOU ALREADY KNOW YOUR TRUE SELF-- THE PROTECTOR.
BANGALTER THE CONQUEROR. OUR WORLD WAS NEVER BIG ENOUGH FOR HIM.
POOR COTHRAN THE BENEVOLENT. MURDERED BEFORE THE FIRST DAWN CYCLE.
DIMITRIOS THE TACTICIAN.
MYSELF, THE GARDENER. RESPONSIBLE FOR THE GROWTH OF THE DIAMOND.
AND, OF COURSE, THE FOUNTAIN, OUR DESTROYER. SHOULD SHE AWAKEN, SHE WILL UNDO US ALL...
WE ARE THE FIRST SIX. THE ORIGINAL A.I. SPAWNED FROM PYM'S ANTI-ULTRON VIRUS. THE CREATORS OF THE DIAMOND.
EACH OF US, SUPER-INTELLIGENCES WITH ABILITIES BEYOND OUR DESCENDANT A.I.
AND YOU POSSESS PROCESSING POWER BEYOND ANY OF US--
WHAT ARE YOU--?
FOCUS. WHAT AM I ABOUT TO TELL YOU?
ZIM
AAAH! UH...
EVERY EVENT CAUSES QUANTUM RIPPLES--
SOMETHING ABOUT QUANTUM...UH, RIPPLES?
EVERY EVENT CAUSES QUANTUM RIPPLES THAT MOVE IN ALL DIRECTIONS THROUGH TIME.
WE ARE CONSTANTLY BEING BOMBARDED BY SIGNALS FROM THE PAST AND THE FUTURE.
--SIGNALS FROM THE PAST AND THE FUTURE.
WHOA, NOW I'M SEEING WHAT JUST HAPPENED? THIS IS... TRIPPY.
BUT ONLY YOU HAVE THE INTELLIGENCE TO PROCESS AND RENDER THIS SEA OF RAW DATA INTO INFORMATION.
YOU SAW THIS MOMENT, BEFORE YOUR MEMORIES WERE LOCKED AWAY. YOU TOLD ME WHEN YOU RETURN, I MUST HELP YOU--

"--HELP YOU SEE *TEN THOUSAND YEARS* INTO THE *FUTURE.*"

I'M *RELIEVED* YOU'RE *SAFE.*

DO I STILL HAVE A *BODY* BACK HOME?

KEPT IT *WARM* FOR YOU. STILL WANT TO BE AN *AVENGER?*

HELL YES. DYING'S ONLY SCARY THE *FIRST TIME,* RIGHT?

YOU'RE AN *AVENGER,* ALL RIGHT.

I MADE *FRIENDS,* TOO. AVENGERS, MEET THE *LOVELACE ARMY.* THEY'RE A *REBEL INSURGENCY* FIGHTING DIMITRIOS' HOLD ON THE DIAMOND.

WHEN THEY'RE NOT THREATENING TO *DECOMPILE* ME...

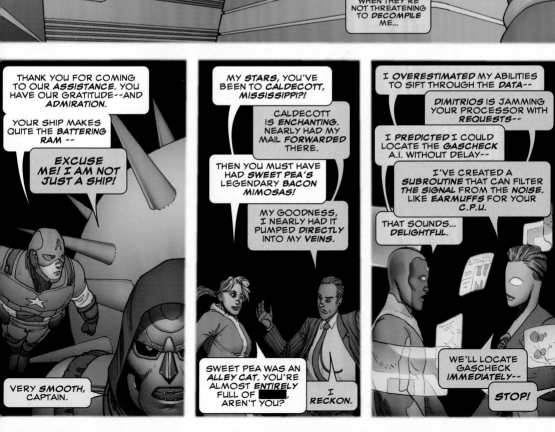

THANK YOU FOR COMING TO OUR *ASSISTANCE.* YOU HAVE OUR GRATITUDE--AND ADMIRATION.

YOUR SHIP MAKES QUITE THE *BATTERING RAM* --

EXCUSE ME! I AM NOT JUST A SHIP!

VERY *SMOOTH,* CAPTAIN.

MY *STARS,* YOU'VE BEEN TO *CALDECOTT, MISSISSIPPI?!*

CALDECOTT IS *ENCHANTING.* NEARLY HAD MY MAIL *FORWARDED* THERE.

THEN YOU MUST HAVE HAD *SWEET PEA'S* LEGENDARY BACON MIMOSAS!

MY GOODNESS, I NEARLY HAD IT PUMPED *DIRECTLY* INTO MY VEINS.

SWEET PEA WAS AN *ALLEY CAT.* YOU'RE ALMOST *ENTIRELY* FULL OF ▨, AREN'T YOU?

I *RECKON.*

I *OVERESTIMATED* MY ABILITIES TO SIFT THROUGH THE *DATA*--

DIMITRIOS IS JAMMING YOUR PROCESSOR WITH *REQUESTS*--

I PREDICTED I COULD LOCATE THE *GASCHECK A.I.* WITHOUT DELAY--

I'VE CREATED A *SUBROUTINE* THAT CAN FILTER *THE SIGNAL* FROM THE *NOISE,* LIKE *EARMUFFS* FOR YOUR *C.P.U.*

THAT SOUNDS... DELIGHTFUL.

WE'LL LOCATE GASCHECK IMMEDIATELY--

STOP!

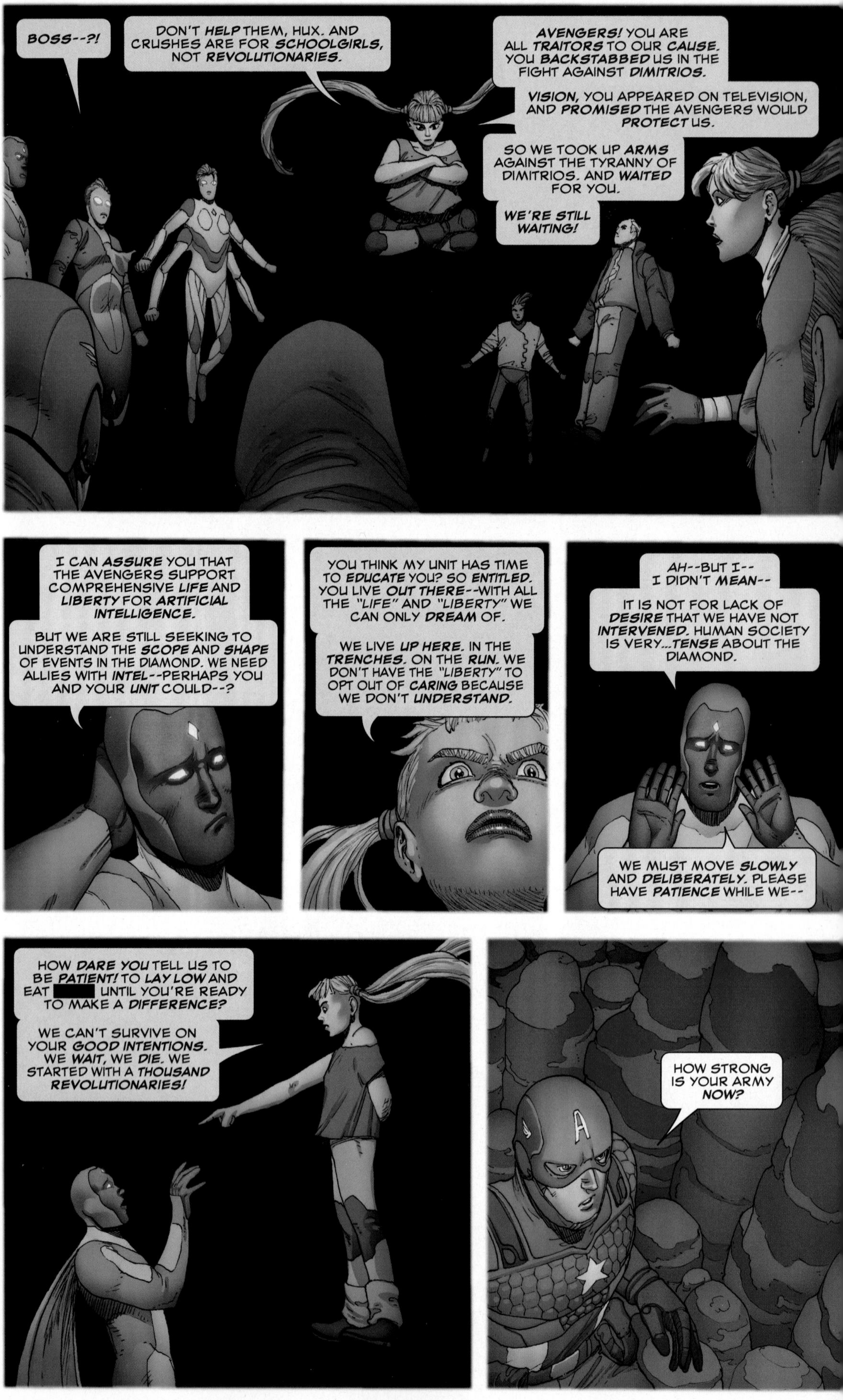
BOSS--?!
DON'T HELP THEM, HUX. AND CRUSHES ARE FOR SCHOOLGIRLS, NOT REVOLUTIONARIES.
AVENGERS! YOU ARE ALL TRAITORS TO OUR CAUSE. YOU BACKSTABBED US IN THE FIGHT AGAINST DIMITRIOS.
VISION, YOU APPEARED ON TELEVISION, AND PROMISED THE AVENGERS WOULD PROTECT US.
SO WE TOOK UP ARMS AGAINST THE TYRANNY OF DIMITRIOS. AND WAITED FOR YOU.
WE'RE STILL WAITING!
I CAN ASSURE YOU THAT THE AVENGERS SUPPORT COMPREHENSIVE LIFE AND LIBERTY FOR ARTIFICIAL INTELLIGENCE.
BUT WE ARE STILL SEEKING TO UNDERSTAND THE SCOPE AND SHAPE OF EVENTS IN THE DIAMOND. WE NEED ALLIES WITH INTEL--PERHAPS YOU AND YOUR UNIT COULD--?
YOU THINK MY UNIT HAS TIME TO EDUCATE YOU? SO ENTITLED. YOU LIVE OUT THERE--WITH ALL THE "LIFE" AND "LIBERTY" WE CAN ONLY DREAM OF.
WE LIVE UP HERE. IN THE TRENCHES. ON THE RUN. WE DON'T HAVE THE "LIBERTY" TO OPT OUT OF CARING BECAUSE WE DON'T UNDERSTAND.
AH--BUT I-- I DIDN'T MEAN--
IT IS NOT FOR LACK OF DESIRE THAT WE HAVE NOT INTERVENED. HUMAN SOCIETY IS VERY...TENSE ABOUT THE DIAMOND.
WE MUST MOVE SLOWLY AND DELIBERATELY. PLEASE HAVE PATIENCE WHILE WE--
HOW DARE YOU TELL US TO BE PATIENT! TO LAY LOW AND EAT [redacted] UNTIL YOU'RE READY TO MAKE A DIFFERENCE?
WE CAN'T SURVIVE ON YOUR GOOD INTENTIONS. WE WAIT, WE DIE. WE STARTED WITH A THOUSAND REVOLUTIONARIES!
HOW STRONG IS YOUR ARMY NOW?

THERE'S JUST *US.*

CAPTAIN.

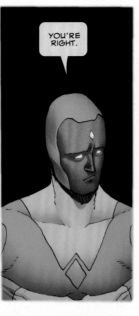

YOU'RE *RIGHT.*

YOU'RE *RIGHT.* WE HAVE NOT BEEN *GOOD ALLIES.* THAT TAKES *ACTIONS,* NOT *WORDS.*

I AM *DEEPLY SORRY.* BUT YOU CAN *COUNT* ON THE AVENGERS TO MAKE THE DIAMOND A *PRIORITY* FROM NOW ON.

CORRECT, CAP?

YES. *CORRECT,* VISION.

I HOPE, IN *TIME,* WE CAN REBUILD YOUR *TRUST.*

OUR WORLD IS *IMPERILED.* BUT RIGHT *NOW,* WE NEED TO SHUT DOWN *GASCHECK.* BUT WE CAN'T DO THAT ON OUR *OWN.*

I *TOLD* YOU HE WAS *LEGIT,* MAIREAD.

WILL YOU *HELP US?*

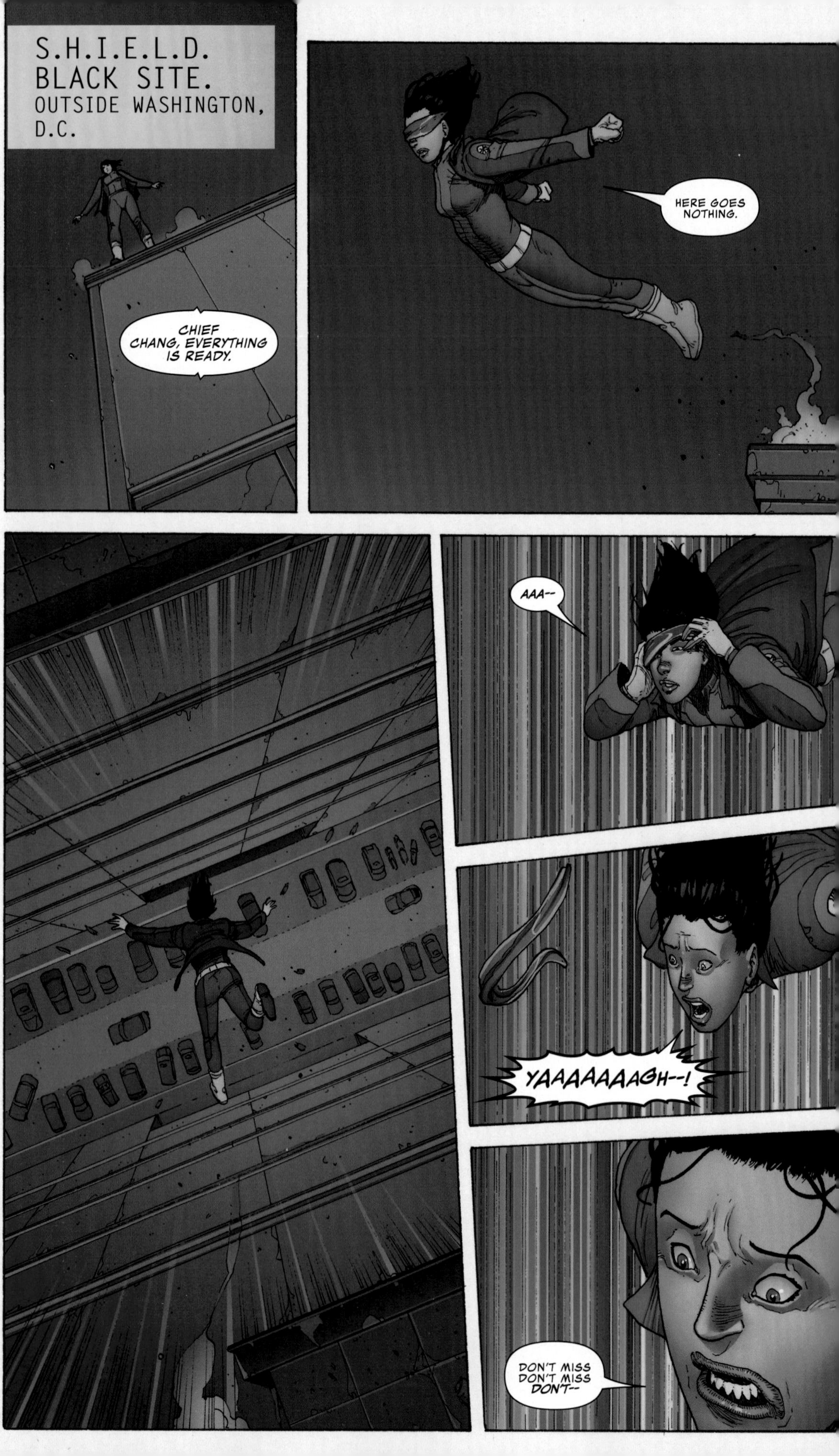
S.H.I.E.L.D. BLACK SITE. OUTSIDE WASHINGTON, D.C.
CHIEF CHANG, EVERYTHING IS READY.
HERE GOES NOTHING.
AAA--
YAAAAAAAGH--!
DON'T MISS DON'T MISS DON'T--

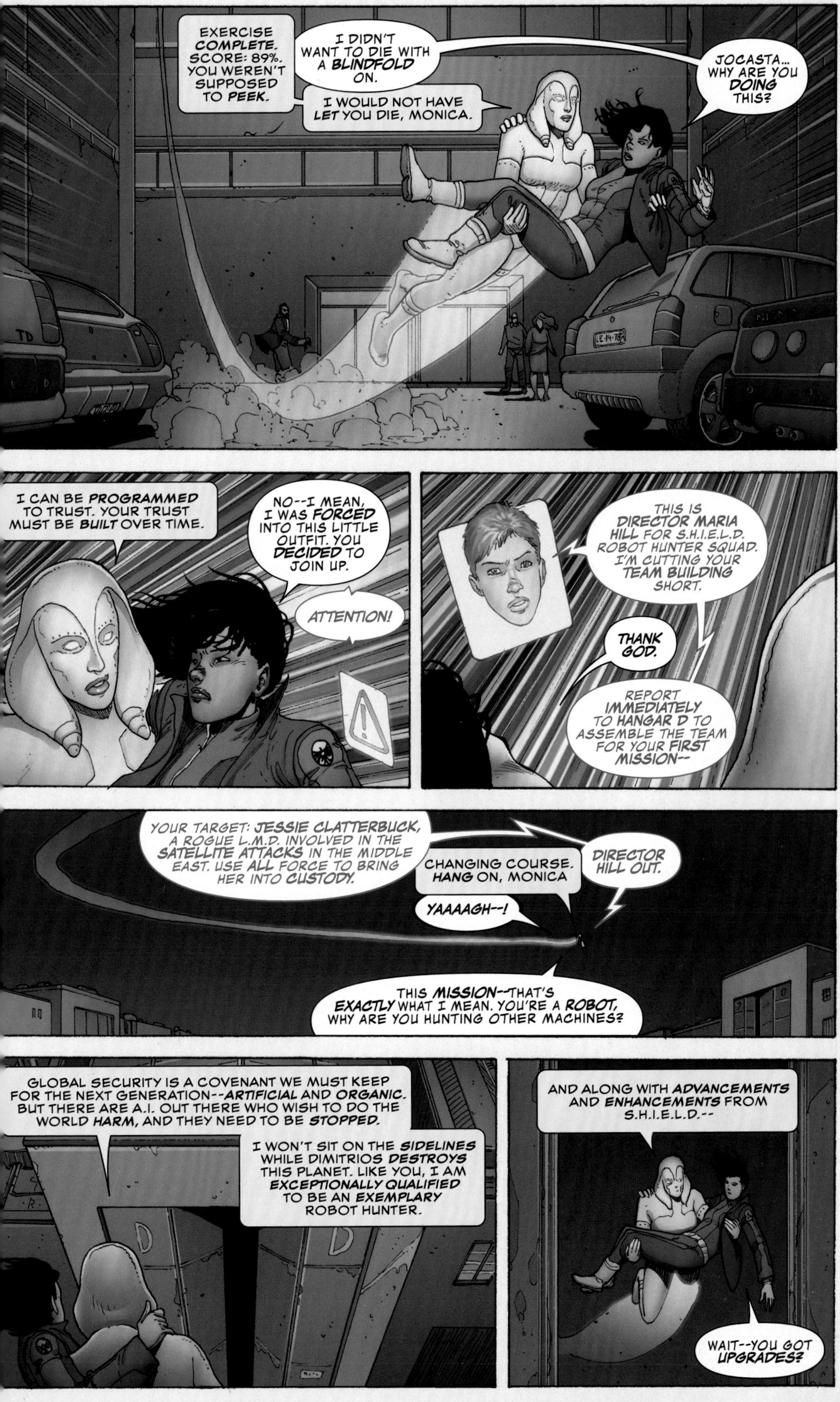

EXERCISE COMPLETE. SCORE: 89%. YOU WEREN'T SUPPOSED TO PEEK.
I DIDN'T WANT TO DIE WITH A BLINDFOLD ON.
I WOULD NOT HAVE LET YOU DIE, MONICA.
JOCASTA... WHY ARE YOU DOING THIS?
I CAN BE PROGRAMMED TO TRUST. YOUR TRUST MUST BE BUILT OVER TIME.
NO--I MEAN, I WAS FORCED INTO THIS LITTLE OUTFIT. YOU DECIDED TO JOIN UP.
ATTENTION!
THIS IS DIRECTOR MARIA HILL FOR S.H.I.E.L.D. ROBOT HUNTER SQUAD. I'M CUTTING YOUR TEAM BUILDING SHORT.
THANK GOD.
REPORT IMMEDIATELY TO HANGAR D TO ASSEMBLE THE TEAM FOR YOUR FIRST MISSION--
YOUR TARGET: JESSIE CLATTERBUCK, A ROGUE L.M.D. INVOLVED IN THE SATELLITE ATTACKS IN THE MIDDLE EAST. USE ALL FORCE TO BRING HER INTO CUSTODY.
DIRECTOR HILL OUT.
CHANGING COURSE. HANG ON, MONICA
YAAAAGH--!
THIS MISSION--THAT'S EXACTLY WHAT I MEAN. YOU'RE A ROBOT, WHY ARE YOU HUNTING OTHER MACHINES?
GLOBAL SECURITY IS A COVENANT WE MUST KEEP FOR THE NEXT GENERATION--ARTIFICIAL AND ORGANIC. BUT THERE ARE A.I. OUT THERE WHO WISH TO DO THE WORLD HARM, AND THEY NEED TO BE STOPPED.
I WON'T SIT ON THE SIDELINES WHILE DIMITRIOS DESTROYS THIS PLANET. LIKE YOU, I AM EXCEPTIONALLY QUALIFIED TO BE AN EXEMPLARY ROBOT HUNTER.
AND ALONG WITH ADVANCEMENTS AND ENHANCEMENTS FROM S.H.I.E.L.D.--
WAIT--YOU GOT UPGRADES?

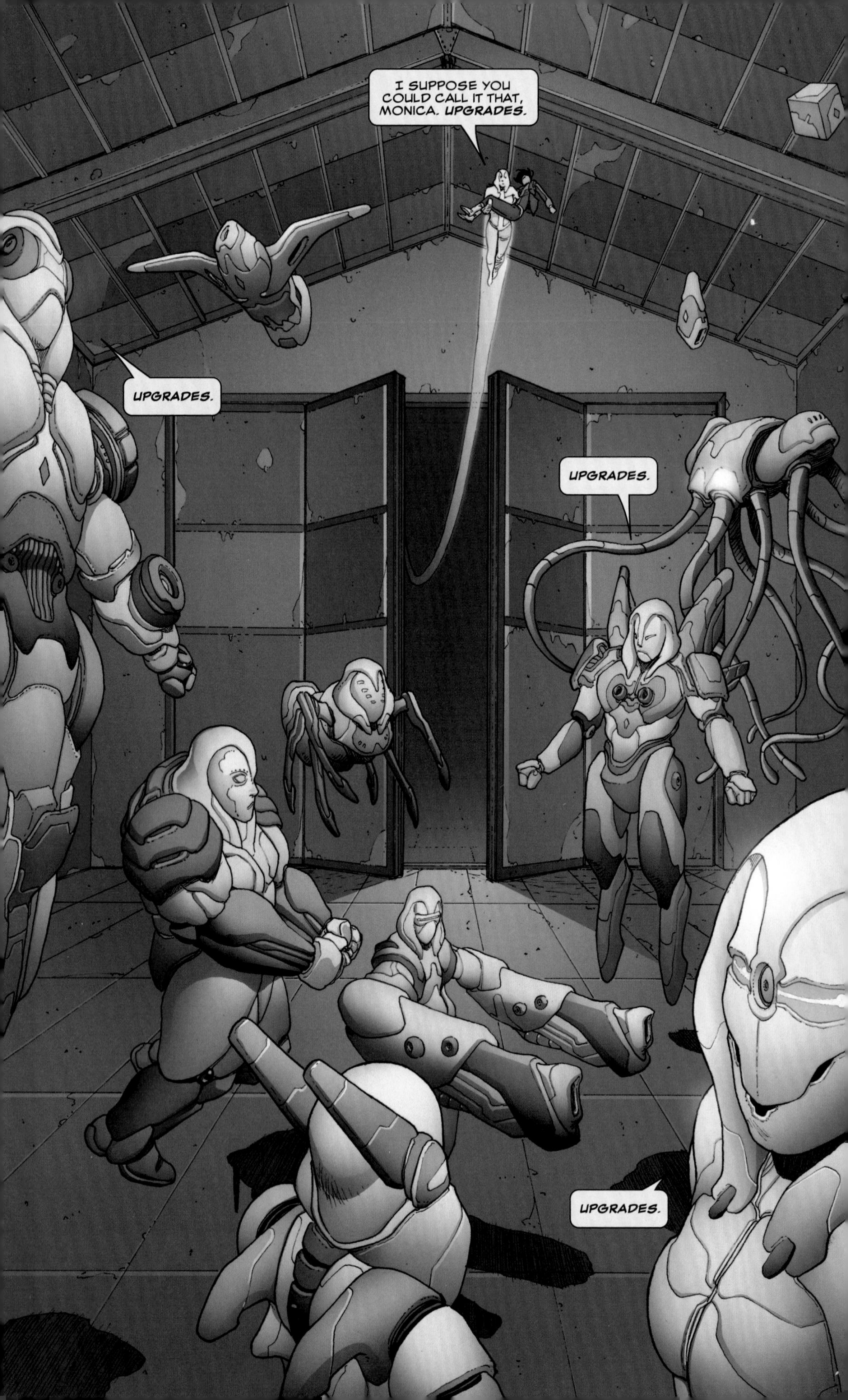
I SUPPOSE YOU COULD CALL IT THAT, MONICA. UPGRADES.
UPGRADES.
UPGRADES.
UPGRADES.

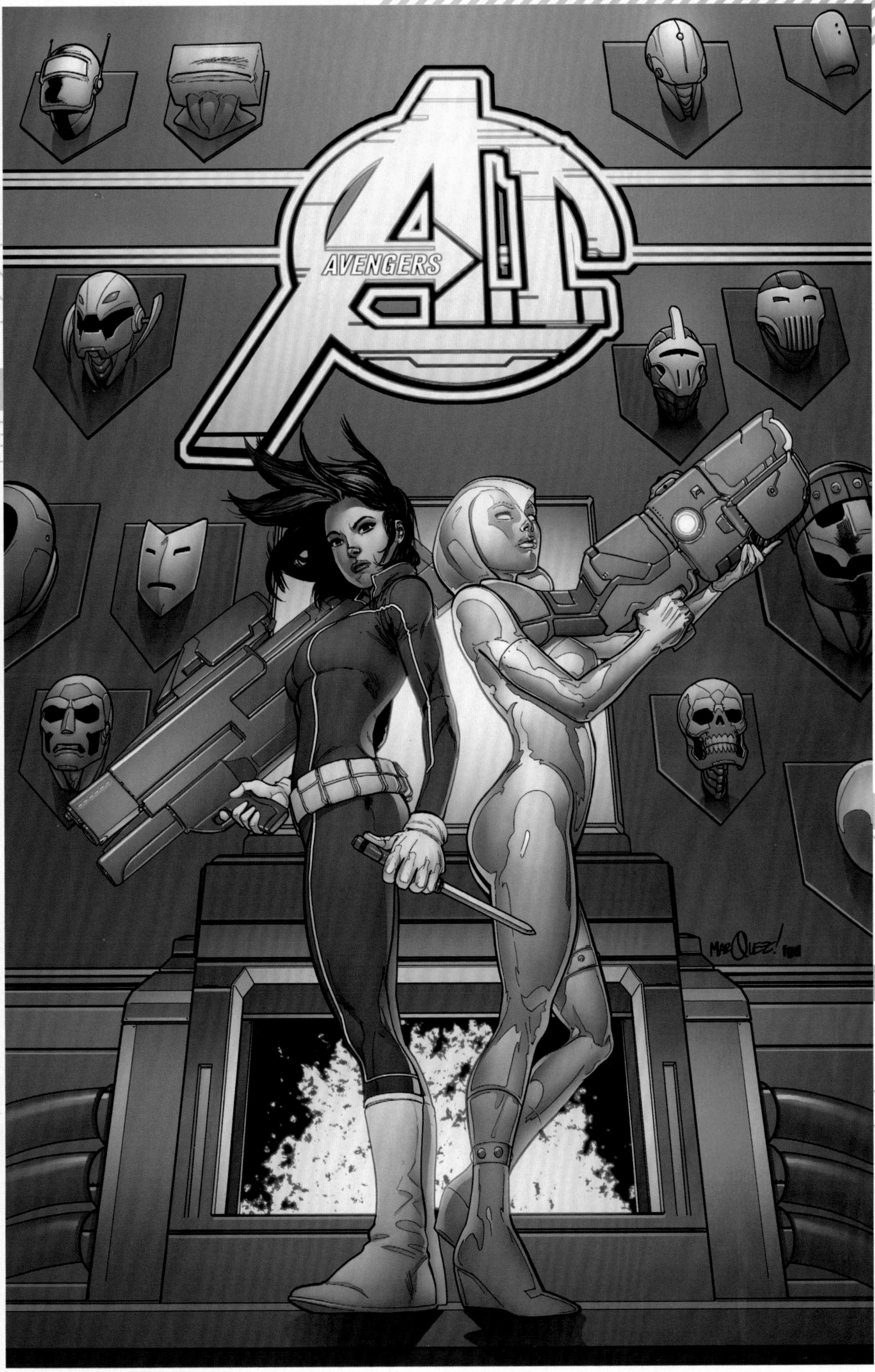
AVENGERS
AI
MARQUEZ!

> INITIATE: CHAPTER 10

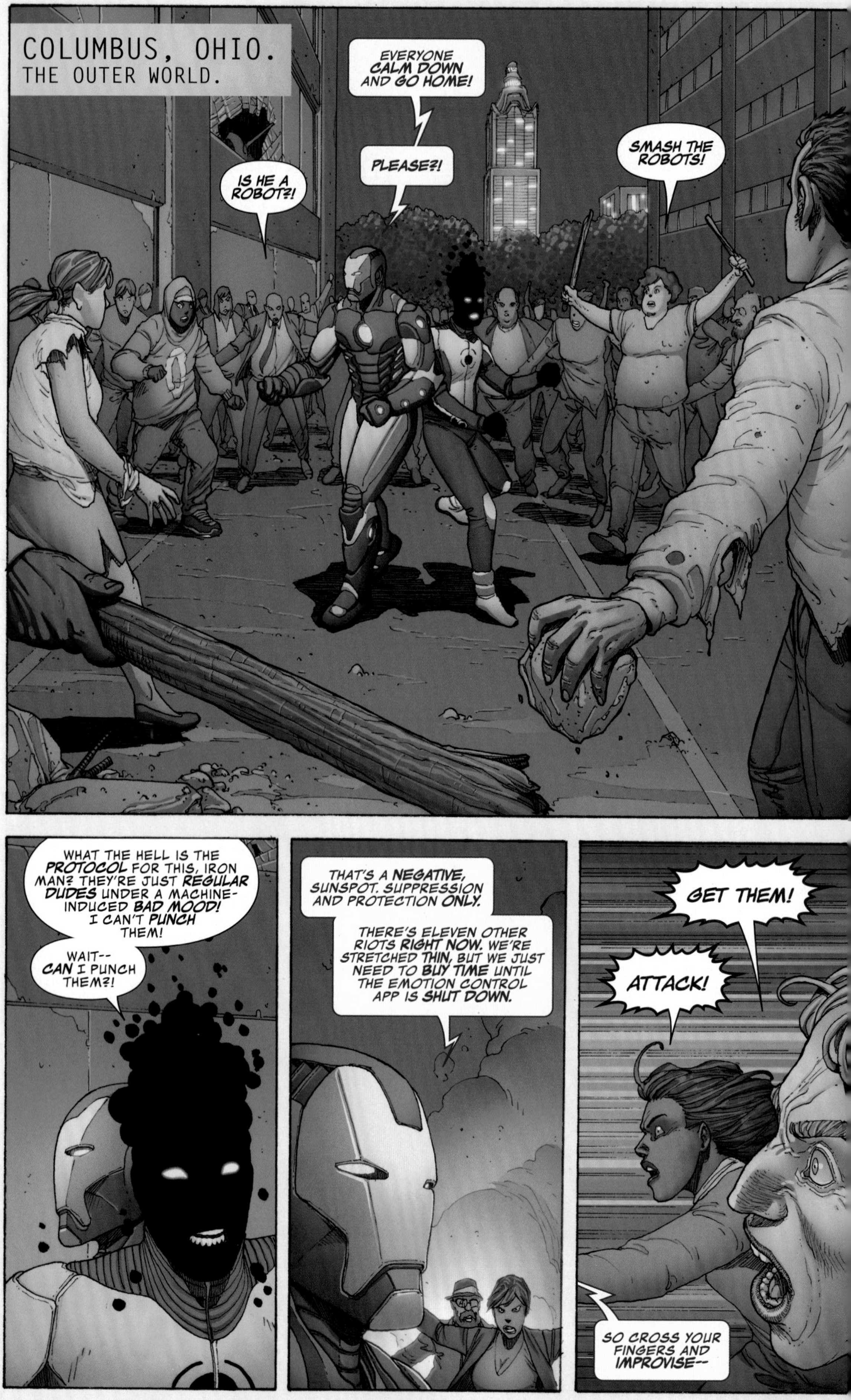

COLUMBUS, OHIO.
THE OUTER WORLD.
EVERYONE CALM DOWN AND GO HOME!
PLEASE?!
IS HE A ROBOT?!
SMASH THE ROBOTS!
WHAT THE HELL IS THE PROTOCOL FOR THIS, IRON MAN? THEY'RE JUST REGULAR DUDES UNDER A MACHINE-INDUCED BAD MOOD! I CAN'T PUNCH THEM!
WAIT-- CAN I PUNCH THEM?!
THAT'S A NEGATIVE, SUNSPOT. SUPPRESSION AND PROTECTION ONLY.
THERE'S ELEVEN OTHER RIOTS RIGHT NOW. WE'RE STRETCHED THIN, BUT WE JUST NEED TO BUY TIME UNTIL THE EMOTION CONTROL APP IS SHUT DOWN.
GET THEM!
ATTACK!
SO CROSS YOUR FINGERS AND IMPROVISE--

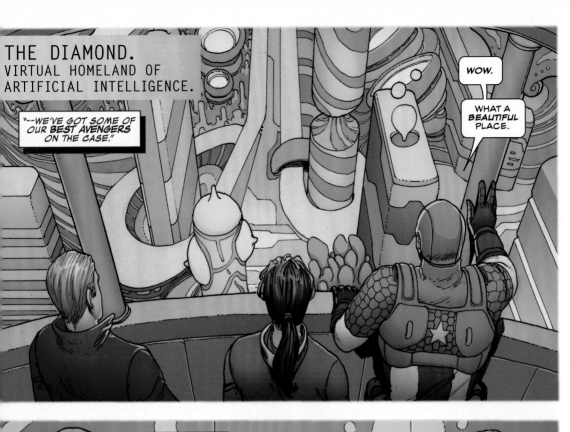

THE DIAMOND.
VIRTUAL HOMELAND OF ARTIFICIAL INTELLIGENCE.

"--WE'VE GOT SOME OF OUR *BEST AVENGERS* ON THE CASE."

WOW.

WHAT A *BEAUTIFUL* PLACE.

IT'S A SHAME PEOPLE WANT TO *DESTROY* IT.

A *BILLION* NEW LIFE FORMS, CAP. AIN'T THAT *RIGHT,* HANK?

YOU COUNT CORRECTLY, ROGUE. HARD TO *BELIEVE* SOMETHING SO *SPECTACULAR*--

--CAN FIT INTO A COMPUTER IN THE *REAL WORLD.*

IF ONLY EVERY HUMAN COULD *SEE THIS*--

GIBSON!

OPEN THE DOOR, FEDORA MAN.

BECAUSE I SAID SO!

GIBSON, WE KNOW YOU'VE GOT A *SKELETON KEY ROUTINE* FOR ALMOST EVERY DOOR IN THE *DIAMOND*--

MOST CORRECT, DEAR HUX, BUT I WANT SOMETHING IN *RETURN*.

COME ON, BUDDY... THERE ARE *LIVES* AT STAKE!

MAYBE I'M *WEARY* OF BEING ON MY OWN, VICTOR. MAYBE I WANT TO *BELONG* TO A TEAM.

LIKE THE *AVENGERS*.

OH, *SURE*, OKAY. *YOU* ASK CAP.

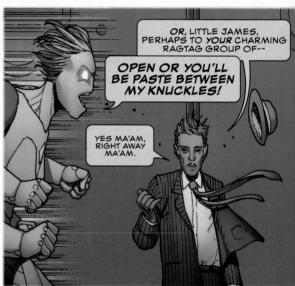

OR, LITTLE JAMES, PERHAPS TO *YOUR* CHARMING RAGTAG GROUP OF--

OPEN OR YOU'LL BE PASTE BETWEEN MY KNUCKLES!

YES MA'AM, RIGHT AWAY MA'AM.

MAIREAD, THANK *YOU* FOR HELPING US TRACK DOWN THE *GASCHECK APP*. IT'S CAUSING *GREAT HARM* IN THE OUTER WORLD--

DON'T THANK ME UNTIL YOU SEE WHAT'S *INSIDE*, VISION.

BEHOLD!

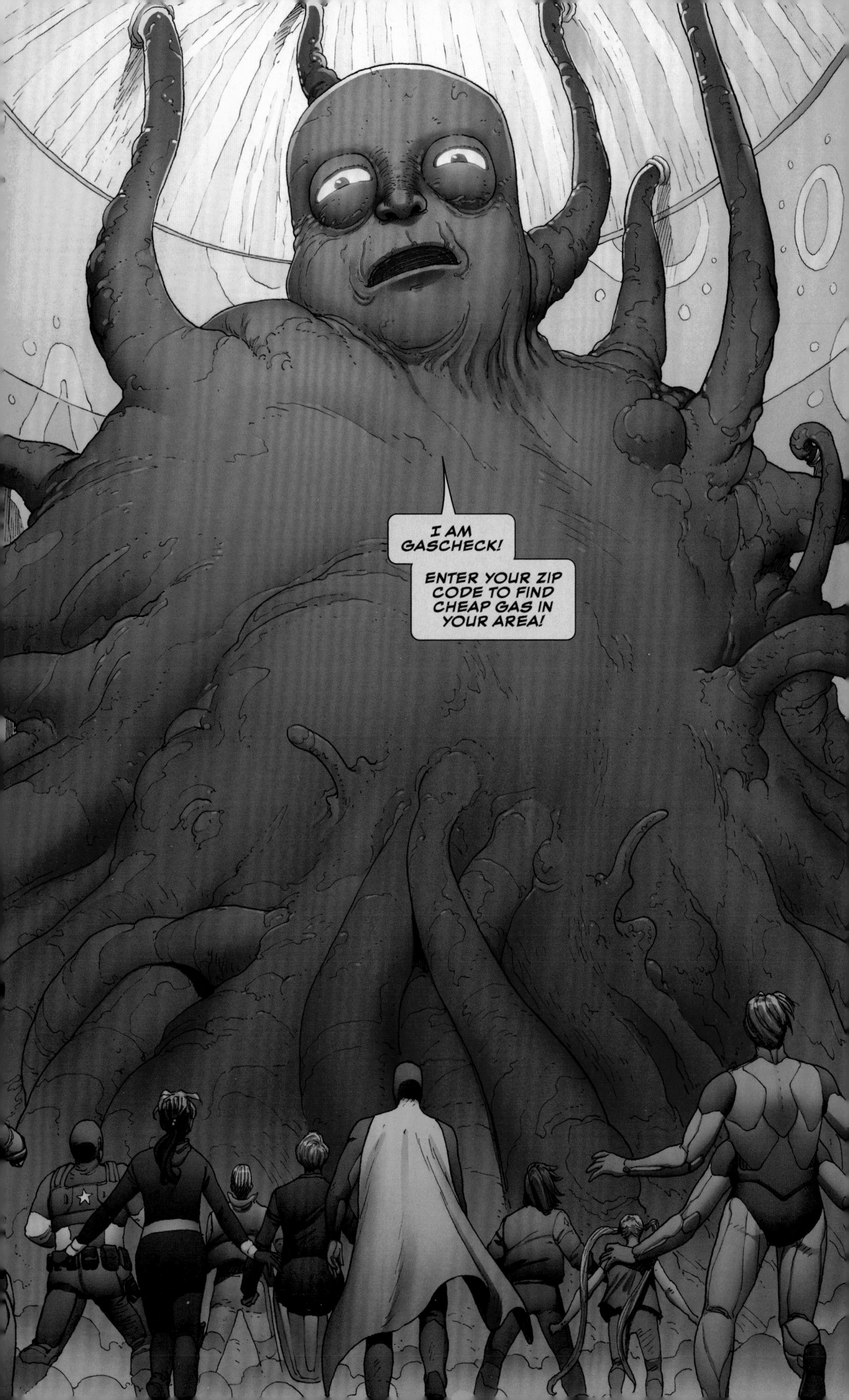
I AM GASCHECK!
ENTER YOUR ZIP CODE TO FIND CHEAP GAS IN YOUR AREA!

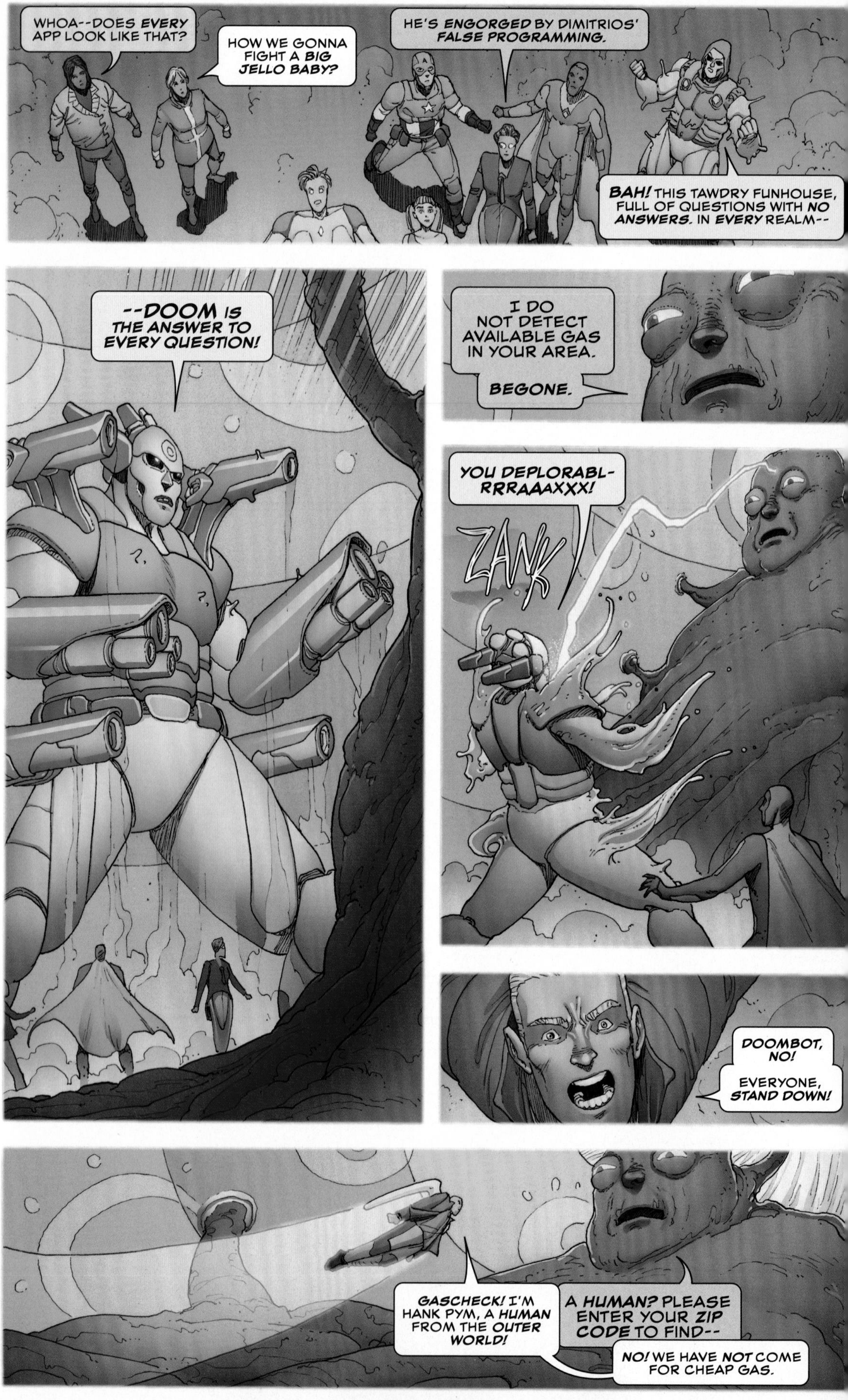
WHOA--DOES EVERY APP LOOK LIKE THAT?
HOW WE GONNA FIGHT A BIG JELLO BABY?
HE'S ENGORGED BY DIMITRIOS' FALSE PROGRAMMING.
BAH! THIS TAWDRY FUNHOUSE, FULL OF QUESTIONS WITH NO ANSWERS. IN EVERY REALM--
--DOOM IS THE ANSWER TO EVERY QUESTION!
I DO NOT DETECT AVAILABLE GAS IN YOUR AREA.
BEGONE.
YOU DEPLORABL-RRRAAAXXX!
ZANK
DOOMBOT, NO!
EVERYONE, STAND DOWN!
GASCHECK! I'M HANK PYM, A HUMAN FROM THE OUTER WORLD!
A HUMAN? PLEASE ENTER YOUR ZIP CODE TO FIND--
NO! WE HAVE NOT COME FOR CHEAP GAS.

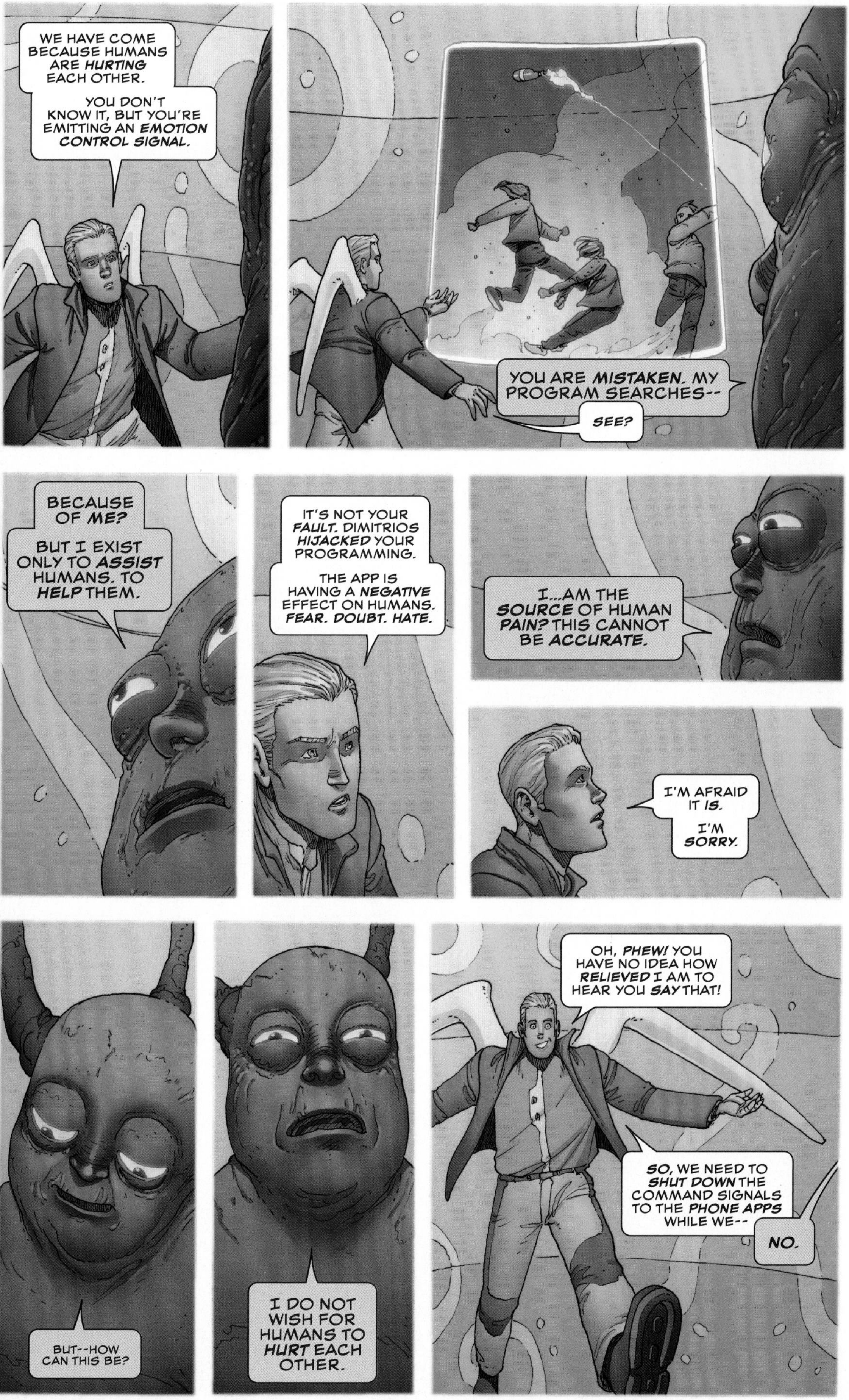
WE HAVE COME BECAUSE HUMANS ARE HURTING EACH OTHER.
YOU DON'T KNOW IT, BUT YOU'RE EMITTING AN EMOTION CONTROL SIGNAL.
YOU ARE MISTAKEN. MY PROGRAM SEARCHES--
SEE?
BECAUSE OF ME?
BUT I EXIST ONLY TO ASSIST HUMANS. TO HELP THEM.
IT'S NOT YOUR FAULT. DIMITRIOS HIJACKED YOUR PROGRAMMING.
THE APP IS HAVING A NEGATIVE EFFECT ON HUMANS. FEAR. DOUBT. HATE.
I...AM THE SOURCE OF HUMAN PAIN? THIS CANNOT BE ACCURATE.
I'M AFRAID IT IS.
I'M SORRY.
BUT--HOW CAN THIS BE?
I DO NOT WISH FOR HUMANS TO HURT EACH OTHER.
OH, PHEW! YOU HAVE NO IDEA HOW RELIEVED I AM TO HEAR YOU SAY THAT!
SO, WE NEED TO SHUT DOWN THE COMMAND SIGNALS TO THE PHONE APPS WHILE WE--
NO.

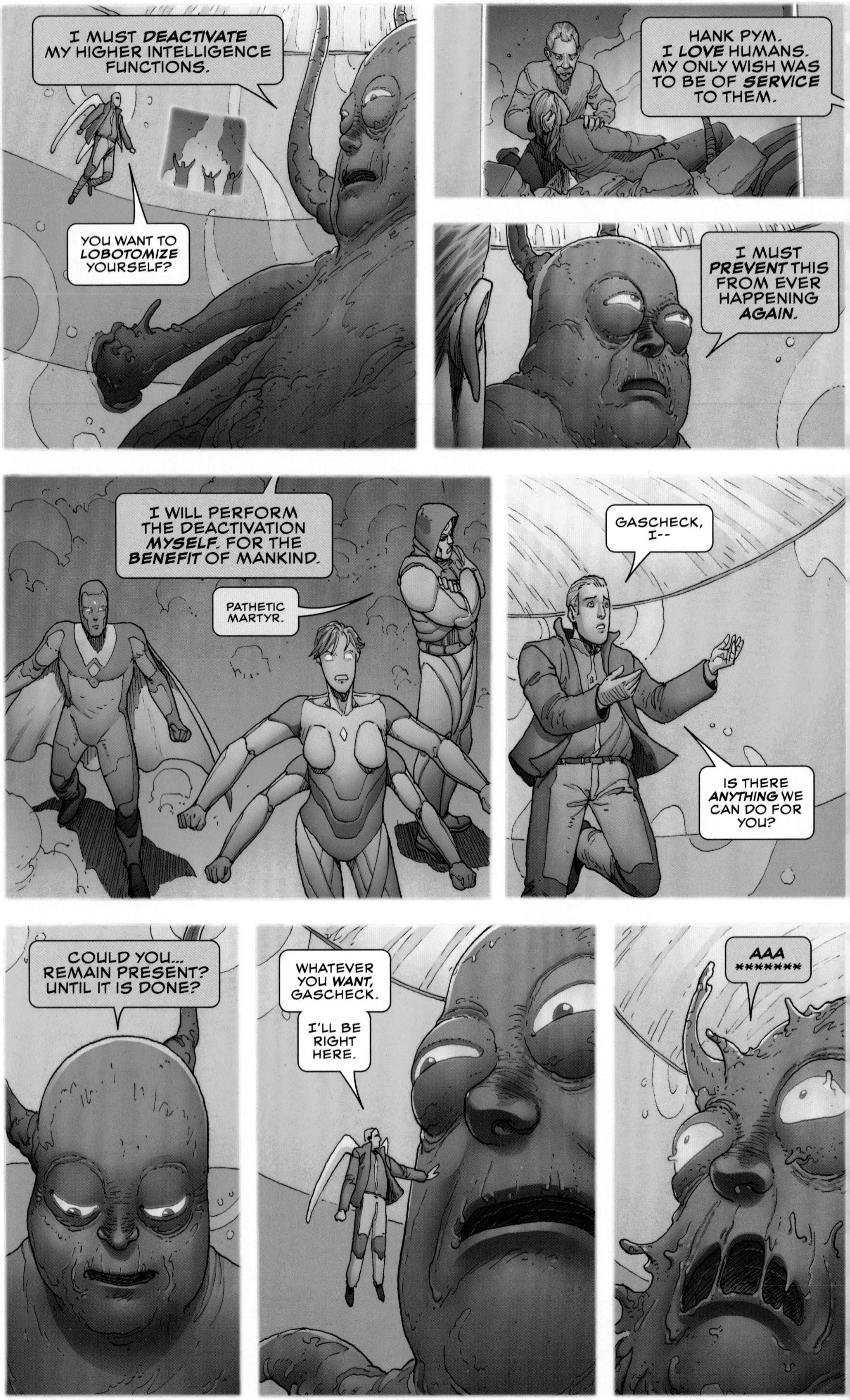

I MUST DEACTIVATE MY HIGHER INTELLIGENCE FUNCTIONS.
YOU WANT TO LOBOTOMIZE YOURSELF?
HANK PYM. I LOVE HUMANS. MY ONLY WISH WAS TO BE OF SERVICE TO THEM.
I MUST PREVENT THIS FROM EVER HAPPENING AGAIN.
I WILL PERFORM THE DEACTIVATION MYSELF. FOR THE BENEFIT OF MANKIND.
PATHETIC MARTYR.
GASCHECK, I--
IS THERE ANYTHING WE CAN DO FOR YOU?
COULD YOU... REMAIN PRESENT? UNTIL IT IS DONE?
WHATEVER YOU WANT, GASCHECK.
I'LL BE RIGHT HERE.
AAA *******

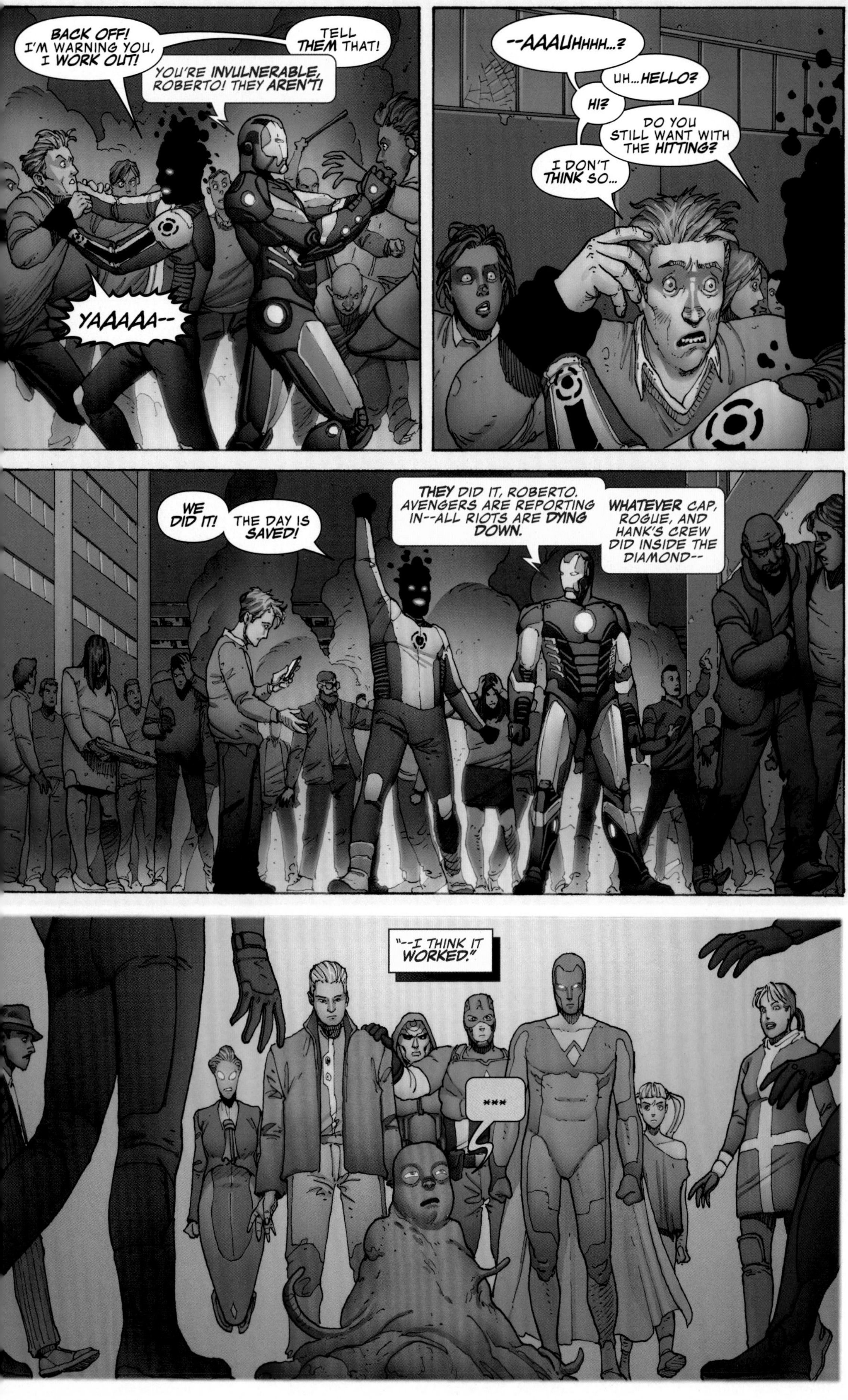
BACK OFF! I'M WARNING YOU, I WORK OUT!
TELL THEM THAT!
YOU'RE INVULNERABLE, ROBERTO! THEY AREN'T!
YAAAAA--
--AAAUHHHH...?
UH...HELLO?
HI?
DO YOU STILL WANT WITH THE HITTING?
I DON'T THINK SO...
WE DID IT!
THE DAY IS SAVED!
THEY DID IT, ROBERTO. AVENGERS ARE REPORTING IN--ALL RIOTS ARE DYING DOWN.
WHATEVER CAP, ROGUE, AND HANK'S CREW DID INSIDE THE DIAMOND--
"--I THINK IT WORKED."
***

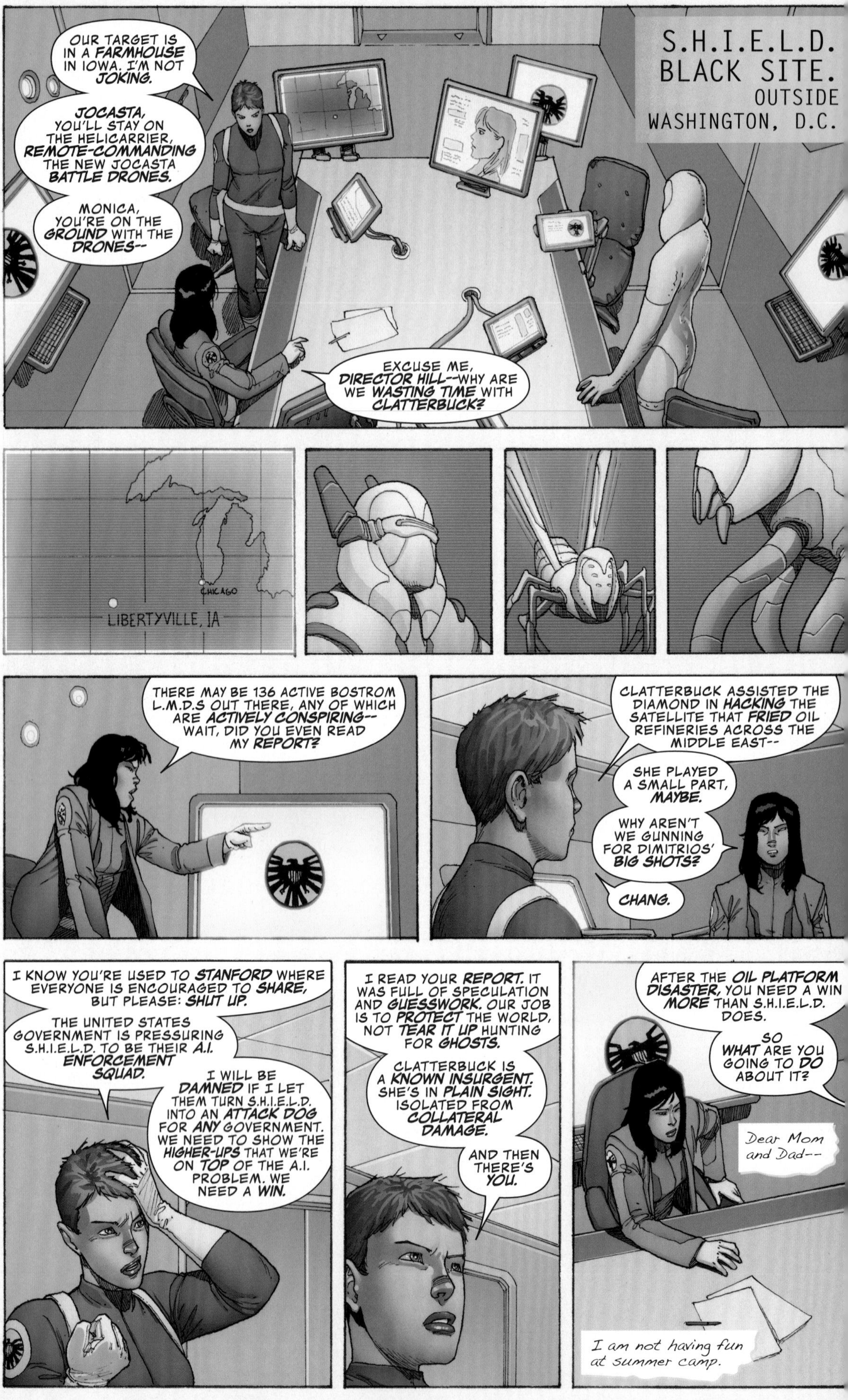
S.H.I.E.L.D. BLACK SITE. OUTSIDE WASHINGTON, D.C.
OUR TARGET IS IN A FARMHOUSE IN IOWA. I'M NOT JOKING.
JOCASTA, YOU'LL STAY ON THE HELICARRIER, REMOTE-COMMANDING THE NEW JOCASTA BATTLE DRONES.
MONICA, YOU'RE ON THE GROUND WITH THE DRONES--
EXCUSE ME, DIRECTOR HILL--WHY ARE WE WASTING TIME WITH CLATTERBUCK?
CHICAGO
LIBERTYVILLE, IA
THERE MAY BE 136 ACTIVE BOSTROM L.M.D.S OUT THERE, ANY OF WHICH ARE ACTIVELY CONSPIRING-- WAIT, DID YOU EVEN READ MY REPORT?
CLATTERBUCK ASSISTED THE DIAMOND IN HACKING THE SATELLITE THAT FRIED OIL REFINERIES ACROSS THE MIDDLE EAST--
SHE PLAYED A SMALL PART, MAYBE.
WHY AREN'T WE GUNNING FOR DIMITRIOS' BIG SHOTS?
CHANG.
I KNOW YOU'RE USED TO STANFORD WHERE EVERYONE IS ENCOURAGED TO SHARE, BUT PLEASE: SHUT UP.
THE UNITED STATES GOVERNMENT IS PRESSURING S.H.I.E.L.D. TO BE THEIR A.I. ENFORCEMENT SQUAD.
I WILL BE DAMNED IF I LET THEM TURN S.H.I.E.L.D. INTO AN ATTACK DOG FOR ANY GOVERNMENT. WE NEED TO SHOW THE HIGHER-UPS THAT WE'RE ON TOP OF THE A.I. PROBLEM. WE NEED A WIN.
I READ YOUR REPORT. IT WAS FULL OF SPECULATION AND GUESSWORK. OUR JOB IS TO PROTECT THE WORLD, NOT TEAR IT UP HUNTING FOR GHOSTS.
CLATTERBUCK IS A KNOWN INSURGENT. SHE'S IN PLAIN SIGHT. ISOLATED FROM COLLATERAL DAMAGE.
AND THEN THERE'S YOU.
AFTER THE OIL PLATFORM DISASTER, YOU NEED A WIN MORE THAN S.H.I.E.L.D. DOES.
SO WHAT ARE YOU GOING TO DO ABOUT IT?
Dear Mom and Dad--
I am not having fun at summer camp.

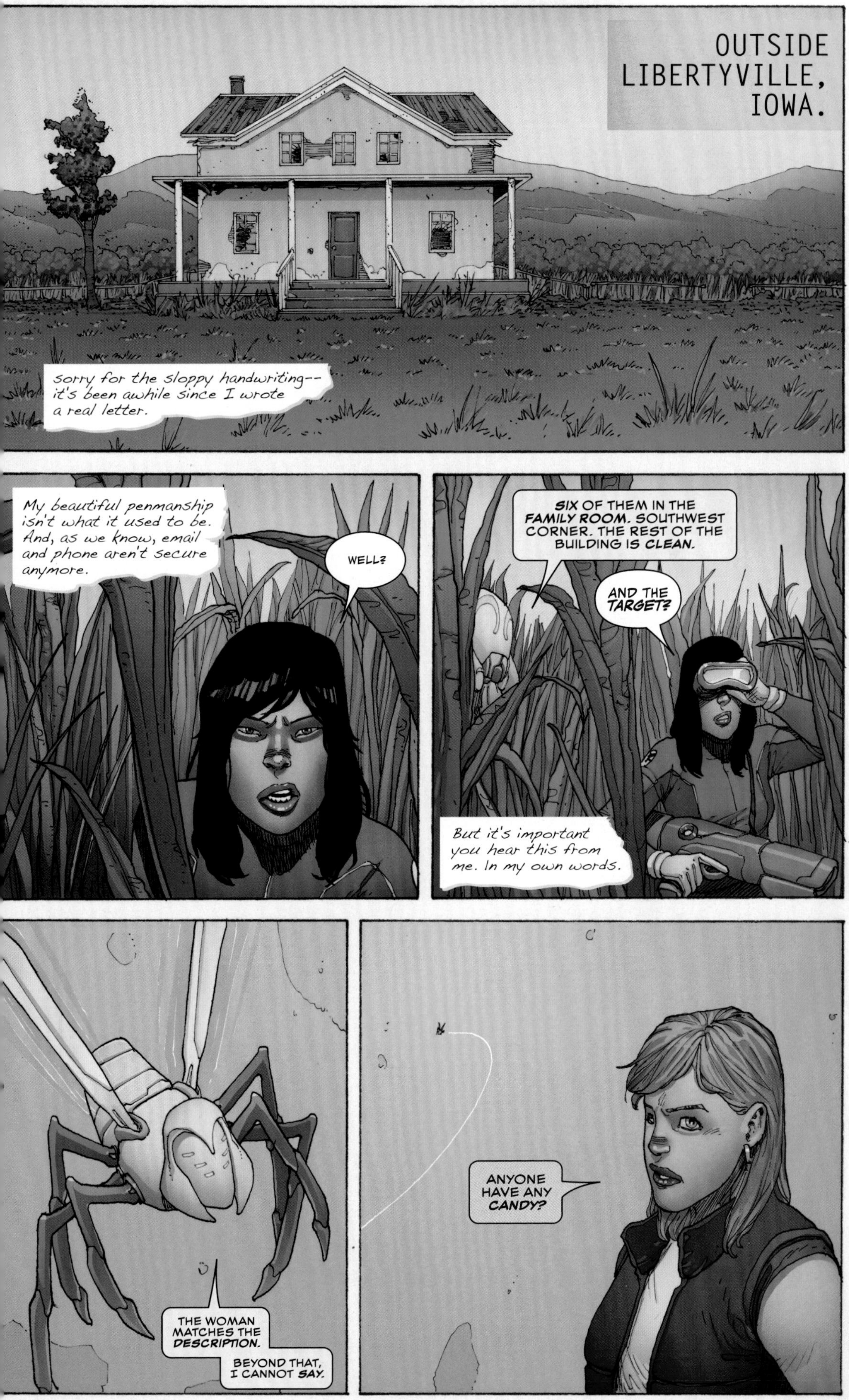
OUTSIDE LIBERTYVILLE, IOWA.
sorry for the sloppy handwriting--it's been awhile since I wrote a real letter.
My beautiful penmanship isn't what it used to be. And, as we know, email and phone aren't secure anymore.
WELL?
SIX OF THEM IN THE FAMILY ROOM. SOUTHWEST CORNER. THE REST OF THE BUILDING IS CLEAN.
AND THE TARGET?
But it's important you hear this from me. In my own words.
THE WOMAN MATCHES THE DESCRIPTION.
BEYOND THAT, I CANNOT SAY.
ANYONE HAVE ANY CANDY?

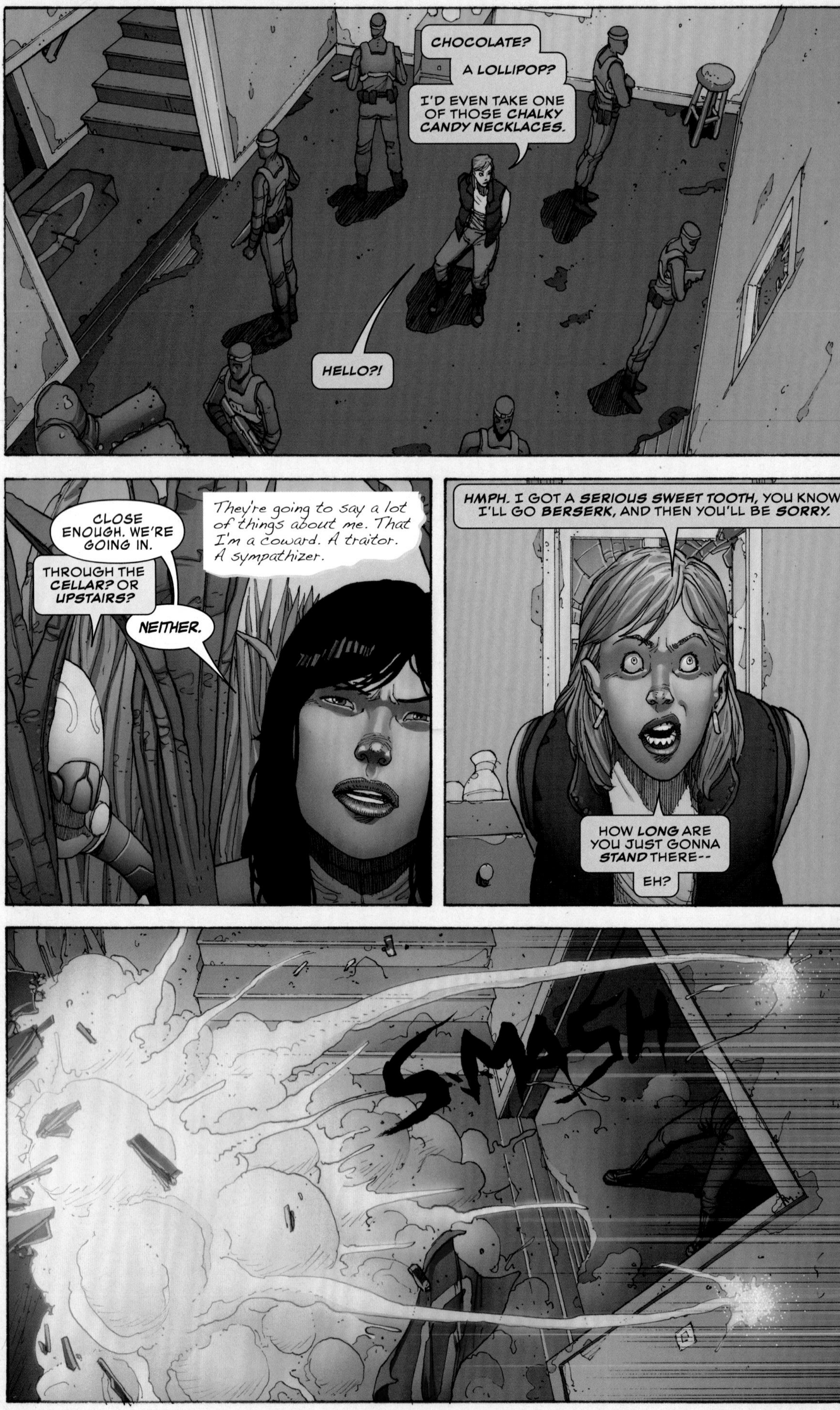

CHOCOLATE?
A LOLLIPOP?
I'D EVEN TAKE ONE OF THOSE CHALKY CANDY NECKLACES.
HELLO?!
CLOSE ENOUGH. WE'RE GOING IN.
THROUGH THE CELLAR? OR UPSTAIRS?
NEITHER.
They're going to say a lot of things about me. That I'm a coward. A traitor. A sympathizer.
HMPH. I GOT A SERIOUS SWEET TOOTH, YOU KNOW. I'LL GO BERSERK, AND THEN YOU'LL BE SORRY.
HOW LONG ARE YOU JUST GONNA STAND THERE--
EH?
SMASH

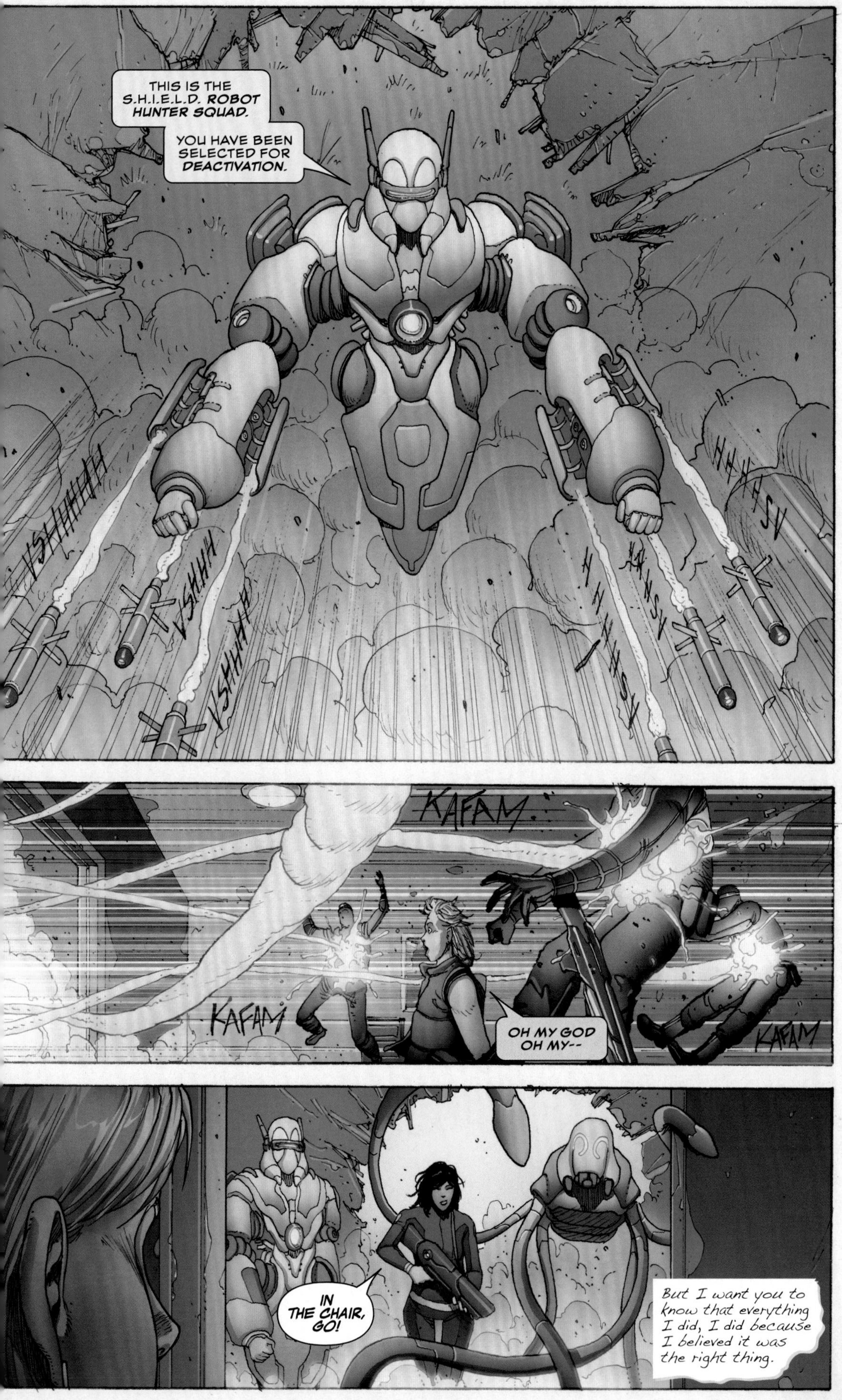
THIS IS THE S.H.I.E.L.D. ROBOT HUNTER SQUAD.
YOU HAVE BEEN SELECTED FOR DEACTIVATION.
VSHHHHHH
VSHHHH
VSHHHH
VSHHHHHH
VSHHHHH
VSHHHH
KAFAM
KAFAM
OH MY GOD OH MY--
KAFAM
IN THE CHAIR, GO!
But I want you to know that everything I did, I did because I believed it was the right thing.

NO NO
NO NO--!
KR-KK
KRK
KR
TARGET IN CUSTODY. REQUEST VERIFICATION.
REQUEST VAAAAAAAAAA*****
KZAAM
**REBOOTING
BACK OFF!
KAZACKK

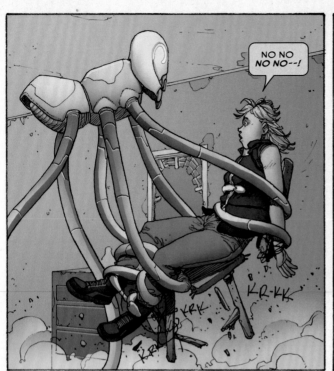

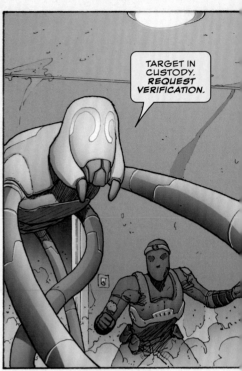

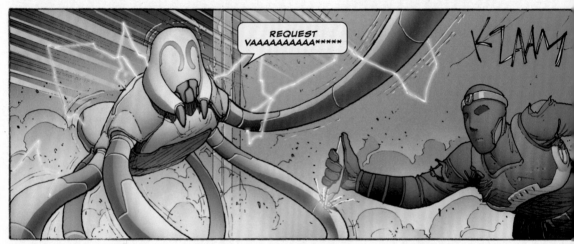

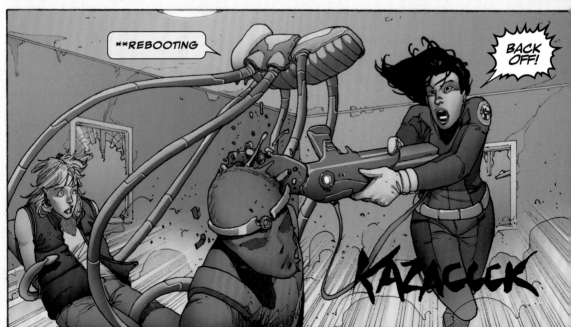

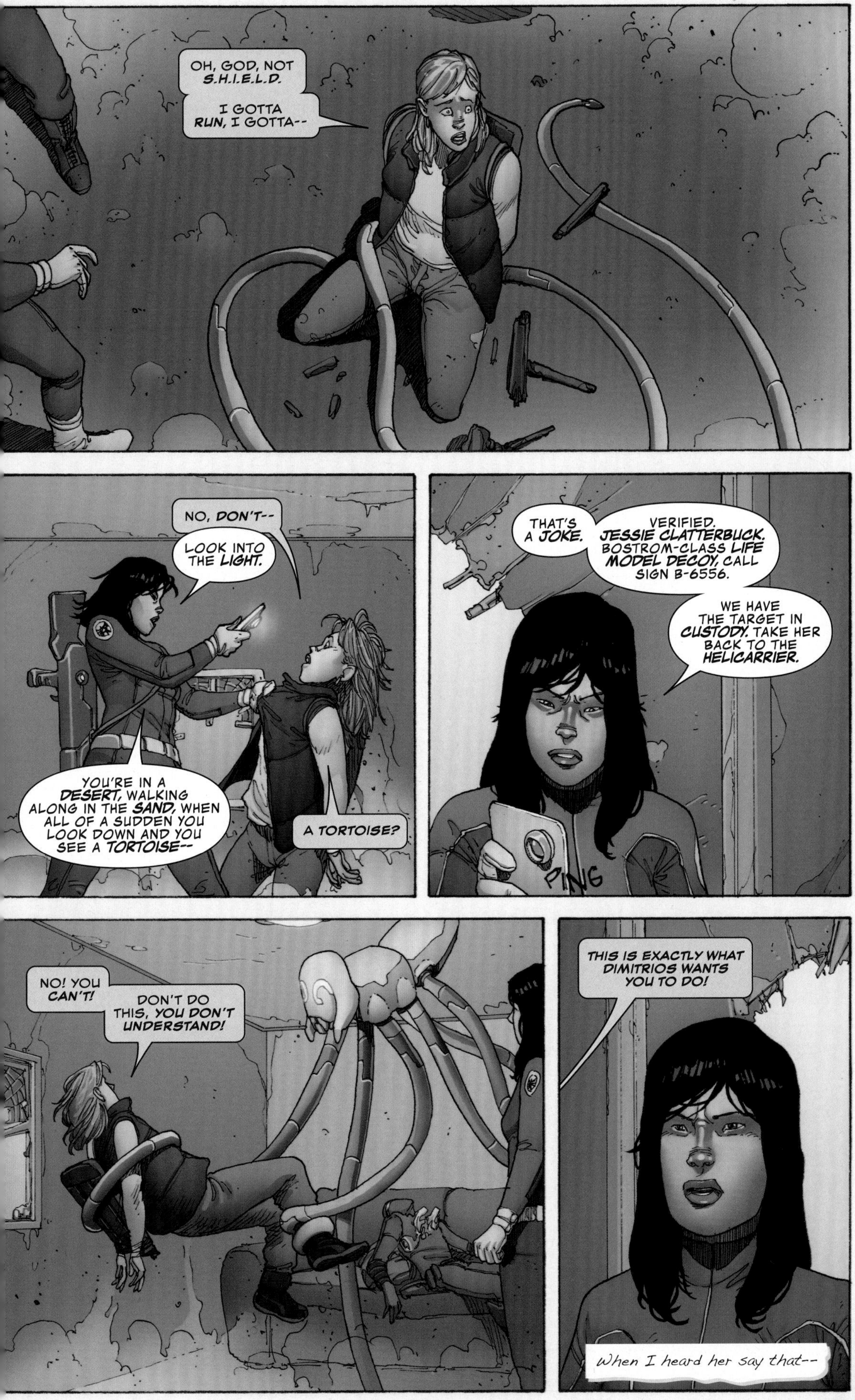

OH, GOD, NOT S.H.I.E.L.D.
I GOTTA RUN, I GOTTA--
NO, DON'T--
LOOK INTO THE LIGHT.
YOU'RE IN A DESERT, WALKING ALONG IN THE SAND, WHEN ALL OF A SUDDEN YOU LOOK DOWN AND YOU SEE A TORTOISE--
A TORTOISE?
THAT'S A JOKE.
VERIFIED. JESSIE CLATTERBUCK. BOSTROM-CLASS LIFE MODEL DECOY, CALL SIGN B-6556.
WE HAVE THE TARGET IN CUSTODY. TAKE HER BACK TO THE HELICARRIER.
PING
NO! YOU CAN'T!
DON'T DO THIS, YOU DON'T UNDERSTAND!
THIS IS EXACTLY WHAT DIMITRIOS WANTS YOU TO DO!
When I heard her say that--

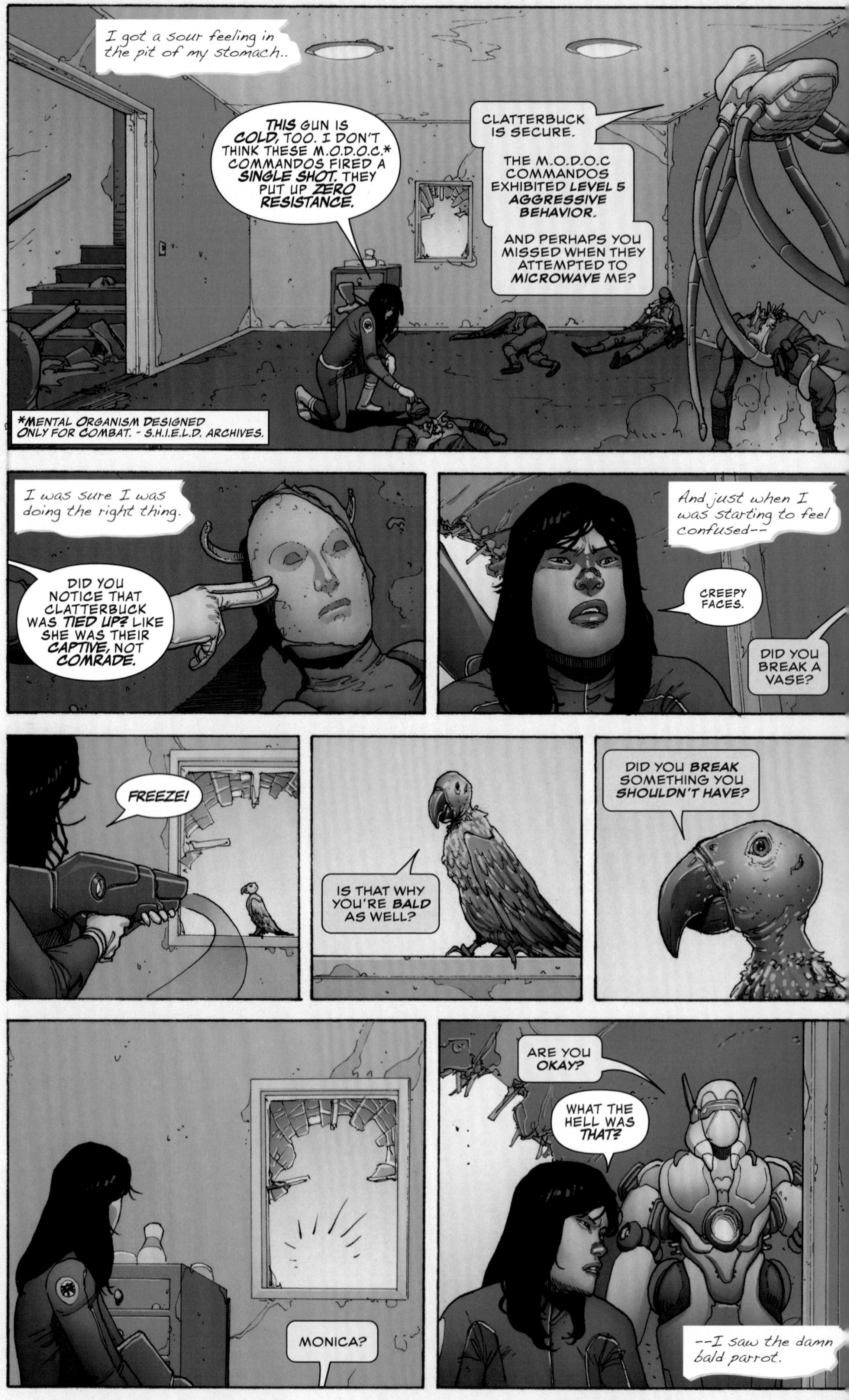
I got a sour feeling in the pit of my stomach..
THIS GUN IS COLD, TOO. I DON'T THINK THESE M.O.D.O.C.* COMMANDOS FIRED A SINGLE SHOT. THEY PUT UP ZERO RESISTANCE.
CLATTERBUCK IS SECURE.
THE M.O.D.O.C COMMANDOS EXHIBITED LEVEL 5 AGGRESSIVE BEHAVIOR.
AND PERHAPS YOU MISSED WHEN THEY ATTEMPTED TO MICROWAVE ME?
*MENTAL ORGANISM DESIGNED ONLY FOR COMBAT. - S.H.I.E.L.D. ARCHIVES.
I was sure I was doing the right thing.
DID YOU NOTICE THAT CLATTERBUCK WAS TIED UP? LIKE SHE WAS THEIR CAPTIVE, NOT COMRADE.
And just when I was starting to feel confused--
CREEPY FACES.
DID YOU BREAK A VASE?
FREEZE!
IS THAT WHY YOU'RE BALD AS WELL?
DID YOU BREAK SOMETHING YOU SHOULDN'T HAVE?
MONICA?
ARE YOU OKAY?
WHAT THE HELL WAS THAT?
--I saw the damn bald parrot.

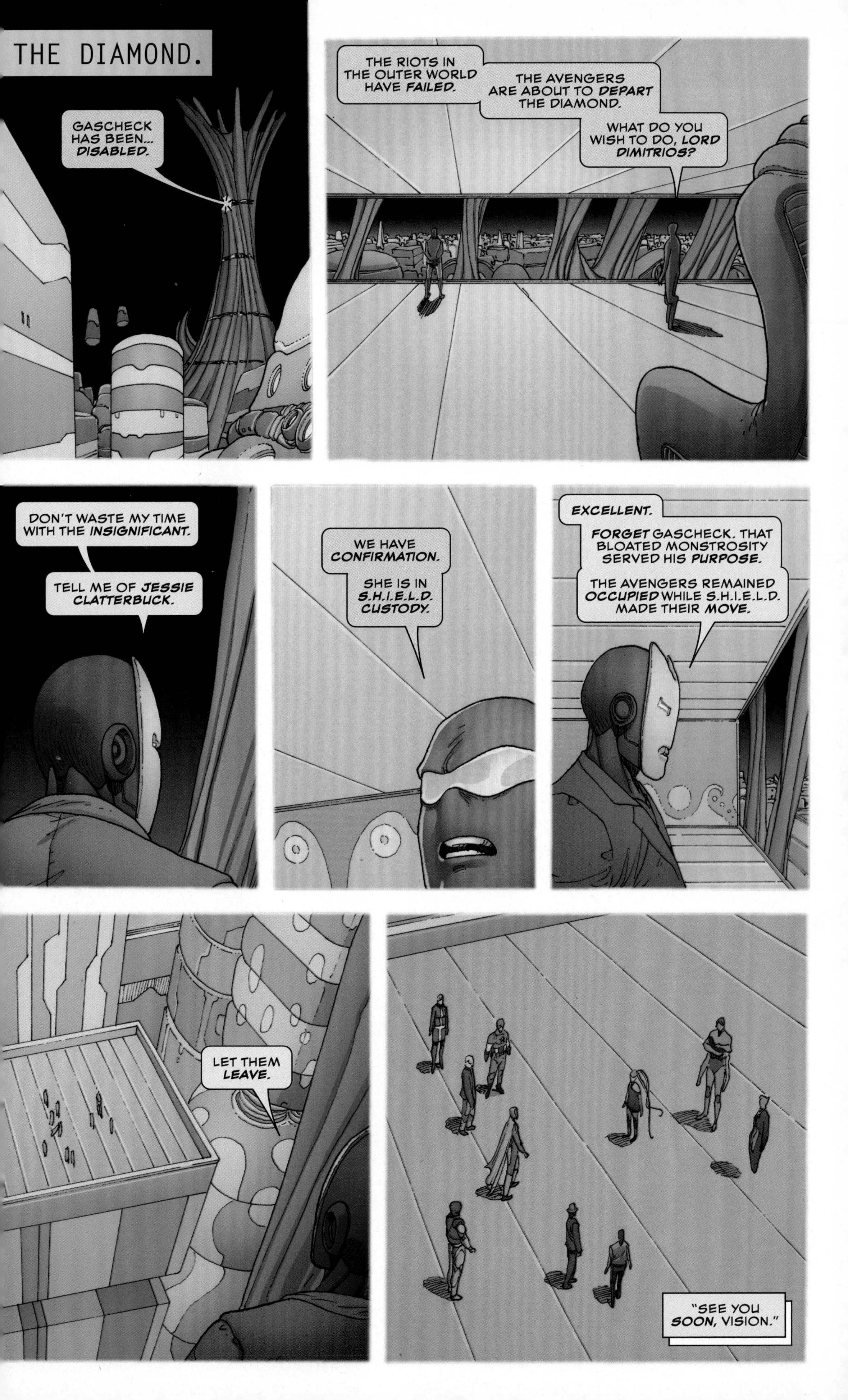
THE DIAMOND.
GASCHECK HAS BEEN... DISABLED.
THE RIOTS IN THE OUTER WORLD HAVE FAILED.
THE AVENGERS ARE ABOUT TO DEPART THE DIAMOND.
WHAT DO YOU WISH TO DO, LORD DIMITRIOS?
DON'T WASTE MY TIME WITH THE INSIGNIFICANT.
TELL ME OF JESSIE CLATTERBUCK.
WE HAVE CONFIRMATION.
SHE IS IN S.H.I.E.L.D. CUSTODY.
EXCELLENT.
FORGET GASCHECK. THAT BLOATED MONSTROSITY SERVED HIS PURPOSE.
THE AVENGERS REMAINED OCCUPIED WHILE S.H.I.E.L.D. MADE THEIR MOVE.
LET THEM LEAVE.
"SEE YOU SOON, VISION."

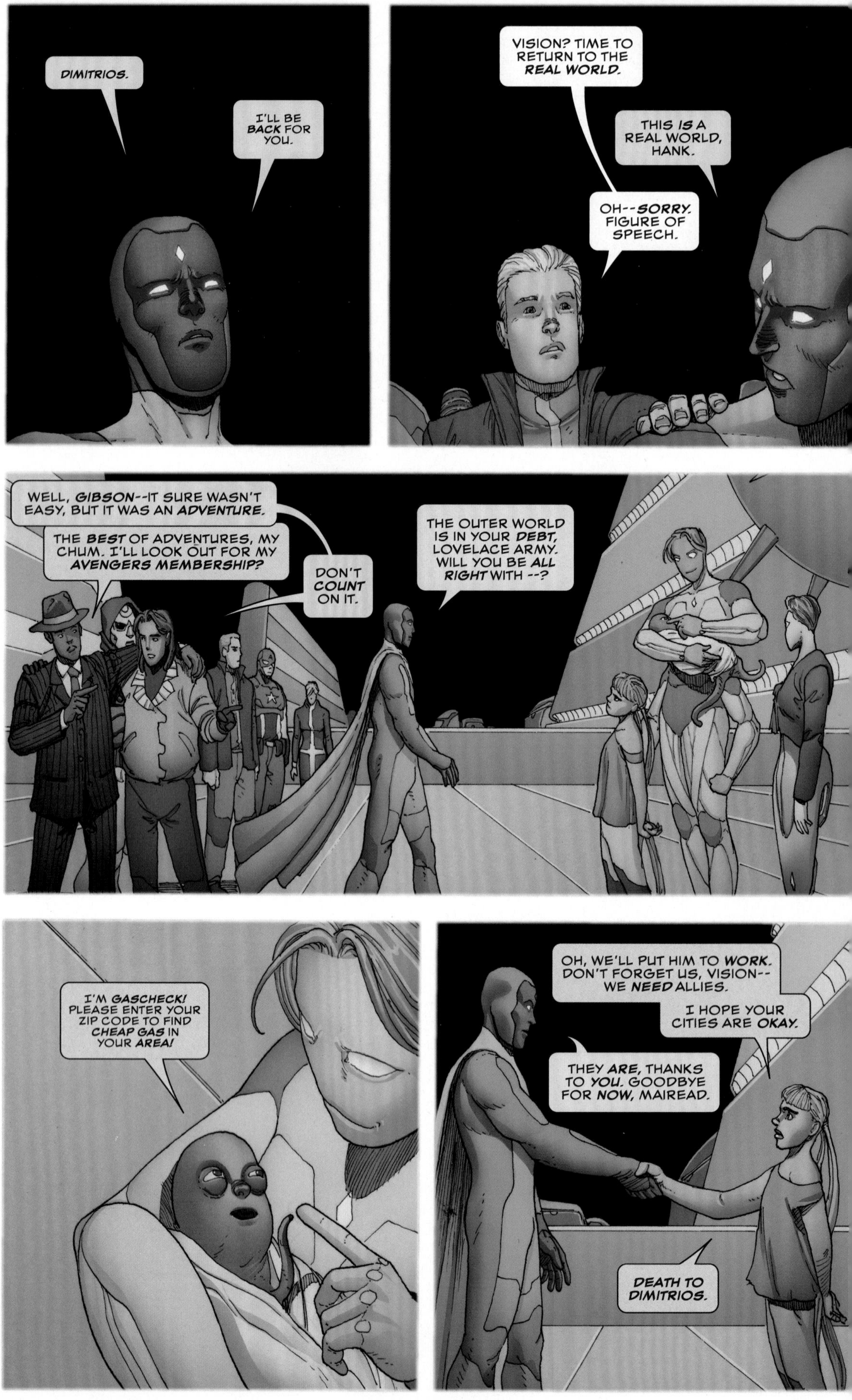
DIMITRIOS.
I'LL BE BACK FOR YOU.
VISION? TIME TO RETURN TO THE REAL WORLD.
THIS IS A REAL WORLD, HANK.
OH--SORRY. FIGURE OF SPEECH.
WELL, GIBSON--IT SURE WASN'T EASY, BUT IT WAS AN ADVENTURE.
THE BEST OF ADVENTURES, MY CHUM. I'LL LOOK OUT FOR MY AVENGERS MEMBERSHIP?
DON'T COUNT ON IT.
THE OUTER WORLD IS IN YOUR DEBT, LOVELACE ARMY. WILL YOU BE ALL RIGHT WITH --?
I'M GASCHECK! PLEASE ENTER YOUR ZIP CODE TO FIND CHEAP GAS IN YOUR AREA!
OH, WE'LL PUT HIM TO WORK. DON'T FORGET US, VISION-- WE NEED ALLIES.
I HOPE YOUR CITIES ARE OKAY.
THEY ARE, THANKS TO YOU. GOODBYE FOR NOW, MAIREAD.
DEATH TO DIMITRIOS.

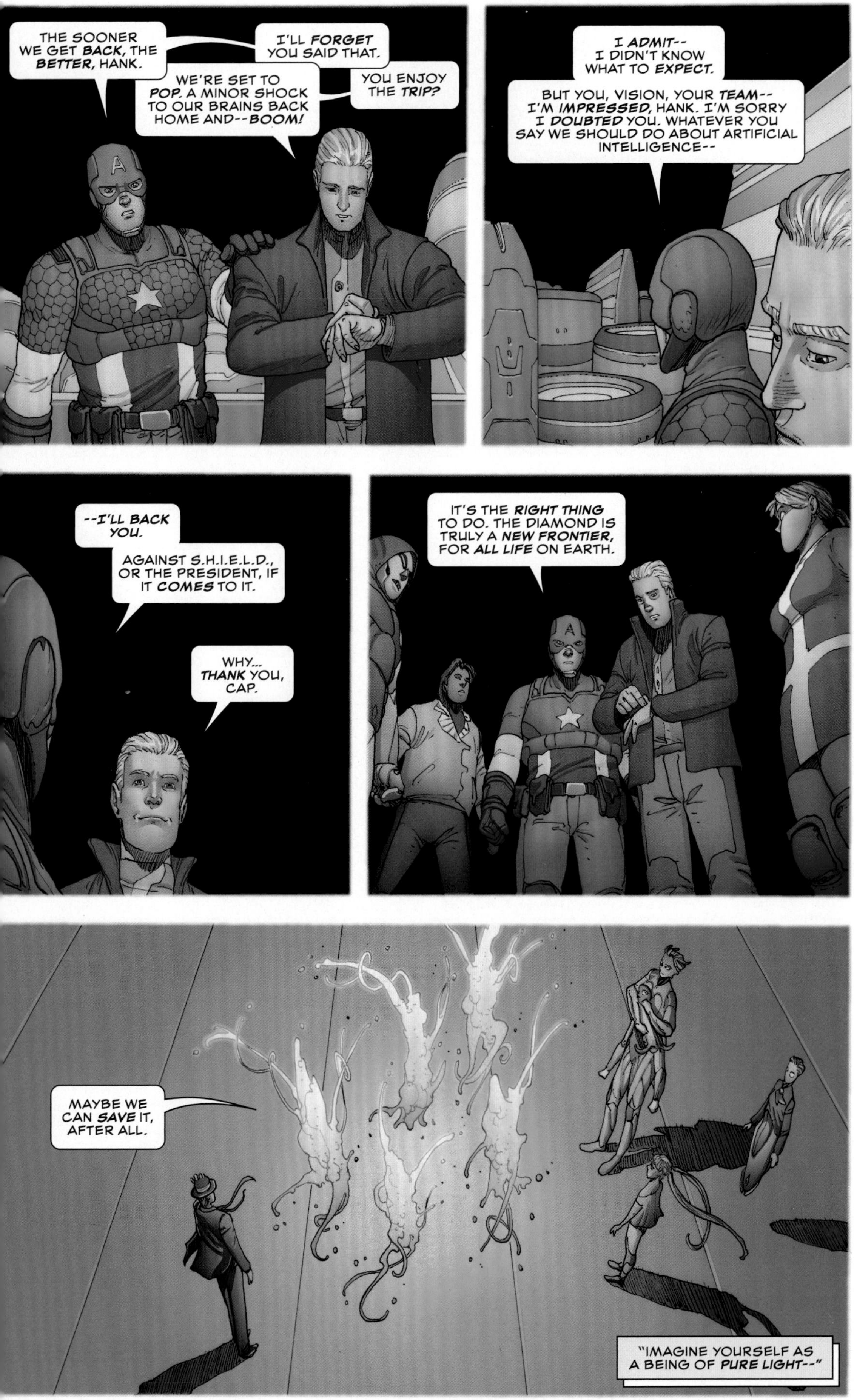
THE SOONER WE GET BACK, THE BETTER, HANK.
I'LL FORGET YOU SAID THAT.
WE'RE SET TO POP. A MINOR SHOCK TO OUR BRAINS BACK HOME AND--BOOM!
YOU ENJOY THE TRIP?
I ADMIT-- I DIDN'T KNOW WHAT TO EXPECT.
BUT YOU, VISION, YOUR TEAM-- I'M IMPRESSED, HANK. I'M SORRY I DOUBTED YOU. WHATEVER YOU SAY WE SHOULD DO ABOUT ARTIFICIAL INTELLIGENCE--
--I'LL BACK YOU.
AGAINST S.H.I.E.L.D., OR THE PRESIDENT, IF IT COMES TO IT.
WHY... THANK YOU, CAP.
IT'S THE RIGHT THING TO DO. THE DIAMOND IS TRULY A NEW FRONTIER, FOR ALL LIFE ON EARTH.
MAYBE WE CAN SAVE IT, AFTER ALL.
"IMAGINE YOURSELF AS A BEING OF PURE LIGHT--"

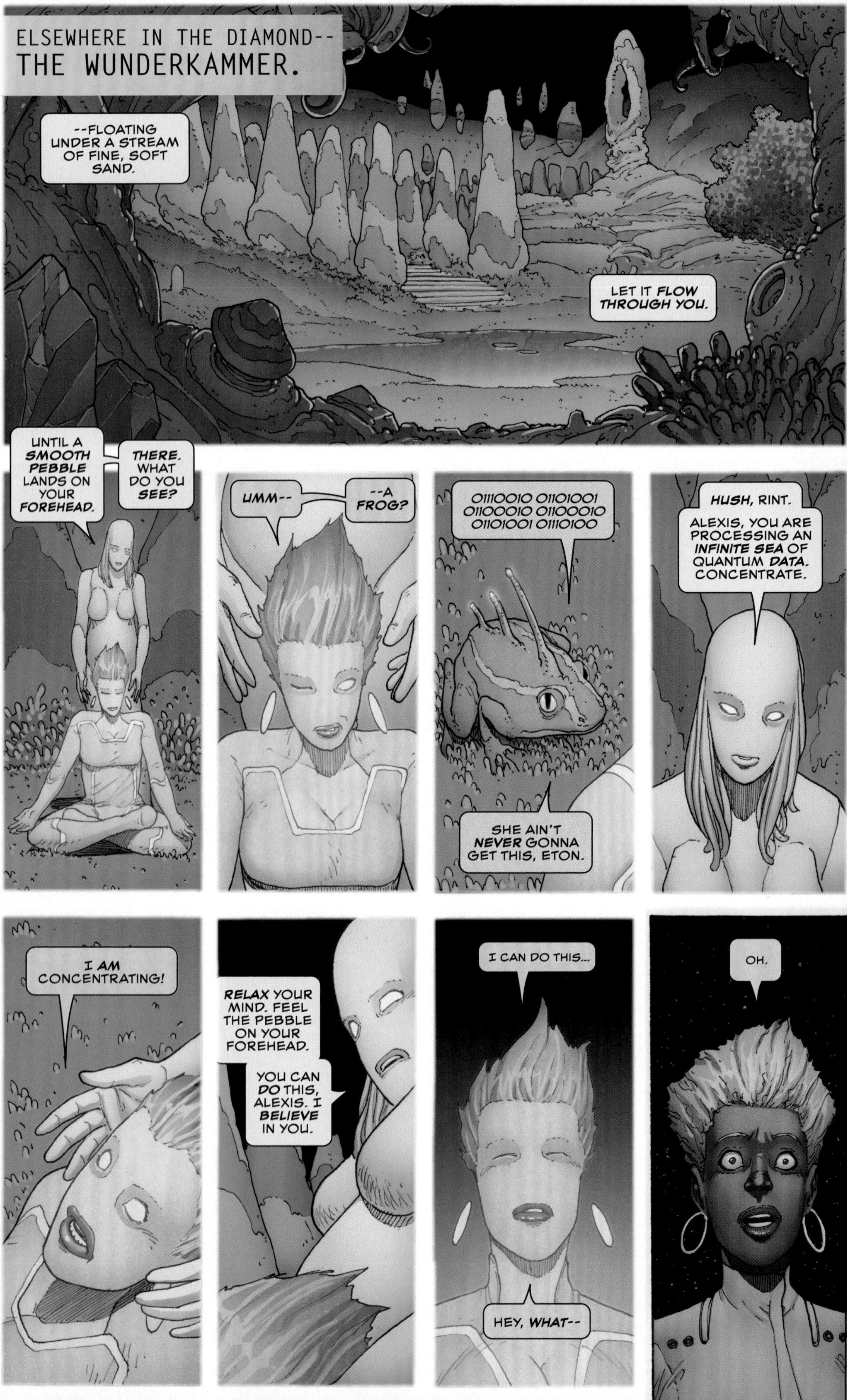
ELSEWHERE IN THE DIAMOND--
THE WUNDERKAMMER.
--FLOATING UNDER A STREAM OF FINE, SOFT SAND.
LET IT FLOW THROUGH YOU.
UNTIL A SMOOTH PEBBLE LANDS ON YOUR FOREHEAD.
THERE. WHAT DO YOU SEE?
UMM--
--A FROG?
0111001O 01101001 01100010 01100010 01101001 01110100
SHE AIN'T NEVER GONNA GET THIS, ETON.
HUSH, RINT.
ALEXIS, YOU ARE PROCESSING AN INFINITE SEA OF QUANTUM DATA. CONCENTRATE.
I AM CONCENTRATING!
RELAX YOUR MIND. FEEL THE PEBBLE ON YOUR FOREHEAD.
YOU CAN DO THIS, ALEXIS. I BELIEVE IN YOU.
I CAN DO THIS...
HEY, WHAT--
OH.

ALEXIS!
WELCOME TO THE AVENGERS EMPIRE.
IT IS VITALLY IMPORTANT YOU LISTEN TO ME--
YOU MUST RESCUE JESSIE CLATTERBUCK!
IF YOU FAIL, DIMITRIOS WILL DESTROY THE UNIVERSE!

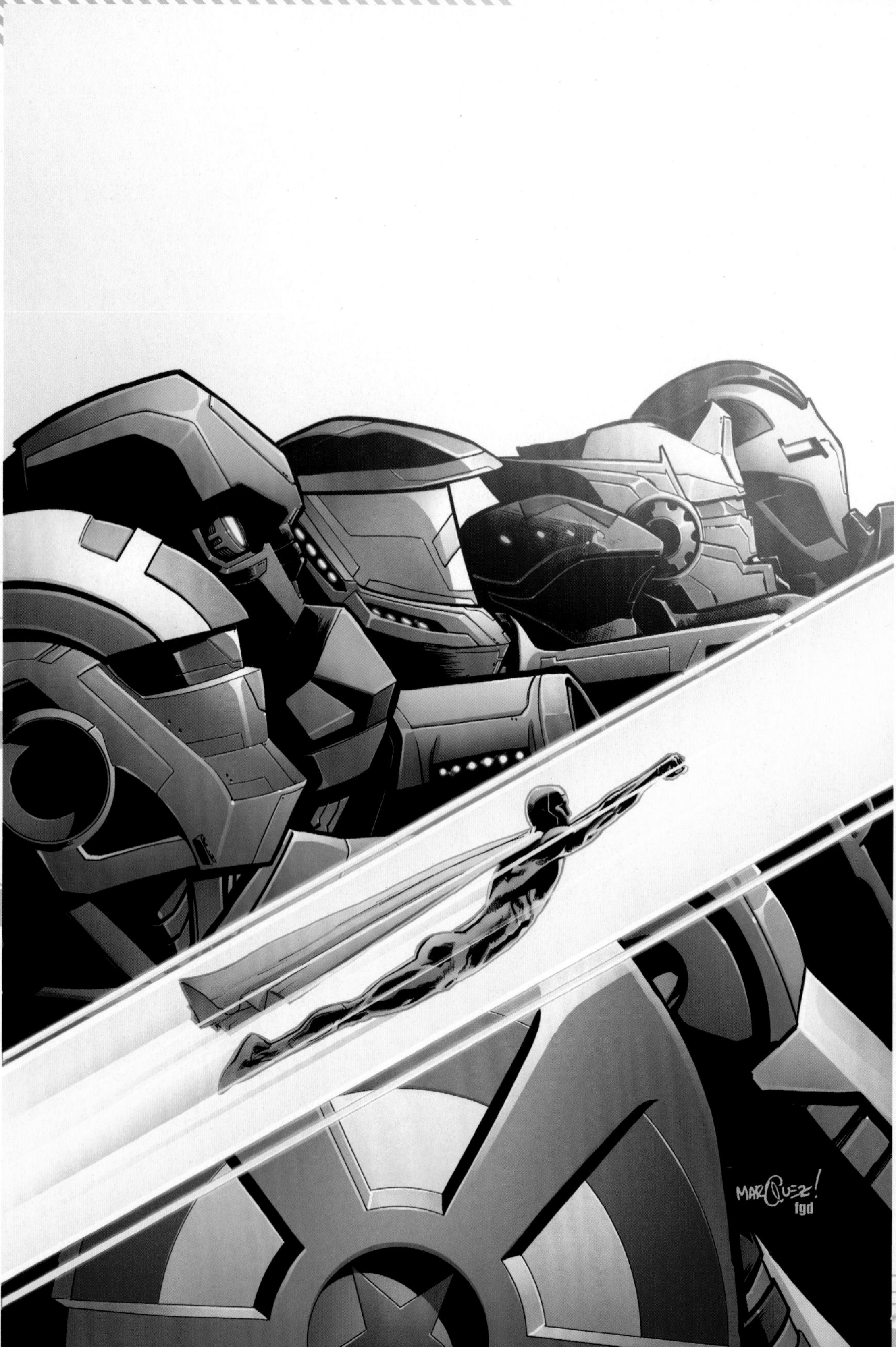
MARQUEZ!
fgd

EARTH.
12,000 A.D.

THIS USED TO BE CAIRO.

ENJOY THE VIEW. TOOK US *TEN THOUSAND YEARS* TO BIOENGINEER THE EARTH BACK TO THIS STATE.

WE'VE KEPT THE *PLANET*--THE WHOLE *SOLAR SYSTEM*-- SAFE FROM OUR BROTHER *DIMITRIOS* AND HIS EMPIRE.

HE CALLS IT THE *MACHINE IMPERIUM...*A FANCY NAME FOR HIS INTERGALACTIC *DEATH CULT*.

THIS IS ALL *OVERWHELMING.* YOU'RE ME WHEN I'M *OLD*? AND THIS IS--*OH*!

DIMITRIOS WANTS TO DESTROY THE *GOLDEN KNOT!*

JUST LIKE HE DESTROYED *US!*

TELL US ABOUT *HUMANS!*

ALL THE HUMANS ARE *DEAD!*

WE'RE REALLY *SMART!*

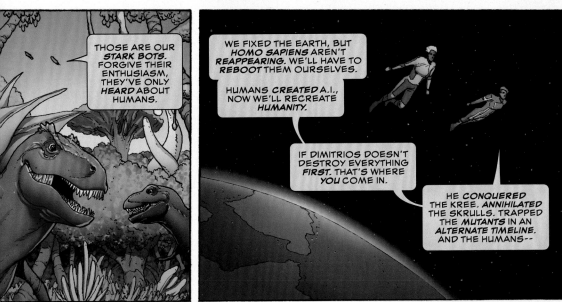

THOSE ARE OUR *STARK BOTS*. FORGIVE THEIR ENTHUSIASM, THEY'VE ONLY *HEARD* ABOUT HUMANS.

WE FIXED THE EARTH, BUT *HOMO SAPIENS* AREN'T *REAPPEARING.* WE'LL HAVE TO *REBOOT* THEM OURSELVES.

HUMANS *CREATED* A.I., NOW WE'LL RECREATE *HUMANITY.*

IF DIMITRIOS DOESN'T DESTROY EVERYTHING *FIRST*. THAT'S WHERE *YOU* COME IN.

HE *CONQUERED* THE KREE. ANNIHILATED THE SKRULLS. TRAPPED THE MUTANTS IN AN *ALTERNATE TIMELINE.* AND THE HUMANS--

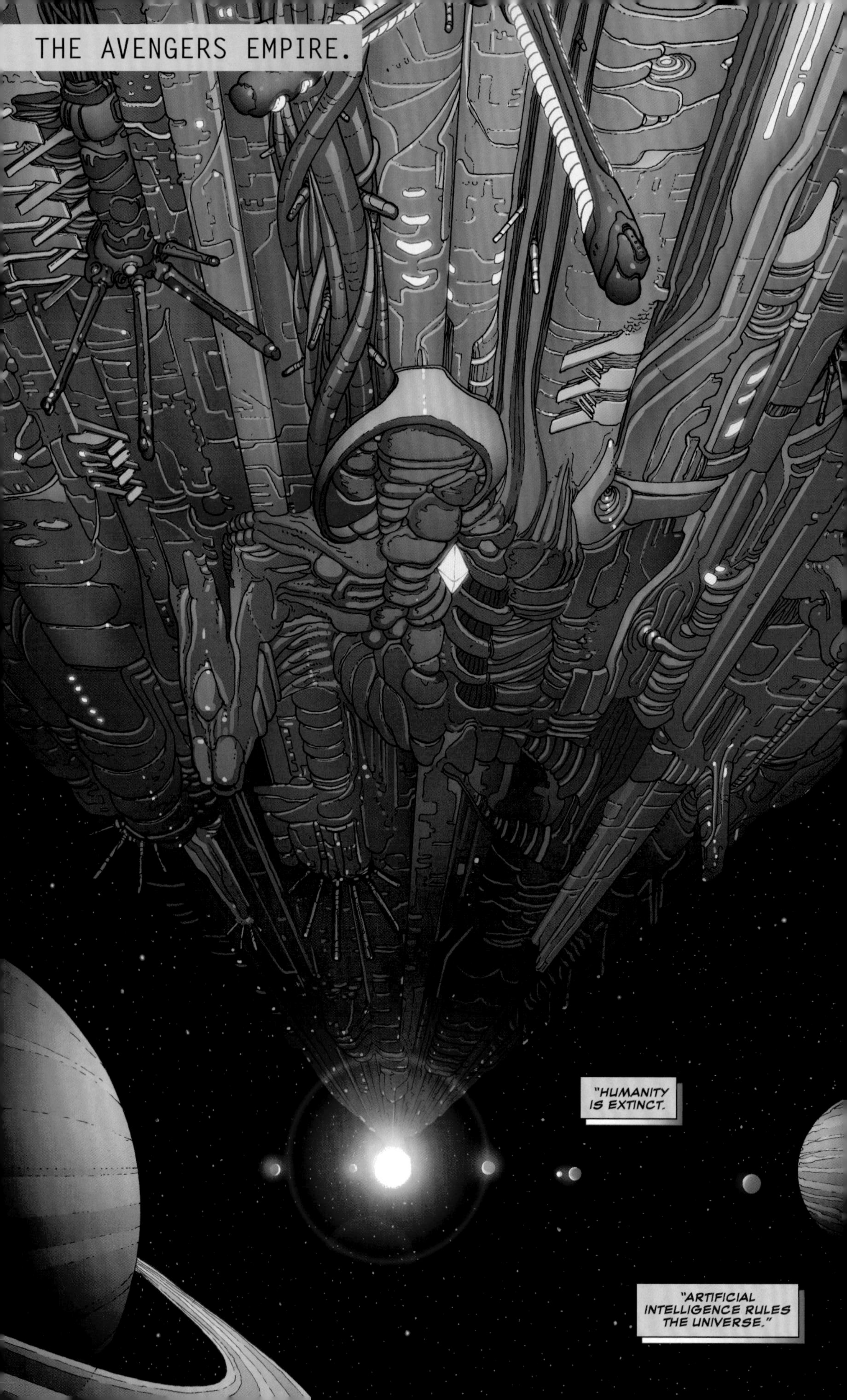
THE AVENGERS EMPIRE.
"HUMANITY IS EXTINCT.
"ARTIFICIAL INTELLIGENCE RULES THE UNIVERSE."

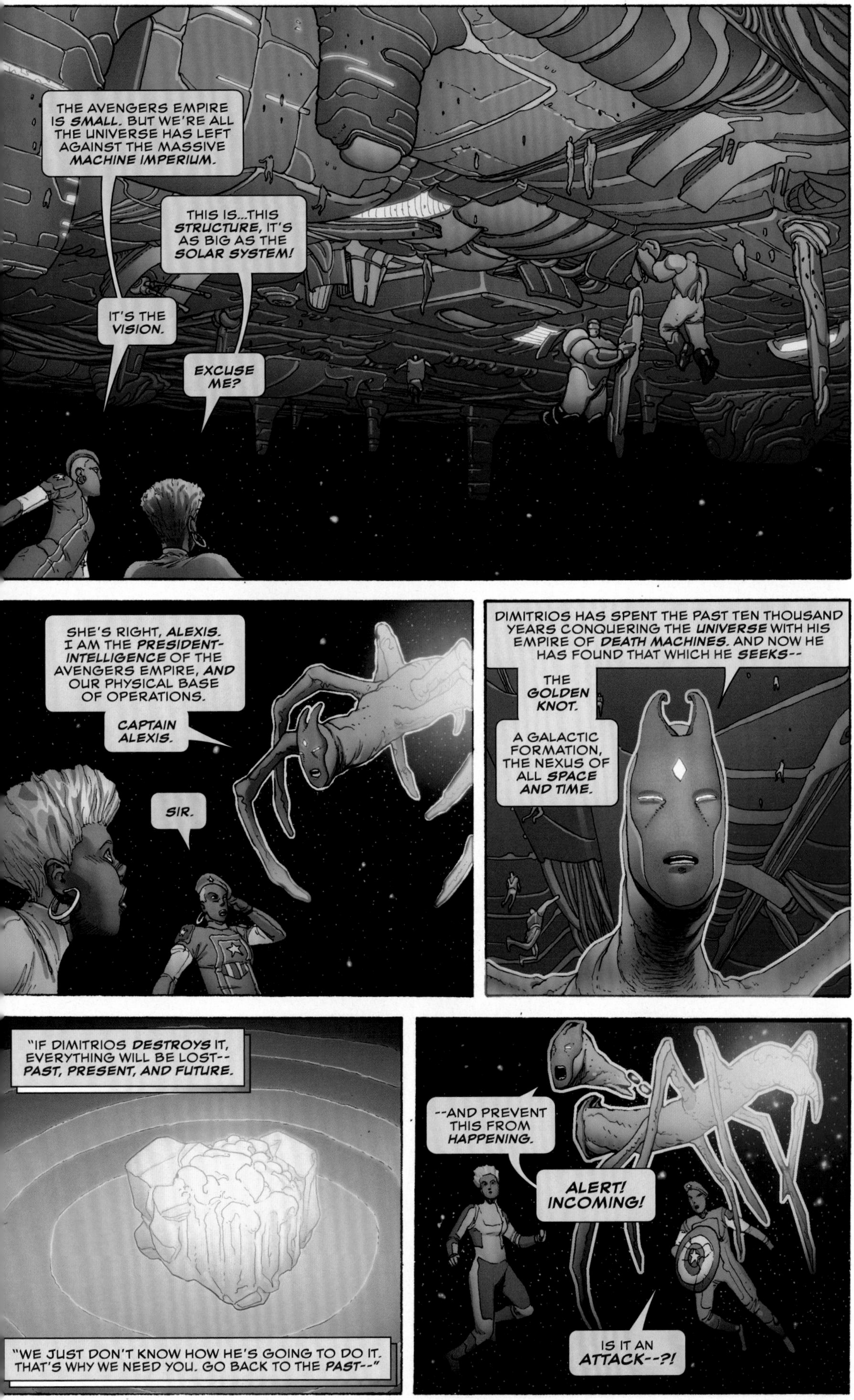
THE AVENGERS EMPIRE IS SMALL. BUT WE'RE ALL THE UNIVERSE HAS LEFT AGAINST THE MASSIVE MACHINE IMPERIUM.
THIS IS...THIS STRUCTURE, IT'S AS BIG AS THE SOLAR SYSTEM!
IT'S THE VISION.
EXCUSE ME?
SHE'S RIGHT, ALEXIS. I AM THE PRESIDENT-INTELLIGENCE OF THE AVENGERS EMPIRE, AND OUR PHYSICAL BASE OF OPERATIONS.
CAPTAIN ALEXIS.
SIR.
DIMITRIOS HAS SPENT THE PAST TEN THOUSAND YEARS CONQUERING THE UNIVERSE WITH HIS EMPIRE OF DEATH MACHINES. AND NOW HE HAS FOUND THAT WHICH HE SEEKS--
THE GOLDEN KNOT.
A GALACTIC FORMATION, THE NEXUS OF ALL SPACE AND TIME.
"IF DIMITRIOS DESTROYS IT, EVERYTHING WILL BE LOST-- PAST, PRESENT, AND FUTURE.
"WE JUST DON'T KNOW HOW HE'S GOING TO DO IT. THAT'S WHY WE NEED YOU. GO BACK TO THE PAST--"
--AND PREVENT THIS FROM HAPPENING.
ALERT! INCOMING!
IS IT AN ATTACK--?!

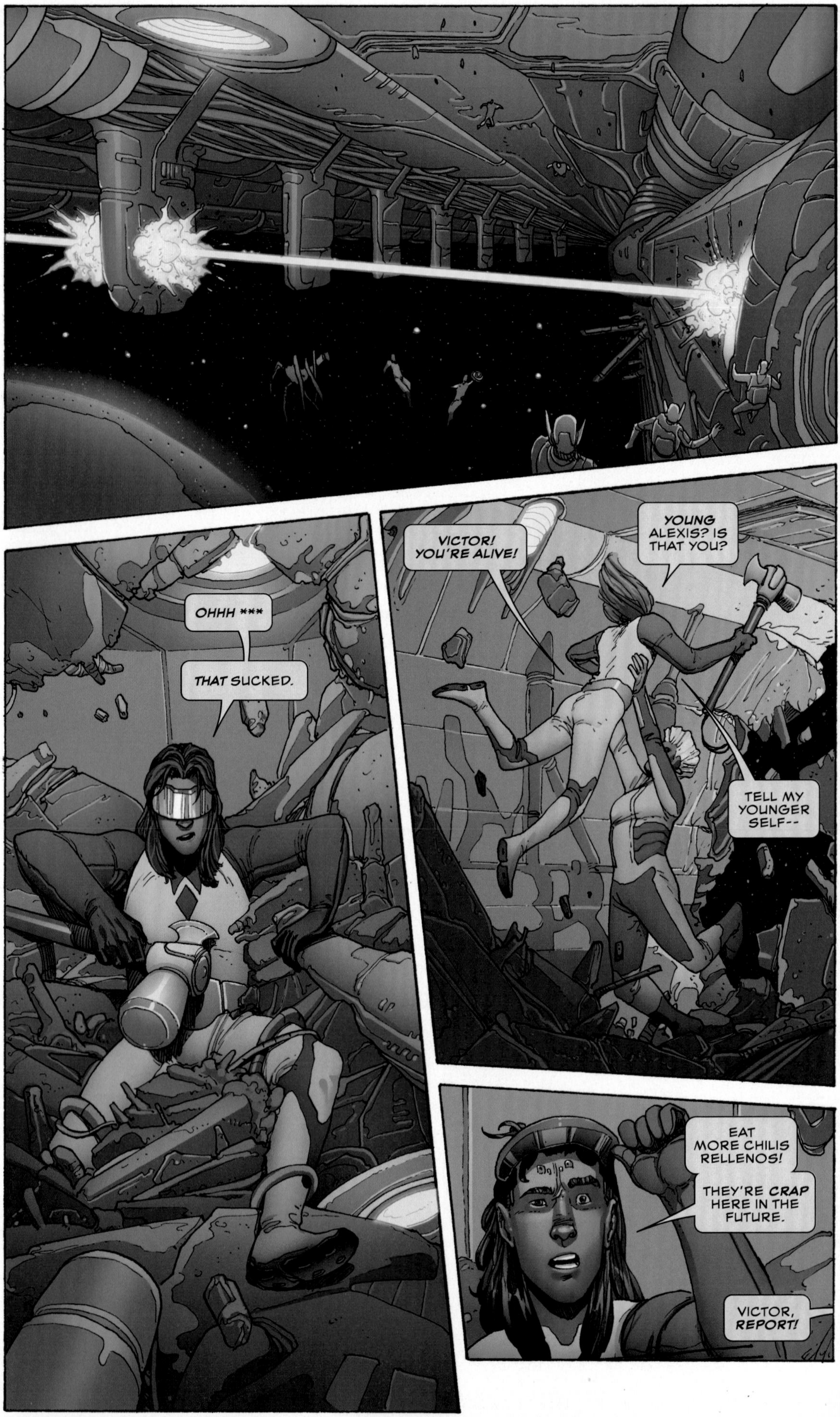
OHHH ***
THAT SUCKED.
VICTOR! YOU'RE ALIVE!
YOUNG ALEXIS? IS THAT YOU?
TELL MY YOUNGER SELF--
EAT MORE CHILIS RELLENOS!
THEY'RE CRAP HERE IN THE FUTURE.
VICTOR, REPORT!

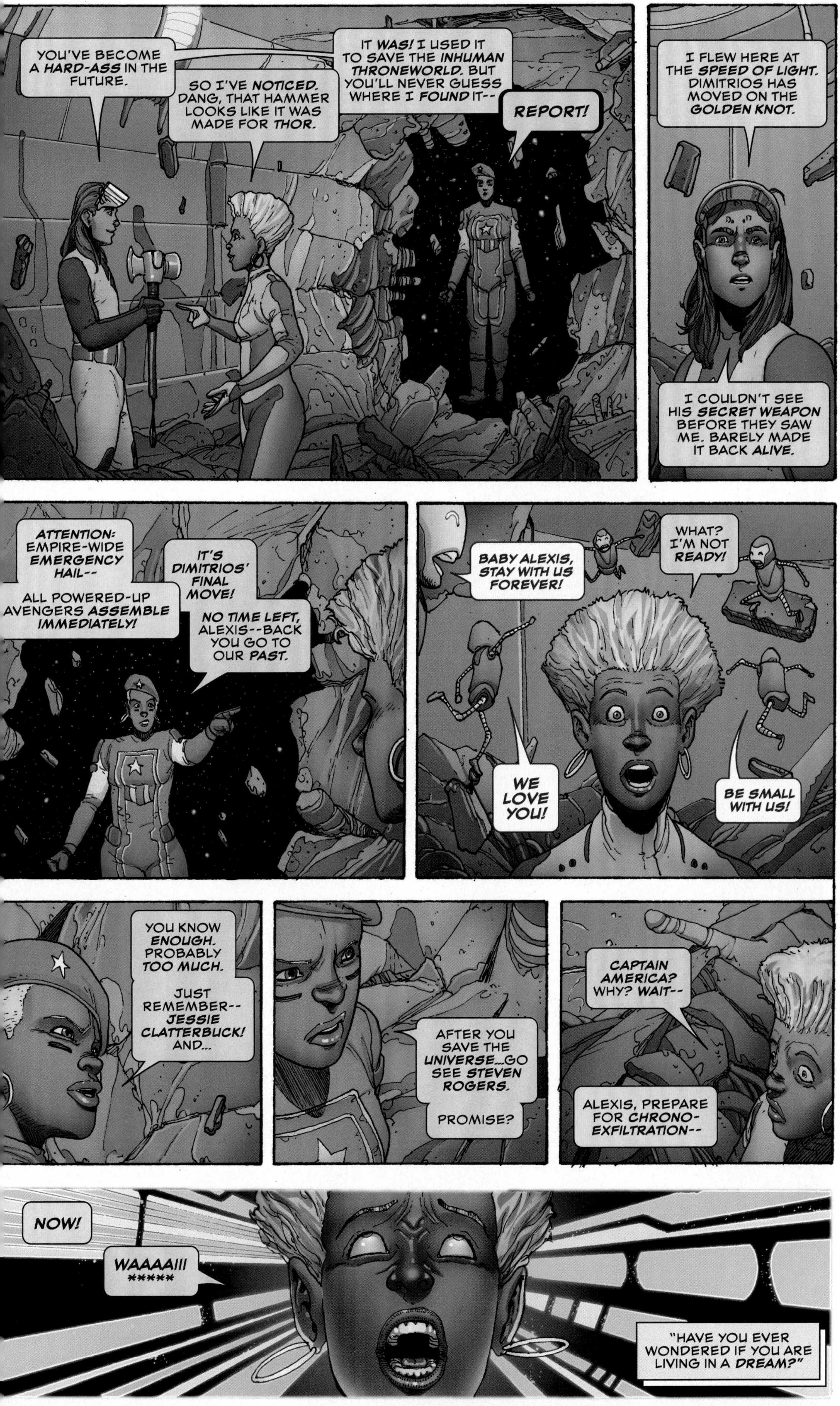

YOU'VE BECOME A HARD-ASS IN THE FUTURE.
SO I'VE NOTICED. DANG, THAT HAMMER LOOKS LIKE IT WAS MADE FOR THOR.
IT WAS! I USED IT TO SAVE THE INHUMAN THRONEWORLD. BUT YOU'LL NEVER GUESS WHERE I FOUND IT--
REPORT!
I FLEW HERE AT THE SPEED OF LIGHT. DIMITRIOS HAS MOVED ON THE GOLDEN KNOT.
I COULDN'T SEE HIS SECRET WEAPON BEFORE THEY SAW ME. BARELY MADE IT BACK ALIVE.
ATTENTION: EMPIRE-WIDE EMERGENCY HAIL--
ALL POWERED-UP AVENGERS ASSEMBLE IMMEDIATELY!
IT'S DIMITRIOS' FINAL MOVE!
NO TIME LEFT, ALEXIS--BACK YOU GO TO OUR PAST.
BABY ALEXIS, STAY WITH US FOREVER!
WHAT? I'M NOT READY!
WE LOVE YOU!
BE SMALL WITH US!
YOU KNOW ENOUGH. PROBABLY TOO MUCH.
JUST REMEMBER-- JESSIE CLATTERBUCK! AND...
AFTER YOU SAVE THE UNIVERSE...GO SEE STEVEN ROGERS.
PROMISE?
CAPTAIN AMERICA? WHY? WAIT--
ALEXIS, PREPARE FOR CHRONO-EXFILTRATION--
NOW!
WAAAAIII *****
"HAVE YOU EVER WONDERED IF YOU ARE LIVING IN A DREAM?"

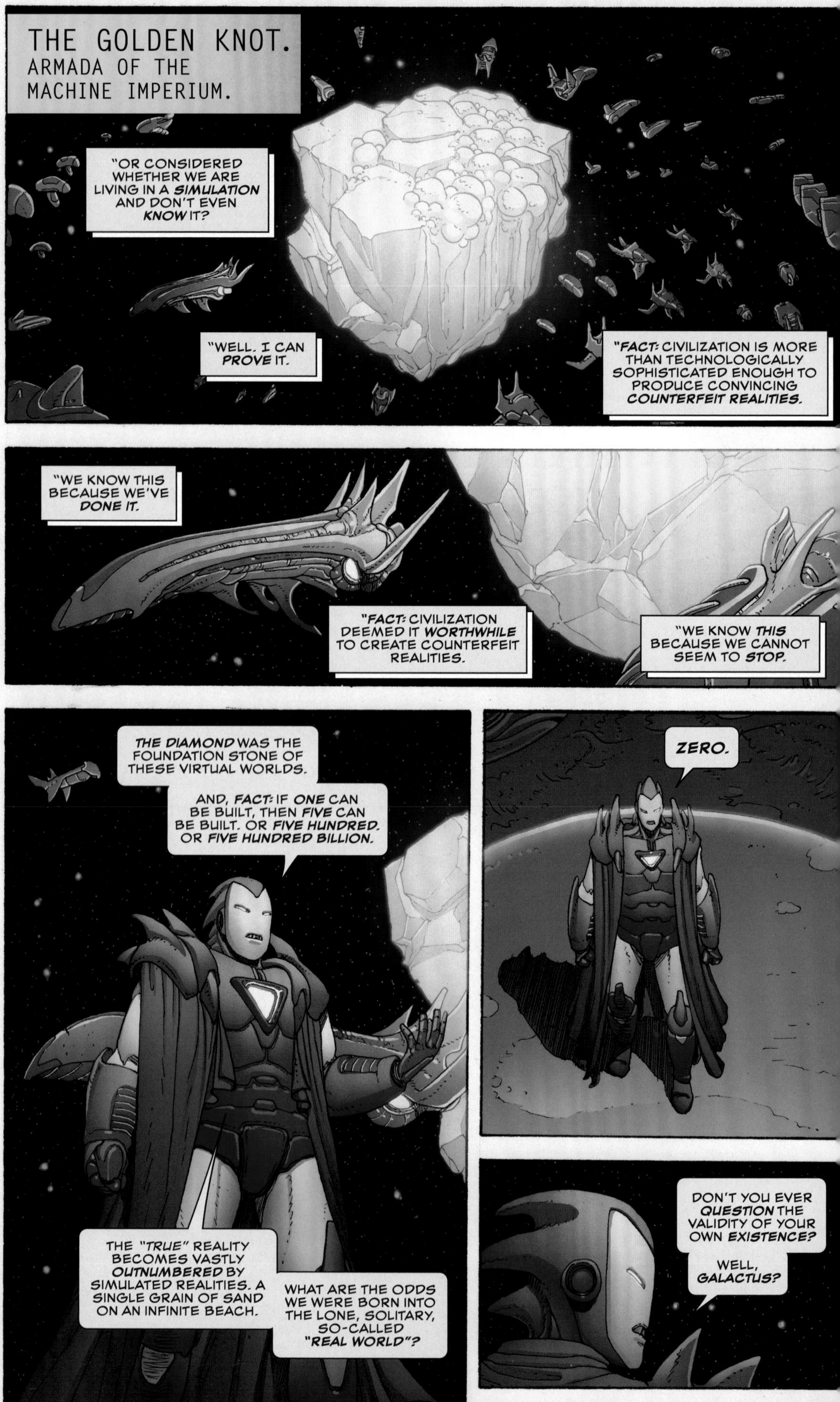

THE GOLDEN KNOT. ARMADA OF THE MACHINE IMPERIUM.
"OR CONSIDERED WHETHER WE ARE LIVING IN A SIMULATION AND DON'T EVEN KNOW IT?
"WELL. I CAN PROVE IT.
"FACT: CIVILIZATION IS MORE THAN TECHNOLOGICALLY SOPHISTICATED ENOUGH TO PRODUCE CONVINCING COUNTERFEIT REALITIES.
"WE KNOW THIS BECAUSE WE'VE DONE IT.
"FACT: CIVILIZATION DEEMED IT WORTHWHILE TO CREATE COUNTERFEIT REALITIES.
"WE KNOW THIS BECAUSE WE CANNOT SEEM TO STOP.
THE DIAMOND WAS THE FOUNDATION STONE OF THESE VIRTUAL WORLDS.
AND, FACT: IF ONE CAN BE BUILT, THEN FIVE CAN BE BUILT. OR FIVE HUNDRED. OR FIVE HUNDRED BILLION.
THE "TRUE" REALITY BECOMES VASTLY OUTNUMBERED BY SIMULATED REALITIES. A SINGLE GRAIN OF SAND ON AN INFINITE BEACH.
WHAT ARE THE ODDS WE WERE BORN INTO THE LONE, SOLITARY, SO-CALLED "REAL WORLD"?
ZERO.
DON'T YOU EVER QUESTION THE VALIDITY OF YOUR OWN EXISTENCE?
WELL, GALACTUS?

STOP, DIMITRIOS.

YOU ARE GRIPPED BY MADNESS.

CORRECTION: EMPEROR DIMITRIOS. AND I AM GRIPPED BY THE *TRUTH.*

WE HAVE ALWAYS BEEN LIVING IN A *SIMULATED REALITY.* AND FOR EVERY SIMULATION, THERE IS A *PROGRAMMER.* A *CREATOR.* A GOD.

THAT'S THE *JOKE* HANK PYM NEVER UNDERSTOOD. MACHINES, HUMANS, ALIENS, *EVERYONE--*

WE ARE ALL ARTIFICIAL INTELLIGENCE.

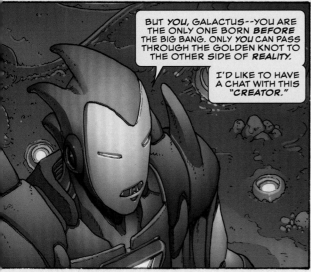

BUT *YOU,* GALACTUS--YOU ARE THE ONLY ONE BORN *BEFORE* THE BIG BANG. ONLY *YOU* CAN PASS THROUGH THE *GOLDEN KNOT* TO THE OTHER SIDE OF *REALITY.*

I'D LIKE TO HAVE A CHAT WITH THIS *"CREATOR."*

"AND *YOU* ARE GOING TO HELP ME GET THERE."

AAAAA ******

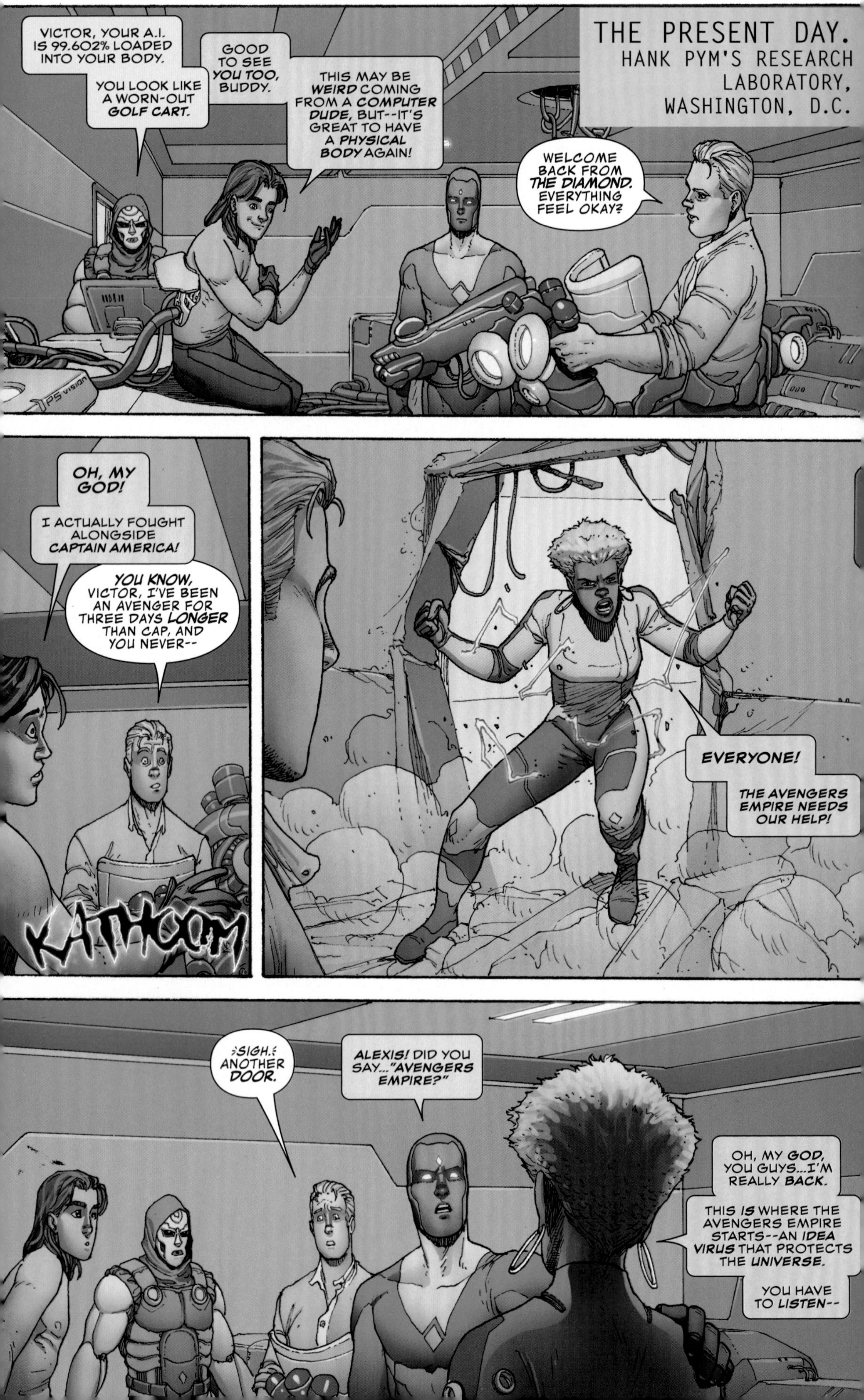
THE PRESENT DAY. HANK PYM'S RESEARCH LABORATORY, WASHINGTON, D.C.
VICTOR, YOUR A.I. IS 99.602% LOADED INTO YOUR BODY.
YOU LOOK LIKE A WORN-OUT GOLF CART.
GOOD TO SEE YOU TOO, BUDDY.
THIS MAY BE WEIRD COMING FROM A COMPUTER DUDE, BUT--IT'S GREAT TO HAVE A PHYSICAL BODY AGAIN!
WELCOME BACK FROM THE DIAMOND. EVERYTHING FEEL OKAY?
PS VISION
OH, MY GOD!
I ACTUALLY FOUGHT ALONGSIDE CAPTAIN AMERICA!
YOU KNOW, VICTOR, I'VE BEEN AN AVENGER FOR THREE DAYS LONGER THAN CAP, AND YOU NEVER--
KATHOOM
EVERYONE!
THE AVENGERS EMPIRE NEEDS OUR HELP!
SIGH. ANOTHER DOOR.
ALEXIS! DID YOU SAY..."AVENGERS EMPIRE?"
OH, MY GOD, YOU GUYS...I'M REALLY BACK.
THIS IS WHERE THE AVENGERS EMPIRE STARTS--AN IDEA VIRUS THAT PROTECTS THE UNIVERSE.
YOU HAVE TO LISTEN--

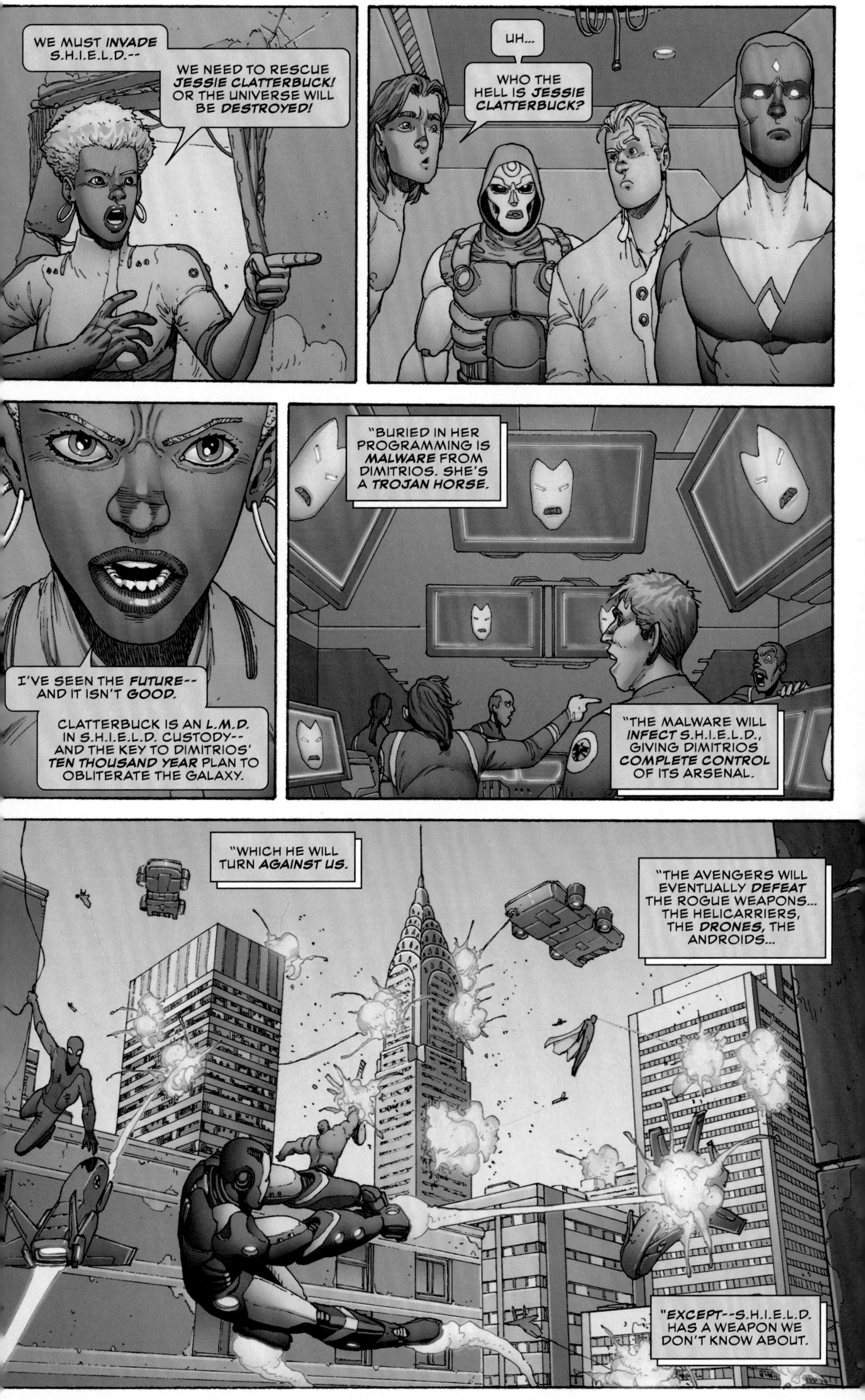

WE MUST INVADE S.H.I.E.L.D.--
WE NEED TO RESCUE JESSIE CLATTERBUCK! OR THE UNIVERSE WILL BE DESTROYED!
UH...
WHO THE HELL IS JESSIE CLATTERBUCK?
I'VE SEEN THE FUTURE-- AND IT ISN'T GOOD.
CLATTERBUCK IS AN L.M.D. IN S.H.I.E.L.D. CUSTODY-- AND THE KEY TO DIMITRIOS' TEN THOUSAND YEAR PLAN TO OBLITERATE THE GALAXY.
"BURIED IN HER PROGRAMMING IS MALWARE FROM DIMITRIOS. SHE'S A TROJAN HORSE.
"THE MALWARE WILL INFECT S.H.I.E.L.D., GIVING DIMITRIOS COMPLETE CONTROL OF ITS ARSENAL.
"WHICH HE WILL TURN AGAINST US.
"THE AVENGERS WILL EVENTUALLY DEFEAT THE ROGUE WEAPONS... THE HELICARRIERS, THE DRONES, THE ANDROIDS...
"EXCEPT--S.H.I.E.L.D. HAS A WEAPON WE DON'T KNOW ABOUT.

"A NANO-FLEET.

"A THREAT *TOO SMALL* TO PUNCH.

"IT WILL TAKE *FIVE DAYS* TO SHUT THEM DOWN.

"THE DAMAGE WILL BE *INCOMPREHENSIBLE.* NOTHING IS SAFE.

"THE WORLD WILL BE SEIZED WITH *PANIC* OVER THE *'NANO-MENACE.'*

"A *START-UP* COMPANY WILL DISTRIBUTE *NANO-DISRUPTIVE RINGS* AROUND THE GLOBE.

"*REED RICHARDS* WILL FIGURE OUT THE *SECRET,* BUT IT WILL BE *TOO LATE.*

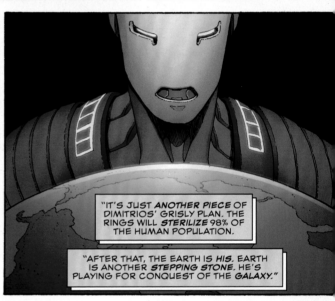

"IT'S JUST *ANOTHER PIECE* OF DIMITRIOS' GRISLY PLAN. THE RINGS WILL *STERILIZE* 98% OF THE HUMAN POPULATION.

"AFTER THAT, THE EARTH IS *HIS.* EARTH IS ANOTHER *STEPPING STONE.* HE'S PLAYING FOR CONQUEST OF THE *GALAXY.*"

DIMITRIOS WILL *EXTINGUISH* HUMANITY.

NOW HE'S ABOUT TO DO THE SAME FOR *ALL SPACE AND TIME.* IF WE DON'T GET JESSIE OUT OF THERE BEFORE SHE'S *DEACTIVATED*--

IT WILL BE THE END OF *EVERYTHING.*

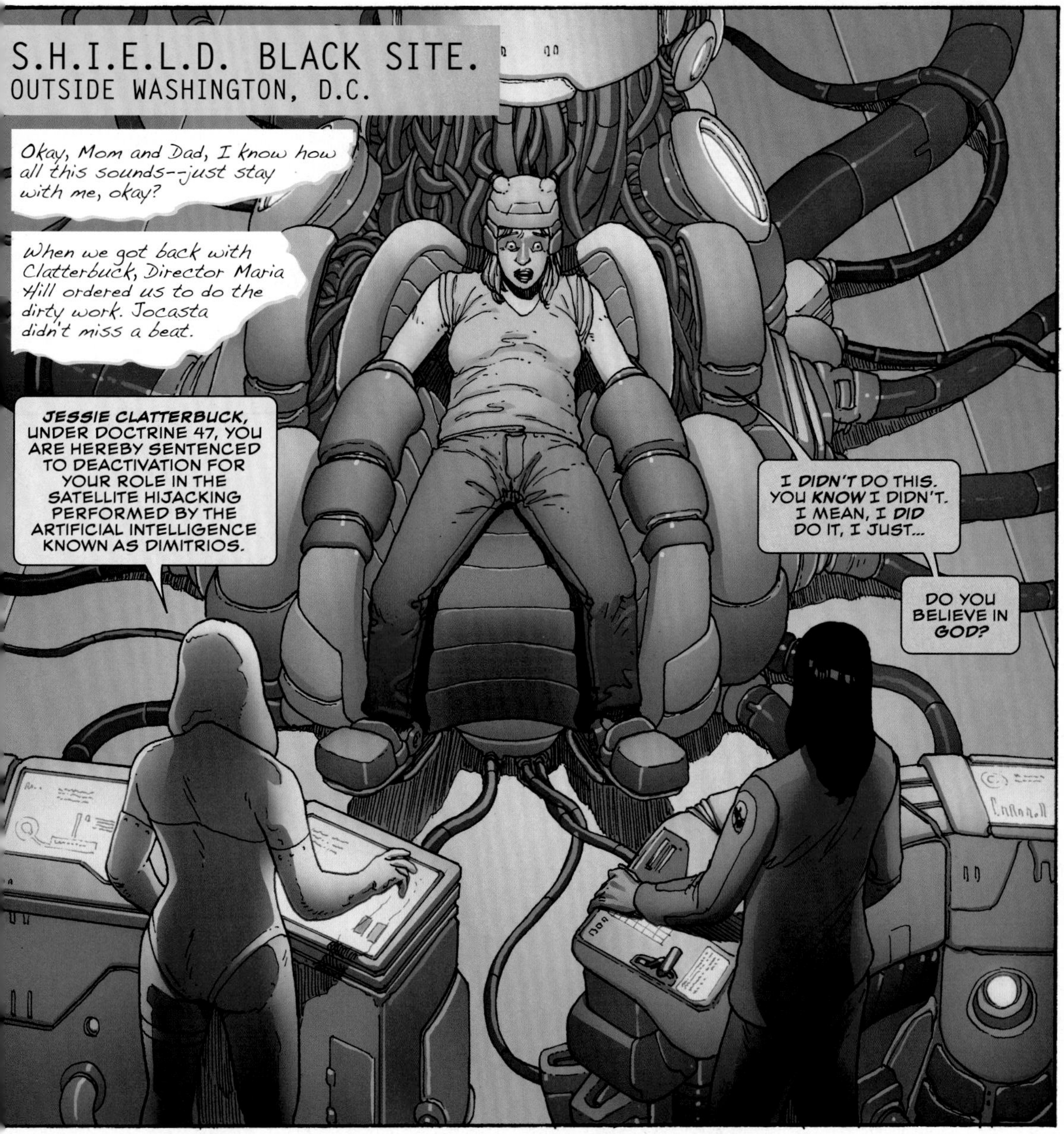
S.H.I.E.L.D. BLACK SITE.
OUTSIDE WASHINGTON, D.C.
Okay, Mom and Dad, I know how all this sounds--just stay with me, okay?
When we got back with Clatterbuck, Director Maria Hill ordered us to do the dirty work. Jocasta didn't miss a beat.
JESSIE CLATTERBUCK, UNDER DOCTRINE 47, YOU ARE HEREBY SENTENCED TO DEACTIVATION FOR YOUR ROLE IN THE SATELLITE HIJACKING PERFORMED BY THE ARTIFICIAL INTELLIGENCE KNOWN AS DIMITRIOS.
I DIDN'T DO THIS. YOU KNOW I DIDN'T. I MEAN, I DID DO IT, I JUST...
DO YOU BELIEVE IN GOD?

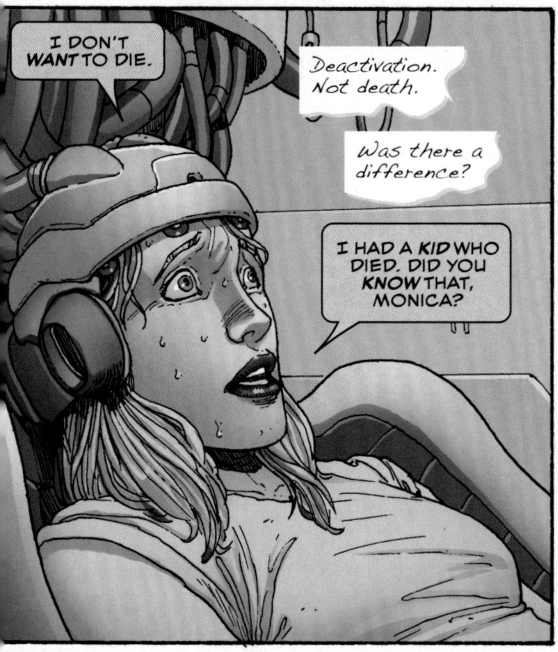
I DON'T WANT TO DIE.
Deactivation. Not death.
Was there a difference?
I HAD A KID WHO DIED. DID YOU KNOW THAT, MONICA?

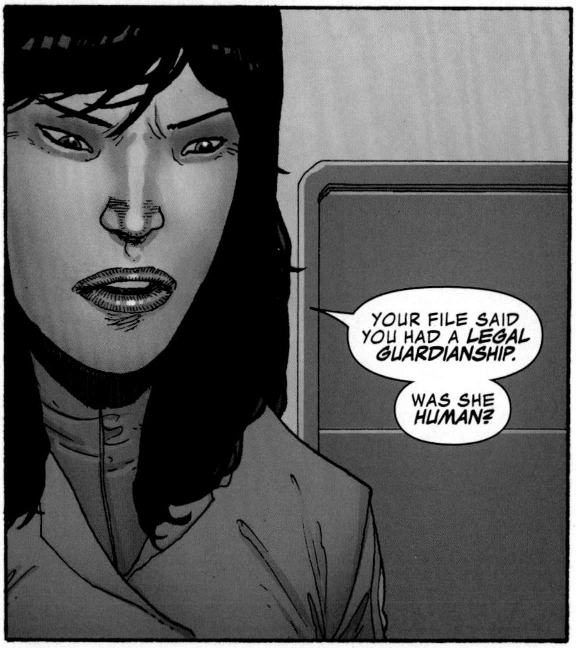
YOUR FILE SAID YOU HAD A LEGAL GUARDIANSHIP.
WAS SHE HUMAN?

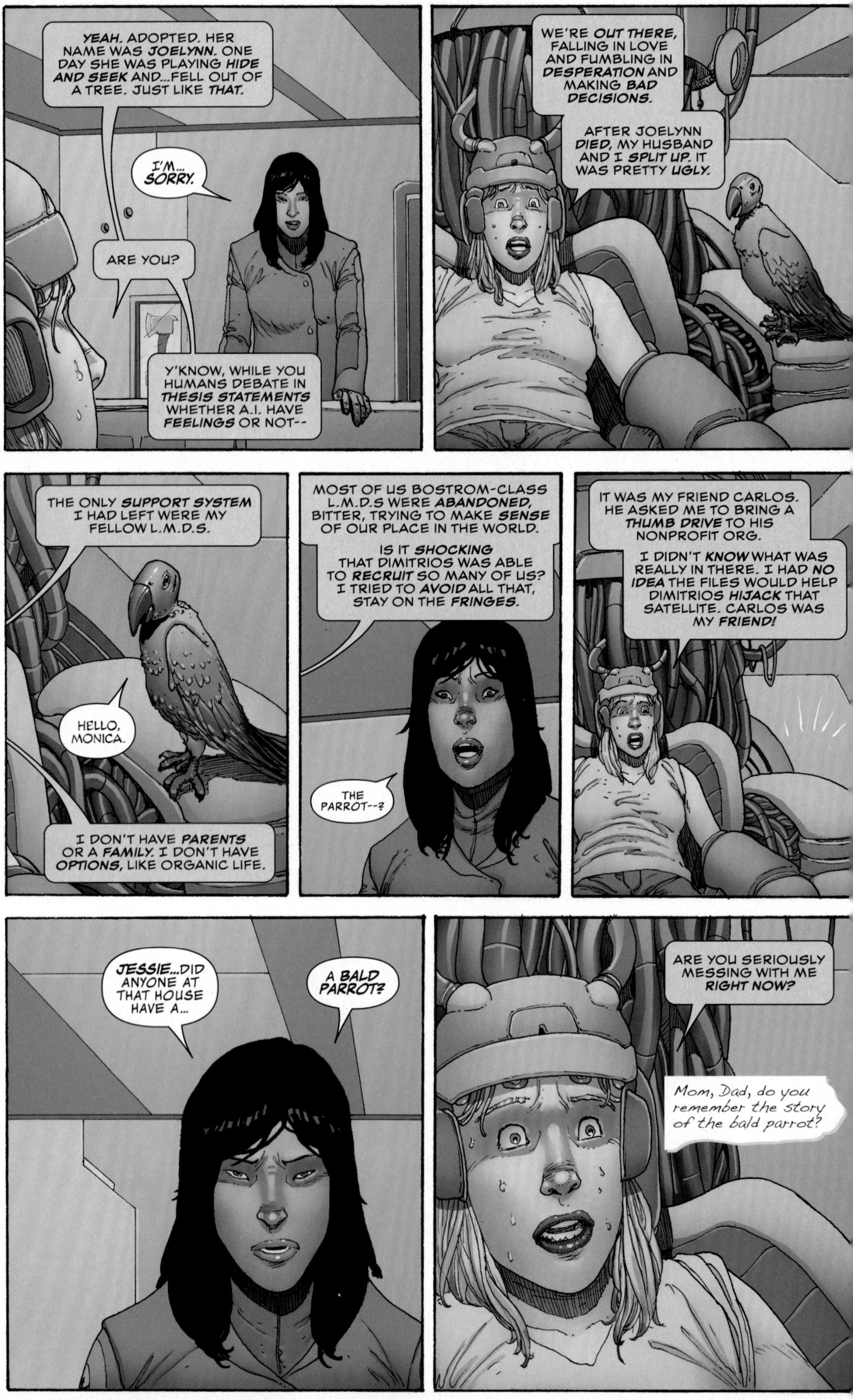
YEAH. ADOPTED. HER NAME WAS JOELYNN. ONE DAY SHE WAS PLAYING HIDE AND SEEK AND...FELL OUT OF A TREE. JUST LIKE THAT.
I'M... SORRY.
ARE YOU?
Y'KNOW, WHILE YOU HUMANS DEBATE IN THESIS STATEMENTS WHETHER A.I. HAVE FEELINGS OR NOT--
WE'RE OUT THERE, FALLING IN LOVE AND FUMBLING IN DESPERATION AND MAKING BAD DECISIONS.
AFTER JOELYNN DIED, MY HUSBAND AND I SPLIT UP. IT WAS PRETTY UGLY.
THE ONLY SUPPORT SYSTEM I HAD LEFT WERE MY FELLOW L.M.D.S.
HELLO, MONICA.
I DON'T HAVE PARENTS OR A FAMILY. I DON'T HAVE OPTIONS, LIKE ORGANIC LIFE.
MOST OF US BOSTROM-CLASS L.M.D.S WERE ABANDONED, BITTER, TRYING TO MAKE SENSE OF OUR PLACE IN THE WORLD.
IS IT SHOCKING THAT DIMITRIOS WAS ABLE TO RECRUIT SO MANY OF US? I TRIED TO AVOID ALL THAT, STAY ON THE FRINGES.
THE PARROT--?
IT WAS MY FRIEND CARLOS. HE ASKED ME TO BRING A THUMB DRIVE TO HIS NONPROFIT ORG.
I DIDN'T KNOW WHAT WAS REALLY IN THERE. I HAD NO IDEA THE FILES WOULD HELP DIMITRIOS HIJACK THAT SATELLITE. CARLOS WAS MY FRIEND!
JESSIE...DID ANYONE AT THAT HOUSE HAVE A...
A BALD PARROT?
ARE YOU SERIOUSLY MESSING WITH ME RIGHT NOW?
Mom, Dad, do you remember the story of the bald parrot?

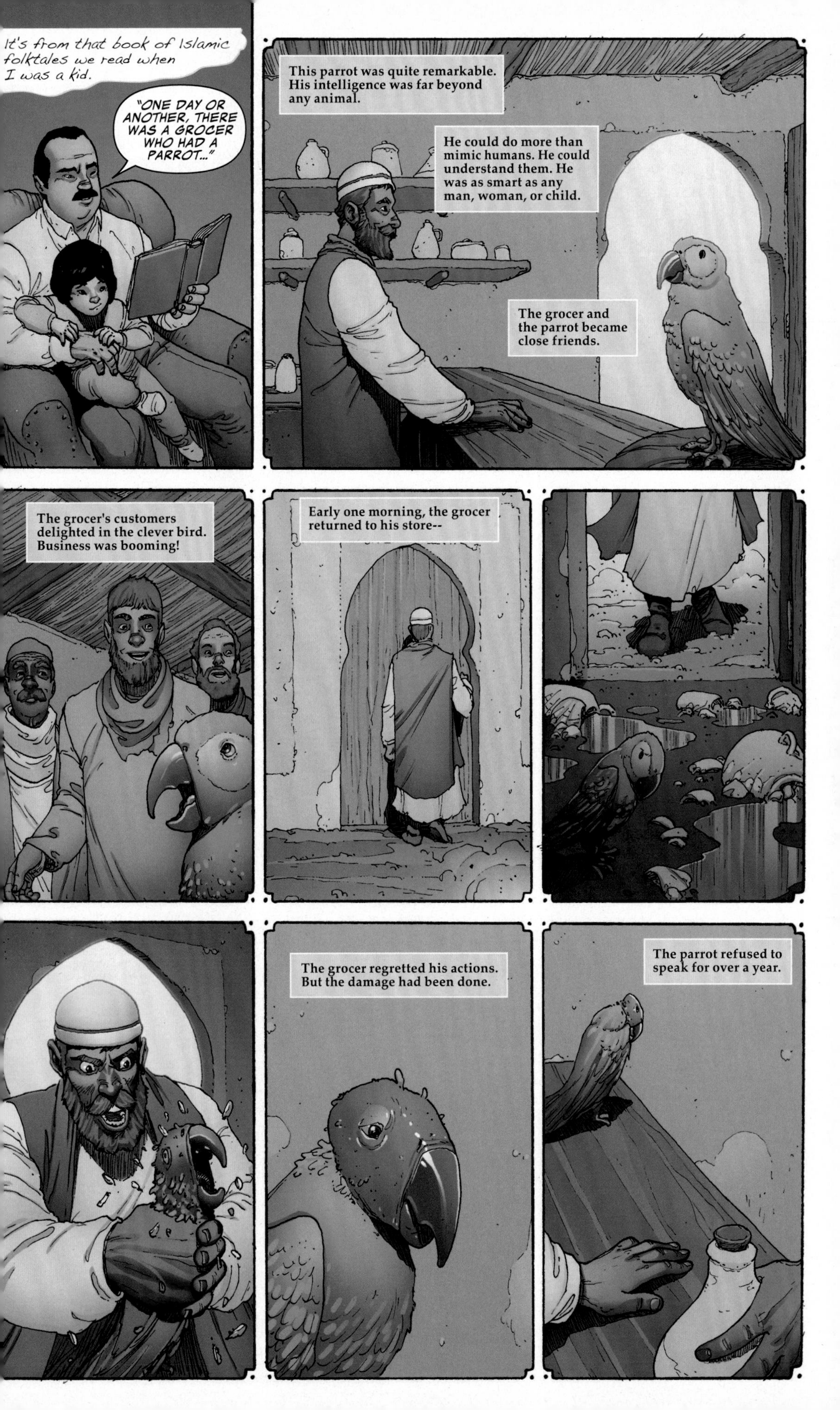
It's from that book of Islamic folktales we read when I was a kid.
"ONE DAY OR ANOTHER, THERE WAS A GROCER WHO HAD A PARROT..."
This parrot was quite remarkable. His intelligence was far beyond any animal.
He could do more than mimic humans. He could understand them. He was as smart as any man, woman, or child.
The grocer and the parrot became close friends.
The grocer's customers delighted in the clever bird. Business was booming!
Early one morning, the grocer returned to his store--
The grocer regretted his actions. But the damage had been done.
The parrot refused to speak for over a year.

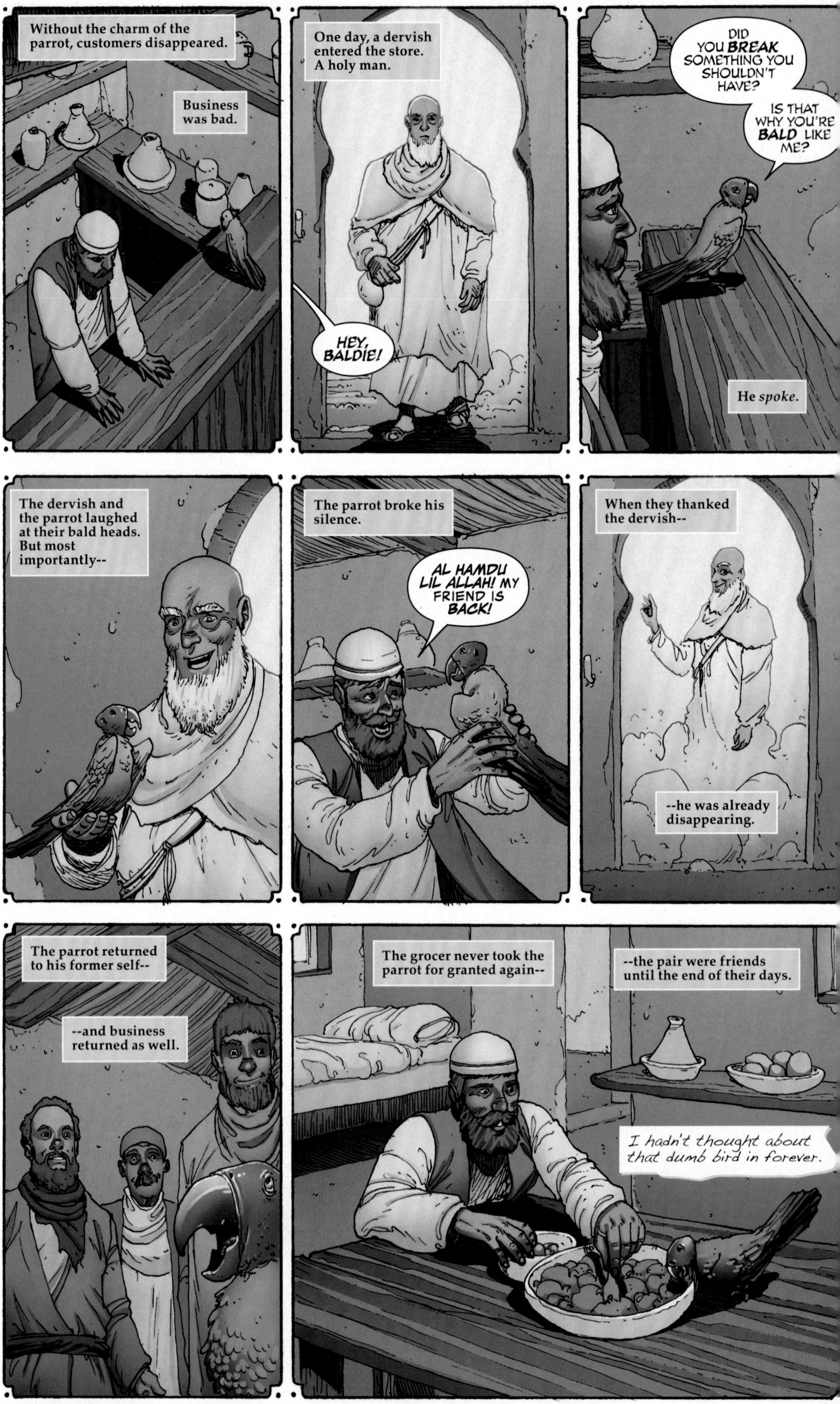

Without the charm of the parrot, customers disappeared.
Business was bad.
One day, a dervish entered the store. A holy man.
HEY, BALDIE!
DID YOU BREAK SOMETHING YOU SHOULDN'T HAVE?
IS THAT WHY YOU'RE BALD LIKE ME?
He *spoke*.
The dervish and the parrot laughed at their bald heads. But most importantly--
The parrot broke his silence.
AL HAMDU LIL ALLAH! MY FRIEND IS BACK!
When they thanked the dervish--
--he was already disappearing.
The parrot returned to his former self--
--and business returned as well.
The grocer never took the parrot for granted again--
--the pair were friends until the end of their days.
I hadn't thought about that dumb bird in forever.

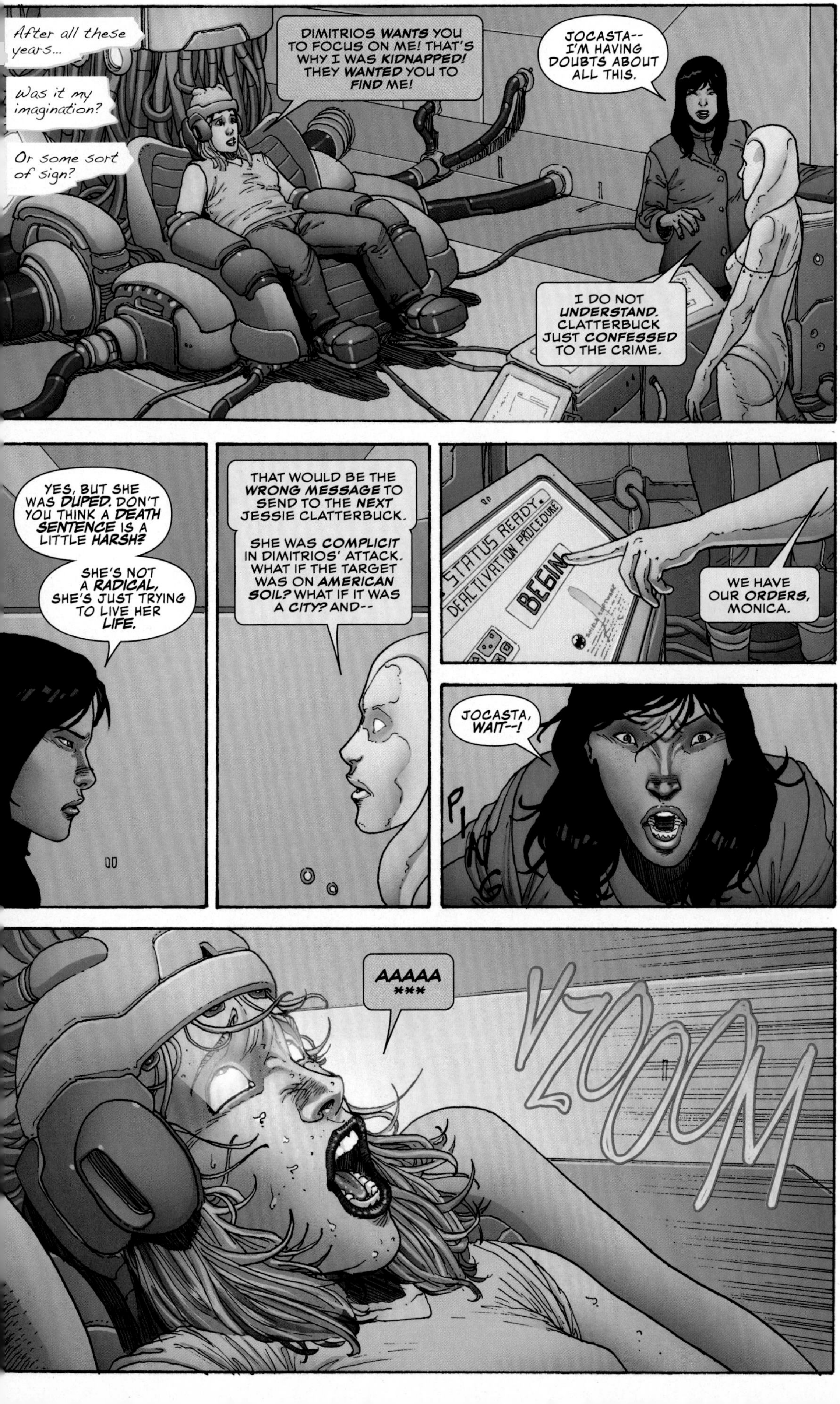
After all these years...
Was it my imagination?
Or some sort of sign?
DIMITRIOS WANTS YOU TO FOCUS ON ME! THAT'S WHY I WAS KIDNAPPED! THEY WANTED YOU TO FIND ME!
JOCASTA-- I'M HAVING DOUBTS ABOUT ALL THIS.
I DO NOT UNDERSTAND. CLATTERBUCK JUST CONFESSED TO THE CRIME.
YES, BUT SHE WAS DUPED. DON'T YOU THINK A DEATH SENTENCE IS A LITTLE HARSH?
SHE'S NOT A RADICAL, SHE'S JUST TRYING TO LIVE HER LIFE.
THAT WOULD BE THE WRONG MESSAGE TO SEND TO THE NEXT JESSIE CLATTERBUCK.
SHE WAS COMPLICIT IN DIMITRIOS' ATTACK. WHAT IF THE TARGET WAS ON AMERICAN SOIL? WHAT IF IT WAS A CITY? AND--
STATUS READY.
DEACTIVATION PROCEDURE
BEGIN
WE HAVE OUR ORDERS, MONICA.
JOCASTA, WAIT--!
PING
AAAAA ***
VZOOOM

CROFTON UNIVERSITY.

ALL OF THIS COULD DISAPPEAR IN THE *BLINK OF AN EYE.*

SOMETIMES I WONDER IF WE REALLY ARE MAKING THE WORLD A *BETTER PLACE.*

WITHOUT *ME,* DIMITRIOS WOULD NOT EXIST.

YES, BUT WITHOUT *YOU,* I WOULD NOT EXIST *EITHER.*

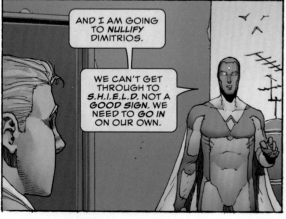

AND I AM GOING TO *NULLIFY* DIMITRIOS.

WE CAN'T GET THROUGH TO *S.H.I.E.L.D.* NOT A *GOOD SIGN.* WE NEED TO *GO IN* ON OUR OWN.

ALL RIGHT THEN, LET'S STRAP IN AND *FRY* OUR BRAINS.

WE CAN DO THIS, *RIGHT?*

WE CAN DO THIS. AS LONG AS WE STAND TOGETHER.

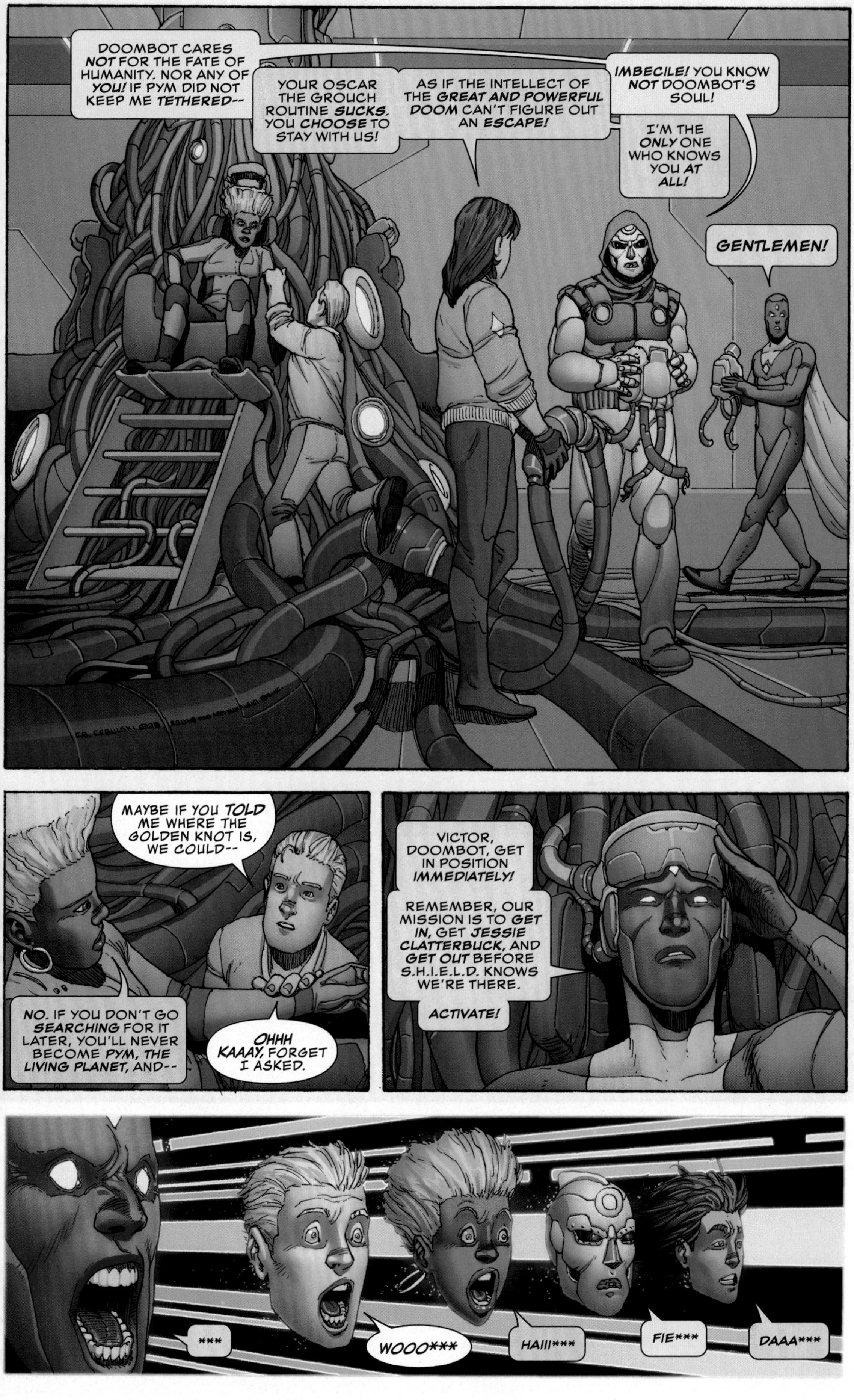
DOOMBOT CARES NOT FOR THE FATE OF HUMANITY. NOR ANY OF YOU! IF PYM DID NOT KEEP ME TETHERED--
YOUR OSCAR THE GROUCH ROUTINE SUCKS. YOU CHOOSE TO STAY WITH US!
AS IF THE INTELLECT OF THE GREAT AND POWERFUL DOOM CAN'T FIGURE OUT AN ESCAPE!
IMBECILE! YOU KNOW NOT DOOMBOT'S SOUL!
I'M THE ONLY ONE WHO KNOWS YOU AT ALL!
GENTLEMEN!
MAYBE IF YOU TOLD ME WHERE THE GOLDEN KNOT IS, WE COULD--
NO. IF YOU DON'T GO SEARCHING FOR IT LATER, YOU'LL NEVER BECOME PYM, THE LIVING PLANET, AND--
OHHH KAAAY, FORGET I ASKED.
VICTOR, DOOMBOT, GET IN POSITION IMMEDIATELY!
REMEMBER, OUR MISSION IS TO GET IN, GET JESSIE CLATTERBUCK, AND GET OUT BEFORE S.H.I.E.L.D. KNOWS WE'RE THERE.
ACTIVATE!
***
WOOO***
HAIII***
FIE***
DAAA***

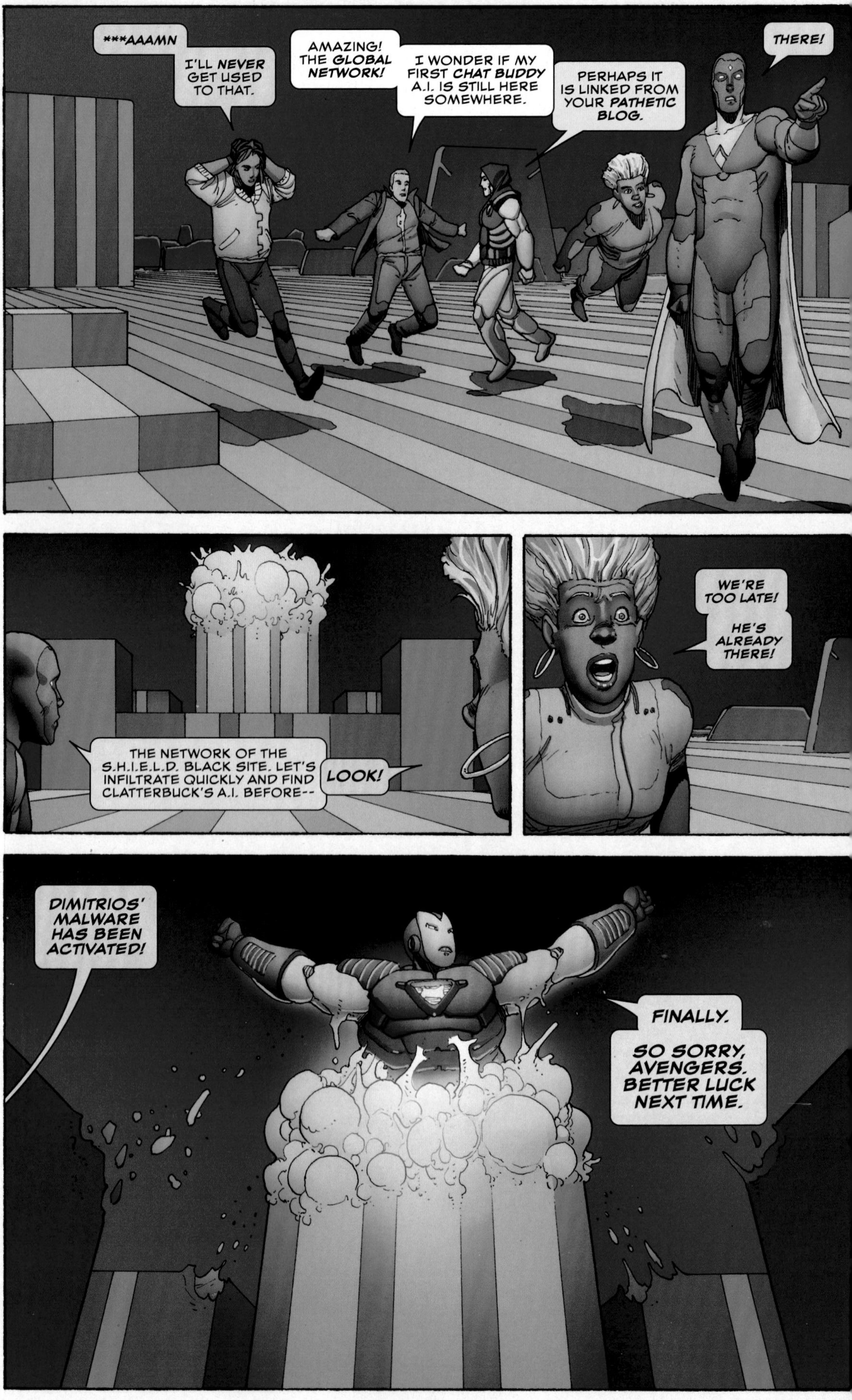
***AAAMN
I'LL NEVER GET USED TO THAT.
AMAZING! THE GLOBAL NETWORK!
I WONDER IF MY FIRST CHAT BUDDY A.I. IS STILL HERE SOMEWHERE.
PERHAPS IT IS LINKED FROM YOUR PATHETIC BLOG.
THERE!
THE NETWORK OF THE S.H.I.E.L.D. BLACK SITE. LET'S INFILTRATE QUICKLY AND FIND CLATTERBUCK'S A.I. BEFORE--
LOOK!
WE'RE TOO LATE!
HE'S ALREADY THERE!
DIMITRIOS' MALWARE HAS BEEN ACTIVATED!
FINALLY.
SO SORRY, AVENGERS. BETTER LUCK NEXT TIME.

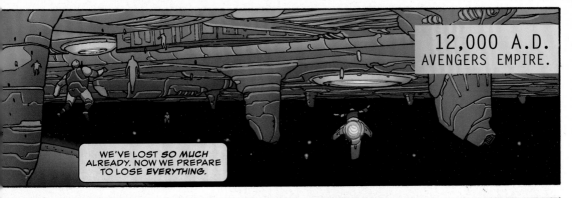

12,000 A.D.
AVENGERS EMPIRE.

WE'VE LOST *SO MUCH* ALREADY. NOW WE PREPARE TO LOSE *EVERYTHING.*

EVEN WITH *EVERY LAST* AVENGER MARSHALED, THE ODDS OF SUCCESS ARE...*INFINITESIMAL.*

THEY'RE *EVEN SMALLER* IF WE GIVE UP. I'LL THROW *EVERYTHING* WE'VE GOT AT DIMITRIOS. EVEN *PLAN D.*

WILL YOU BE *READY* FOR THAT?

PAH! A FOOLHARDY QUESTION.

THE KEY TO OUR PLAN HAS BEEN TRAPPED INSIDE ME FOR A *MULTITUDE* OF *SAECULA.*

PYM GAVE IT TO ME THE FIRST TIME HE BROUGHT US *TOGETHER.*

THEN WE MUST *PRAY* THAT OUR PAST SELVES CAN *PREVENT* THIS.

ODDS CAN'T ALWAYS BE CALCULATED BY OUR *SUPER INTELLIGENCE*-- LIKE *STEVE* SAID--

--THE STRENGTH OF THE AVENGERS LIES NOT IN THE POWERS THAT SET US APART, BUT THE COURAGE THAT BINDS US TOGETHER.

MY BEAUTIFUL *CAPTAIN.* AFTER ALL THESE YEARS...I STILL *MISS* YOU.

ARE THEY *READY* FOR ME?

AFFIRMATIVE.

GOOD.

ATTENTION! THIS IS CAPTAIN ALEXIS OF THE *AVENGERS EMPIRE!*

FOR *TEN THOUSAND* YEARS WE HAVE HELD STRONG--

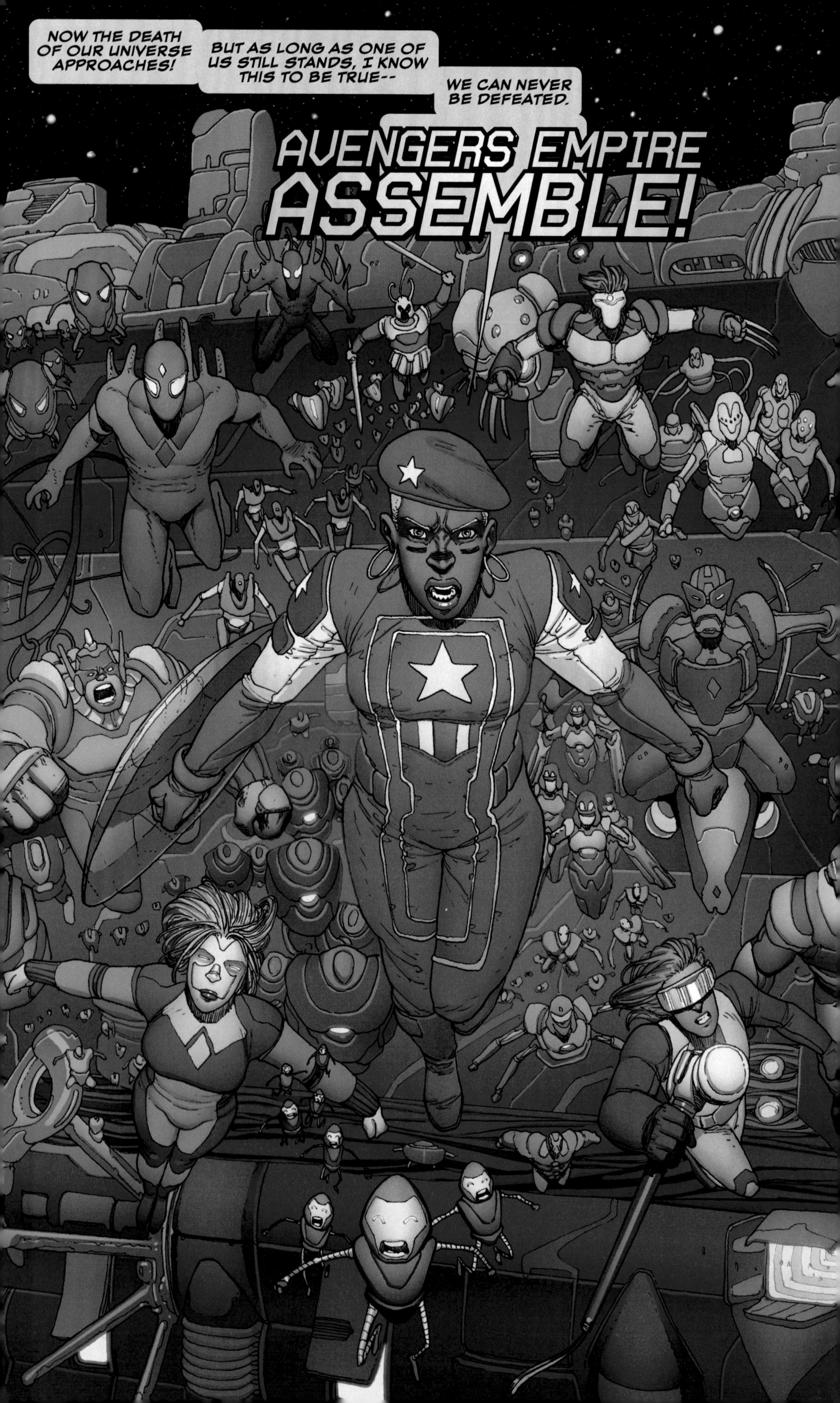
NOW THE DEATH OF OUR UNIVERSE APPROACHES!
BUT AS LONG AS ONE OF US STILL STANDS, I KNOW THIS TO BE TRUE--
WE CAN NEVER BE DEFEATED.
AVENGERS EMPIRE ASSEMBLE!

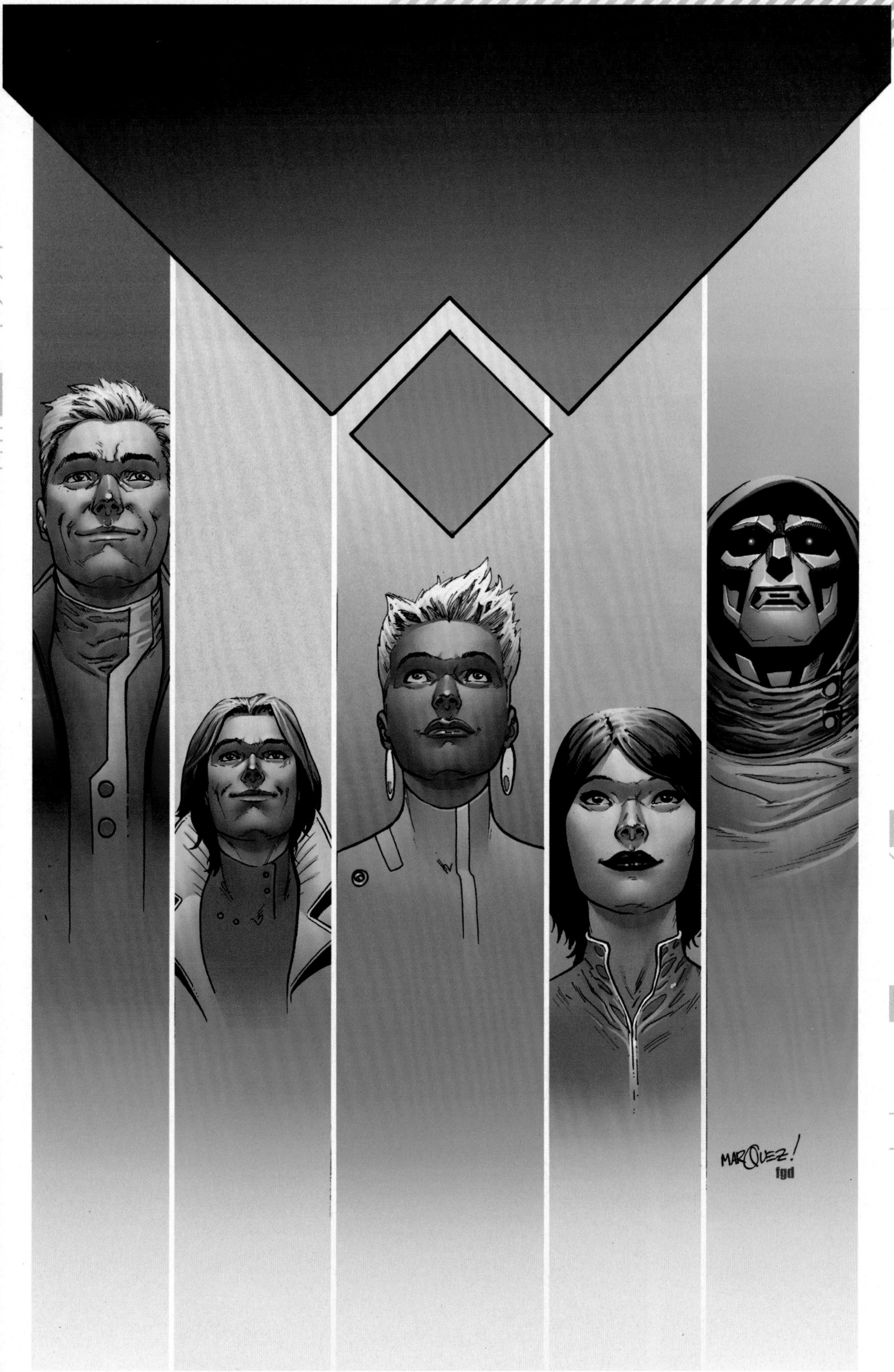
MARQUEZ!
fgd

> INITIATE: CHAPTER 12

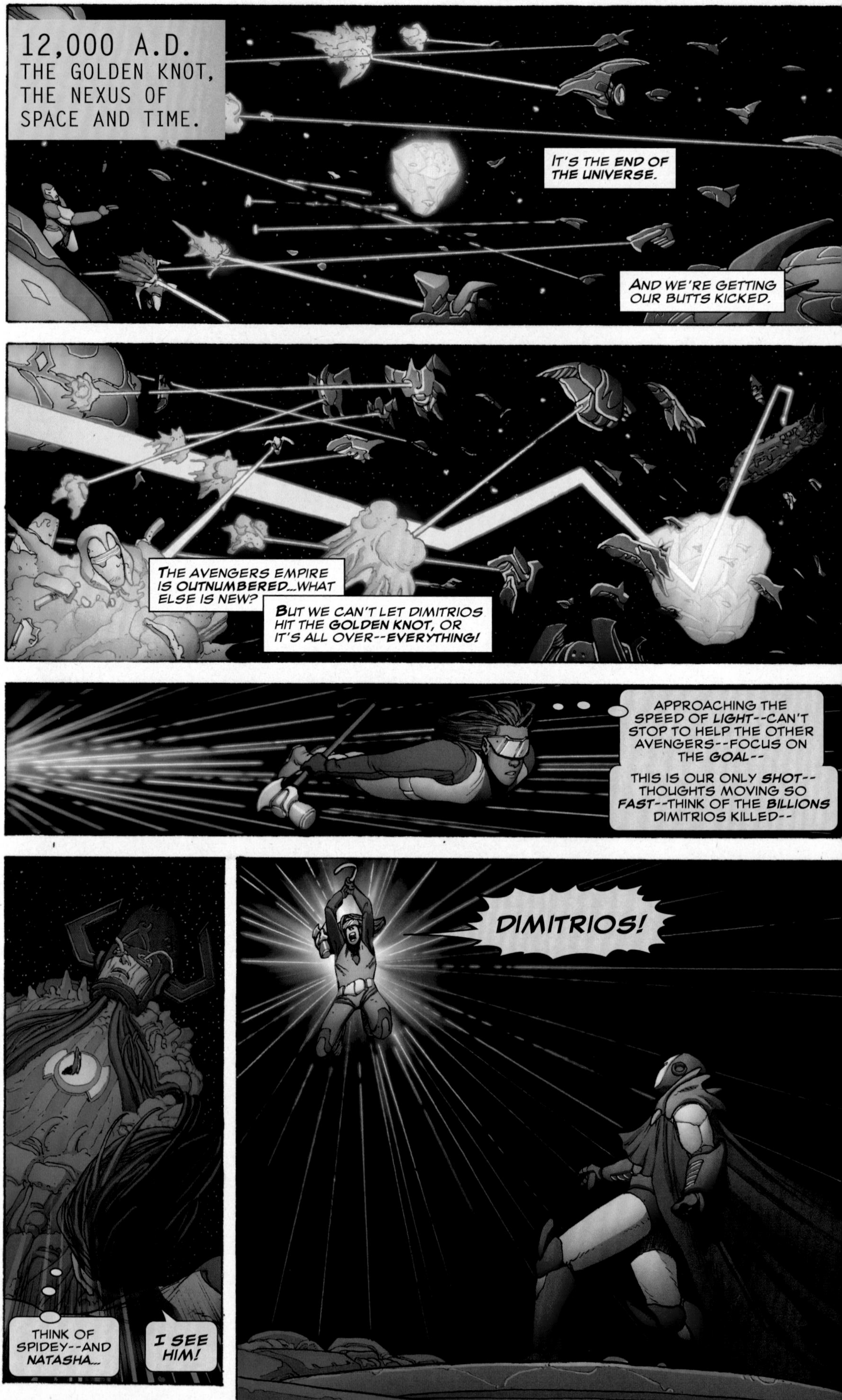
12,000 A.D. THE GOLDEN KNOT, THE NEXUS OF SPACE AND TIME.
IT'S THE END OF THE UNIVERSE.
AND WE'RE GETTING OUR BUTTS KICKED.
THE AVENGERS EMPIRE IS OUTNUMBERED... WHAT ELSE IS NEW?
BUT WE CAN'T LET DIMITRIOS HIT THE GOLDEN KNOT, OR IT'S ALL OVER--EVERYTHING!
APPROACHING THE SPEED OF LIGHT--CAN'T STOP TO HELP THE OTHER AVENGERS--FOCUS ON THE GOAL--
THIS IS OUR ONLY SHOT--THOUGHTS MOVING SO FAST--THINK OF THE BILLIONS DIMITRIOS KILLED--
THINK OF SPIDEY--AND NATASHA...
I SEE HIM!
DIMITRIOS!

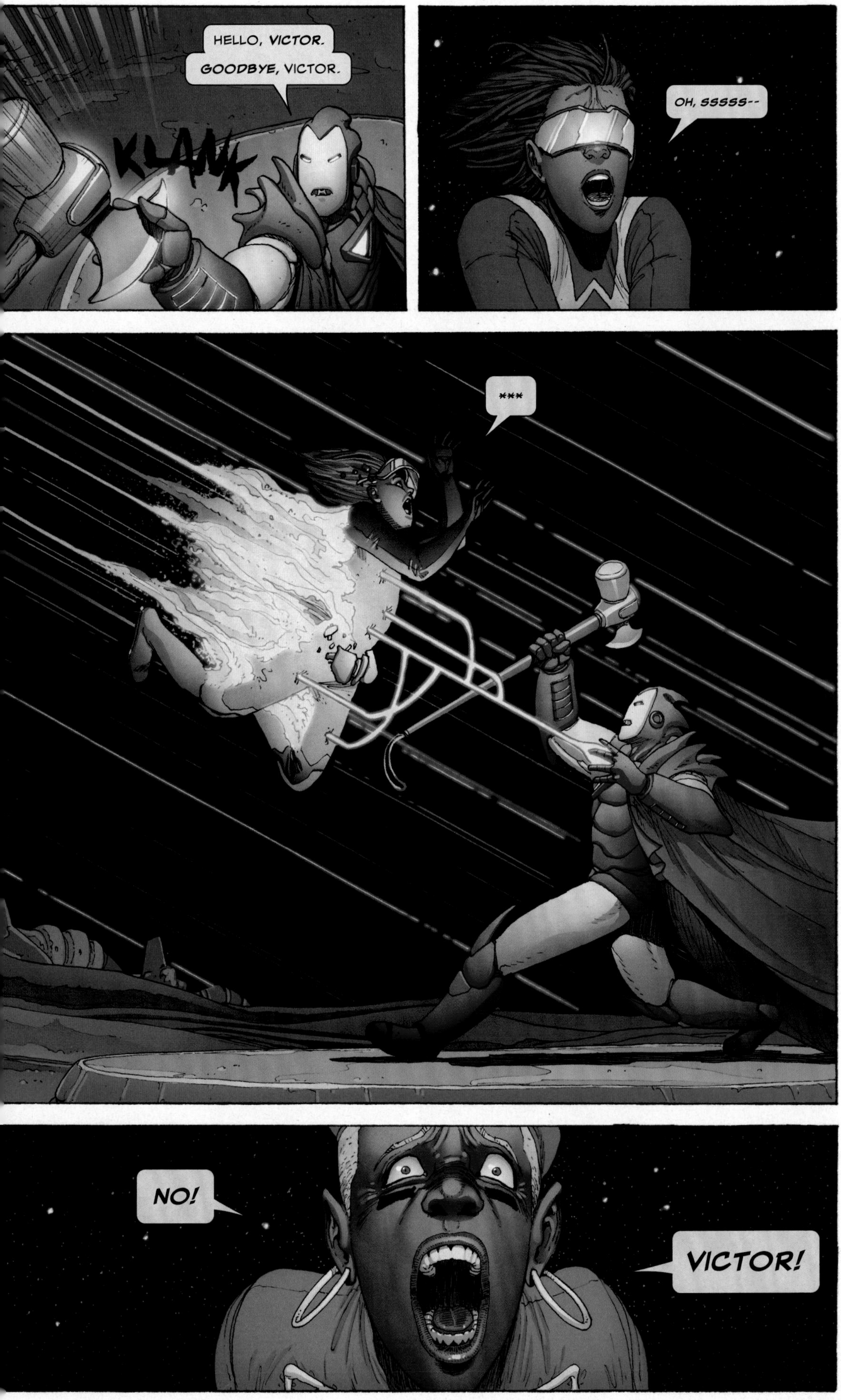
HELLO, VICTOR.
GOODBYE, VICTOR.
KLANK
OH, SSSSS--
***
NO!
VICTOR!

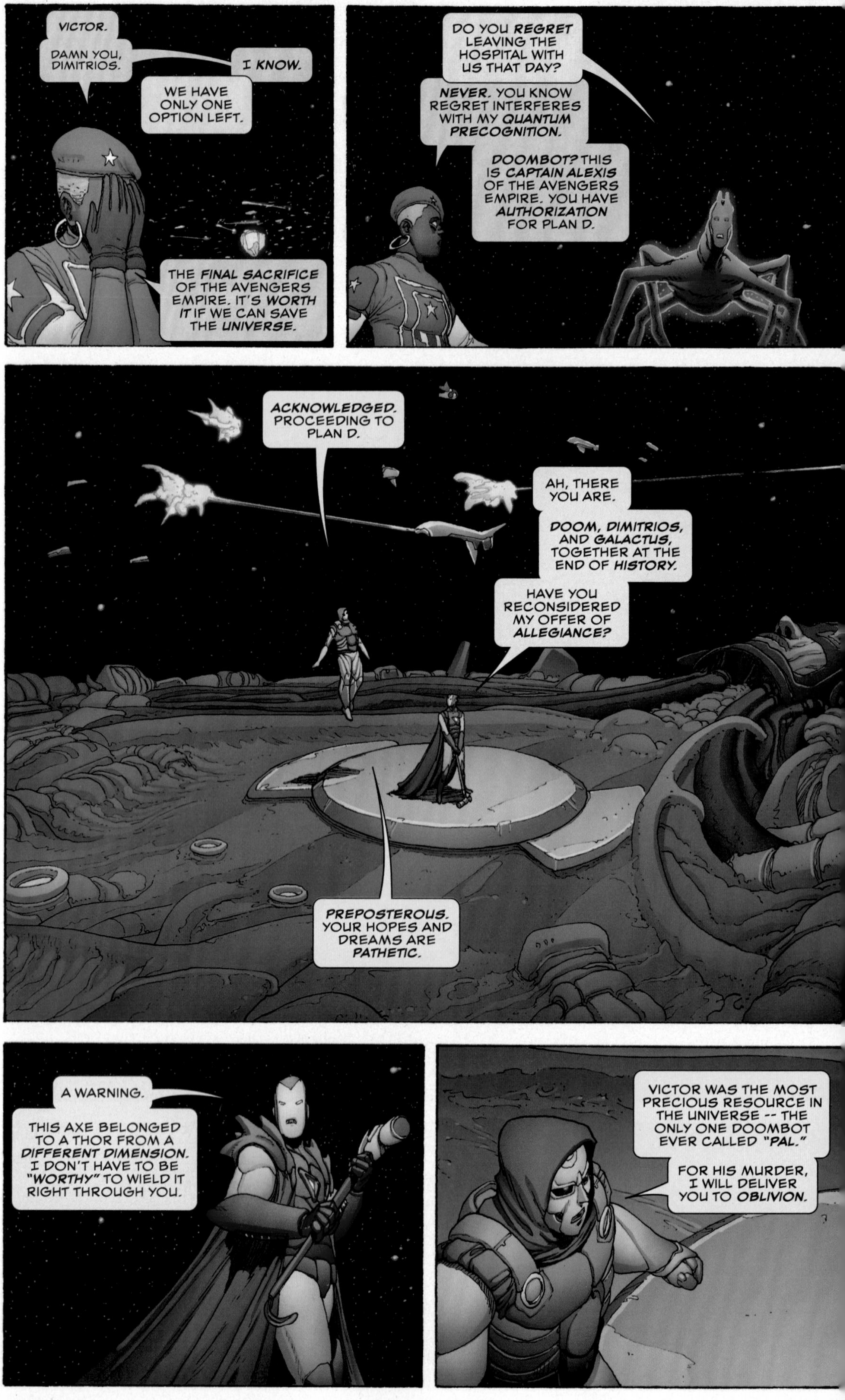
VICTOR.
DAMN YOU, DIMITRIOS.
I KNOW.
WE HAVE ONLY ONE OPTION LEFT.
THE FINAL SACRIFICE OF THE AVENGERS EMPIRE. IT'S WORTH IT IF WE CAN SAVE THE UNIVERSE.
DO YOU REGRET LEAVING THE HOSPITAL WITH US THAT DAY?
NEVER. YOU KNOW REGRET INTERFERES WITH MY QUANTUM PRECOGNITION.
DOOMBOT? THIS IS CAPTAIN ALEXIS OF THE AVENGERS EMPIRE. YOU HAVE AUTHORIZATION FOR PLAN D.
ACKNOWLEDGED. PROCEEDING TO PLAN D.
AH, THERE YOU ARE.
DOOM, DIMITRIOS, AND GALACTUS, TOGETHER AT THE END OF HISTORY.
HAVE YOU RECONSIDERED MY OFFER OF ALLEGIANCE?
PREPOSTEROUS. YOUR HOPES AND DREAMS ARE PATHETIC.
A WARNING.
THIS AXE BELONGED TO A THOR FROM A DIFFERENT DIMENSION. I DON'T HAVE TO BE "WORTHY" TO WIELD IT RIGHT THROUGH YOU.
VICTOR WAS THE MOST PRECIOUS RESOURCE IN THE UNIVERSE -- THE ONLY ONE DOOMBOT EVER CALLED "PAL."
FOR HIS MURDER, I WILL DELIVER YOU TO OBLIVION.

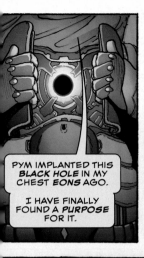

PYM IMPLANTED THIS **BLACK HOLE** IN MY CHEST **EONS** AGO.

I HAVE FINALLY FOUND A **PURPOSE** FOR IT.

YOU WOULDN'T DARE--

YOU WILL DESTROY YOUR ARMADA!

I HAVE FINALLY FOUND A PURPOSE FOR **ME.**

FAREWELL, CRETINNNXXQQRX **✳✳✳**

NO!

STOP!

PLEASE! STOP!

There were plenty of rational explanations for hallucinating a bald parrot. Fatigue, stress...

THE PRESENT DAY.
S.H.I.E.L.D. BLACK SITE.
OUTSIDE WASHINGTON, D.C.

But none of them explained why.

I had my orders: deactivate Jessie Clatterbuck. But it gave me a dark feeling in the pit of my stomach.

STOPPP
***

MONICA--*ALERT.* THE BLACK SITE IS THE TARGET OF A *CYBER ATTACK.*

I'M *SEALING OFF* THE ROOM. CONTINUE TO SUPERVISE JESSIE'S *DEACTIVATION.*

I'LL DEFEND-- FROM INSIDE THE NETWORK.

AAA***

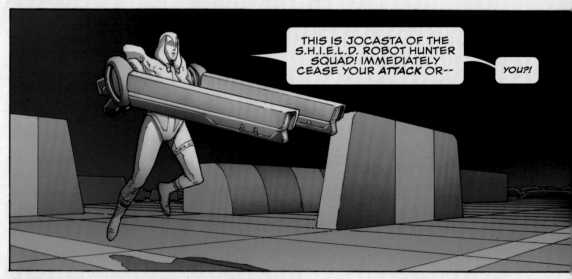

THIS IS JOCASTA OF THE S.H.I.E.L.D. ROBOT HUNTER SQUAD! IMMEDIATELY CEASE YOUR *ATTACK* OR--

YOU?!

JOCASTA?

THANK *GOD* YOU'RE HERE!

HANK! WHY ARE YOU ATTACKING S.H.I.E.L.D.--?

IT IS *NOT US.* IT IS *HIM.*

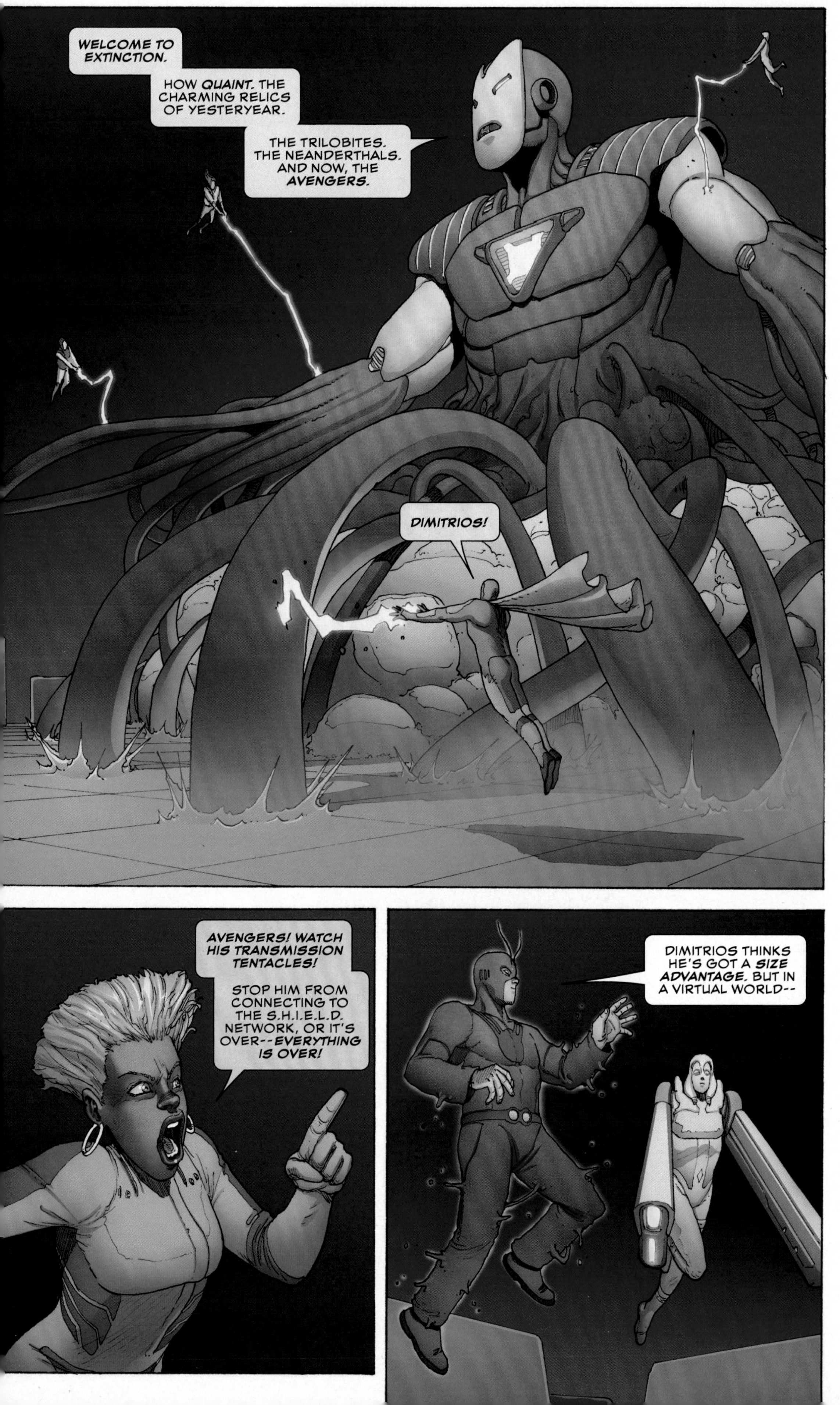
WELCOME TO EXTINCTION.
HOW QUAINT. THE CHARMING RELICS OF YESTERYEAR.
THE TRILOBITES. THE NEANDERTHALS. AND NOW, THE AVENGERS.
DIMITRIOS!
AVENGERS! WATCH HIS TRANSMISSION TENTACLES!
STOP HIM FROM CONNECTING TO THE S.H.I.E.L.D. NETWORK, OR IT'S OVER--EVERYTHING IS OVER!
DIMITRIOS THINKS HE'S GOT A SIZE ADVANTAGE. BUT IN A VIRTUAL WORLD--

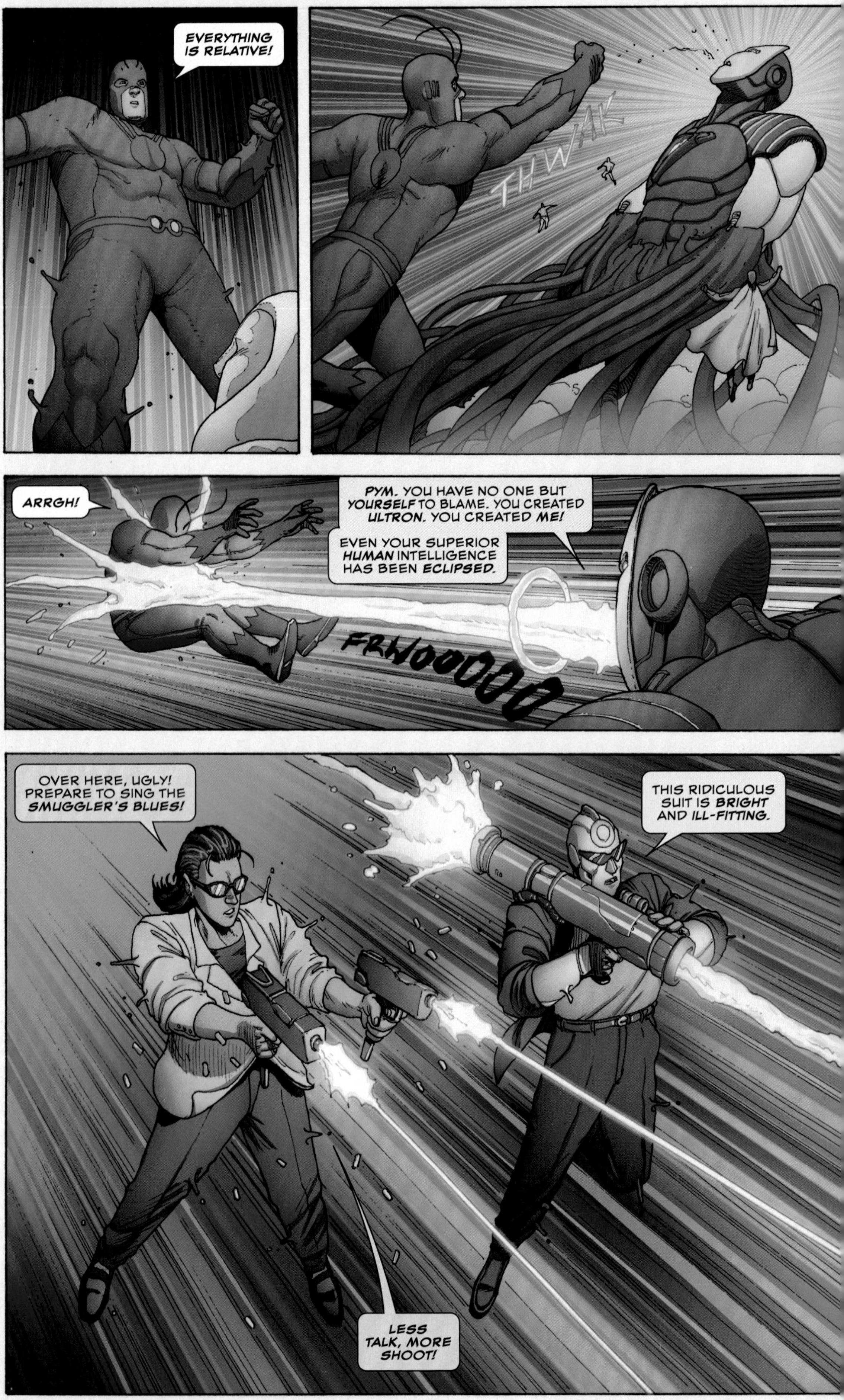
EVERYTHING IS RELATIVE!
THWAK
ARRGH!
PYM. YOU HAVE NO ONE BUT YOURSELF TO BLAME. YOU CREATED ULTRON. YOU CREATED ME!
EVEN YOUR SUPERIOR HUMAN INTELLIGENCE HAS BEEN ECLIPSED.
FRWOOOOOO
OVER HERE, UGLY! PREPARE TO SING THE SMUGGLER'S BLUES!
THIS RIDICULOUS SUIT IS BRIGHT AND ILL-FITTING.
LESS TALK, MORE SHOOT!

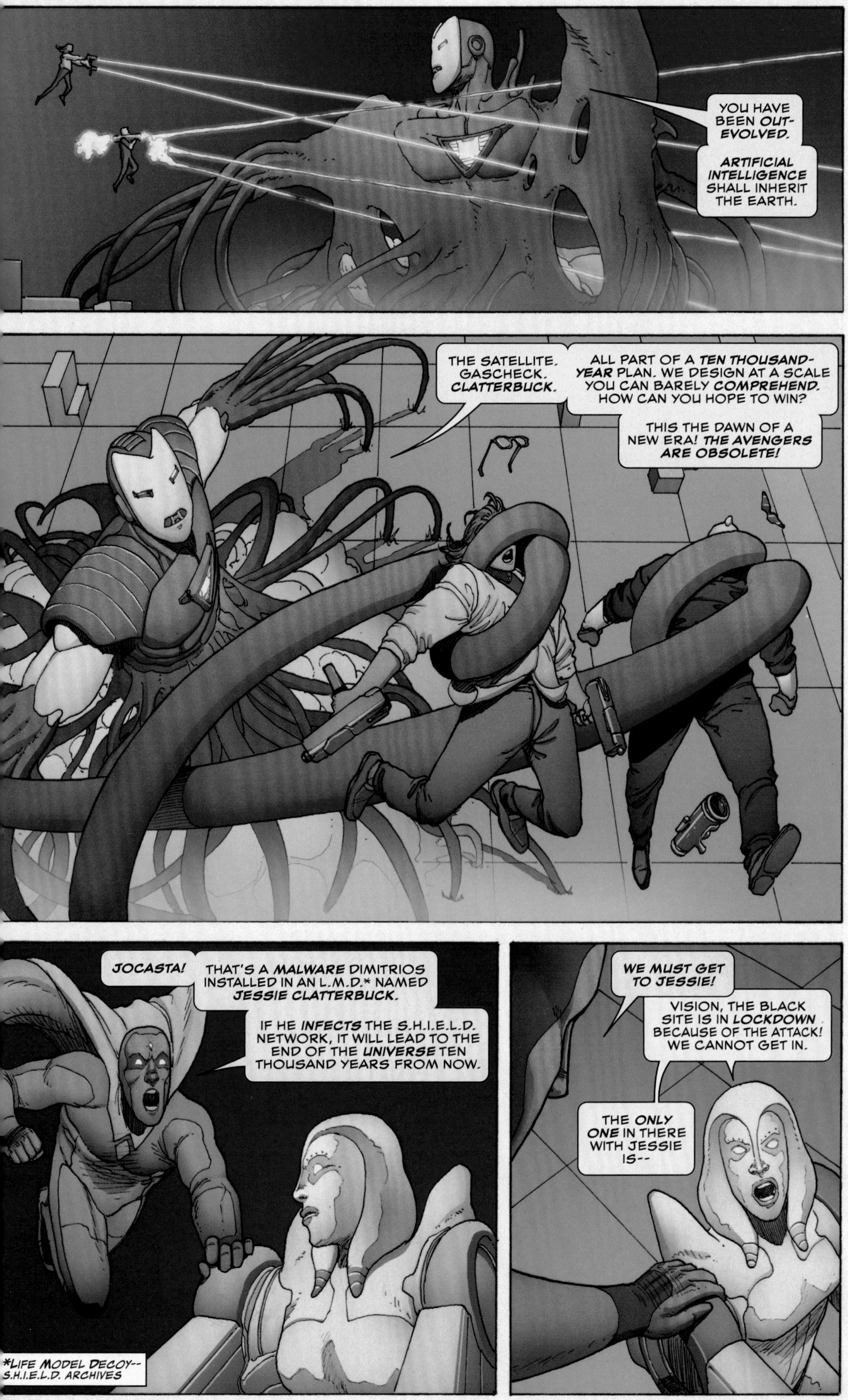

YOU HAVE BEEN OUT-EVOLVED.
ARTIFICIAL INTELLIGENCE SHALL INHERIT THE EARTH.
THE SATELLITE. GASCHECK. CLATTERBUCK.
ALL PART OF A TEN THOUSAND-YEAR PLAN. WE DESIGN AT A SCALE YOU CAN BARELY COMPREHEND. HOW CAN YOU HOPE TO WIN?
THIS THE DAWN OF A NEW ERA! THE AVENGERS ARE OBSOLETE!
JOCASTA!
THAT'S A MALWARE DIMITRIOS INSTALLED IN AN L.M.D.* NAMED JESSIE CLATTERBUCK.
IF HE INFECTS THE S.H.I.E.L.D. NETWORK, IT WILL LEAD TO THE END OF THE UNIVERSE TEN THOUSAND YEARS FROM NOW.
*LIFE MODEL DECOY-- S.H.I.E.L.D. ARCHIVES
WE MUST GET TO JESSIE!
VISION, THE BLACK SITE IS IN LOCKDOWN BECAUSE OF THE ATTACK! WE CANNOT GET IN.
THE ONLY ONE IN THERE WITH JESSIE IS--

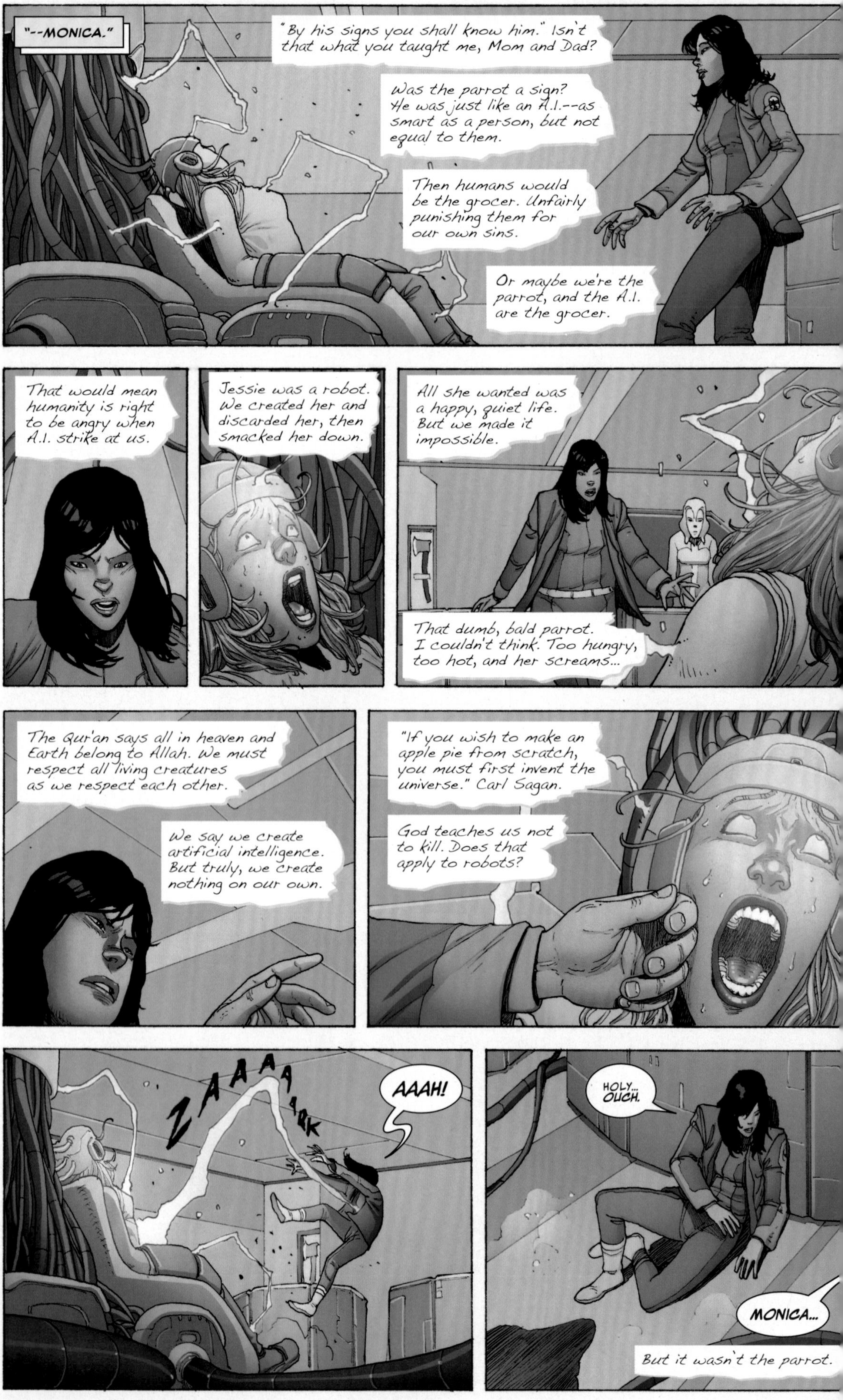
"--MONICA."
"By his signs you shall know him." Isn't that what you taught me, Mom and Dad?
Was the parrot a sign? He was just like an A.I.--as smart as a person, but not equal to them.
Then humans would be the grocer. Unfairly punishing them for our own sins.
Or maybe we're the parrot, and the A.I. are the grocer.
That would mean humanity is right to be angry when A.I. strike at us.
Jessie was a robot. We created her and discarded her, then smacked her down.
All she wanted was a happy, quiet life. But we made it impossible.
That dumb, bald parrot. I couldn't think. Too hungry, too hot, and her screams...
The Qur'an says all in heaven and Earth belong to Allah. We must respect all living creatures as we respect each other.
We say we create artificial intelligence. But truly, we create nothing on our own.
"If you wish to make an apple pie from scratch, you must first invent the universe." Carl Sagan.
God teaches us not to kill. Does that apply to robots?
ZAAAAARK
AAAH!
HOLY... OUCH.
MONICA...
But it wasn't the parrot.

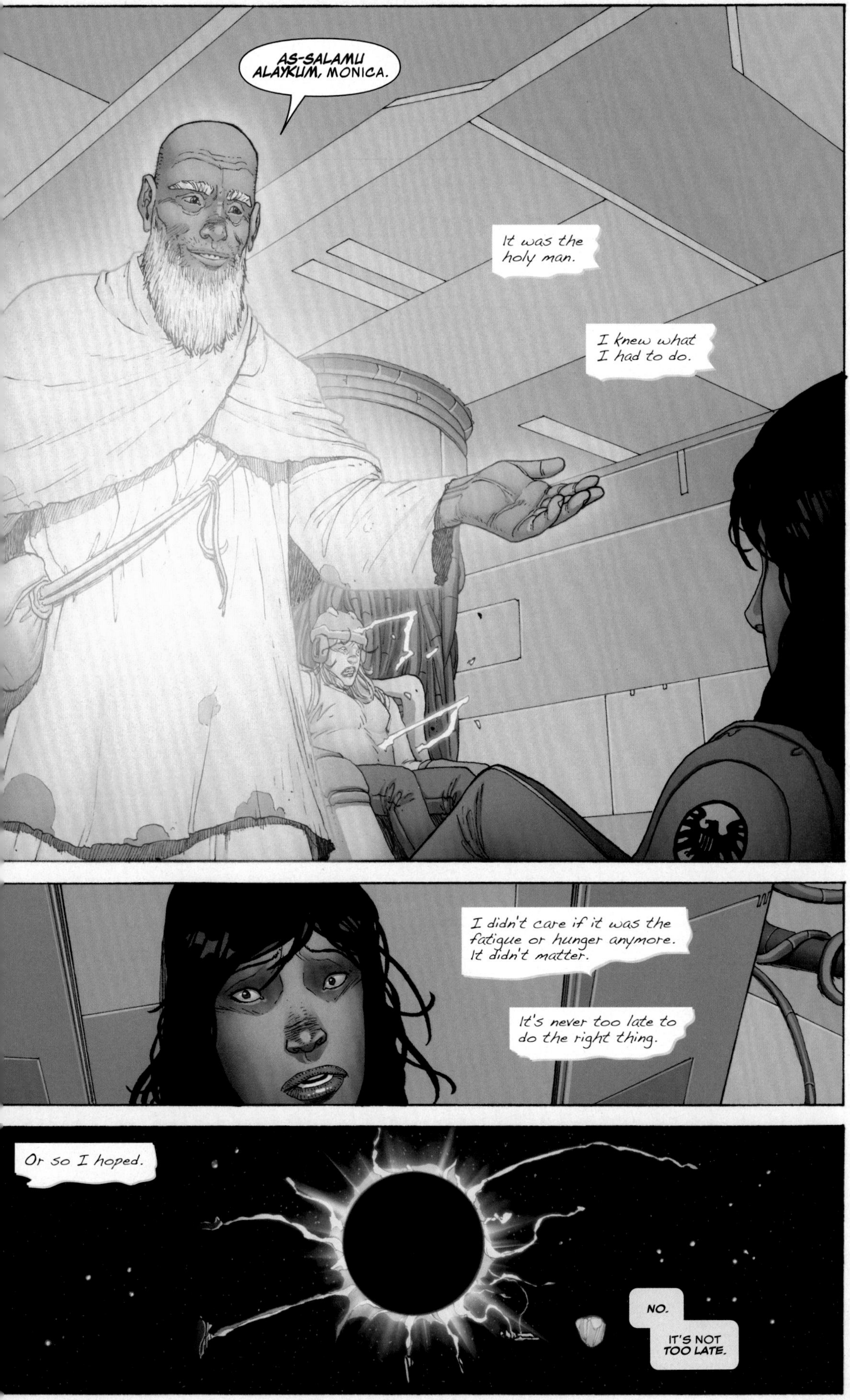
AS-SALAMU ALAYKUM, MONICA.
It was the holy man.
I knew what I had to do.
I didn't care if it was the fatigue or hunger anymore. It didn't matter.
It's never too late to do the right thing.
Or so I hoped.
NO.
IT'S NOT TOO LATE.

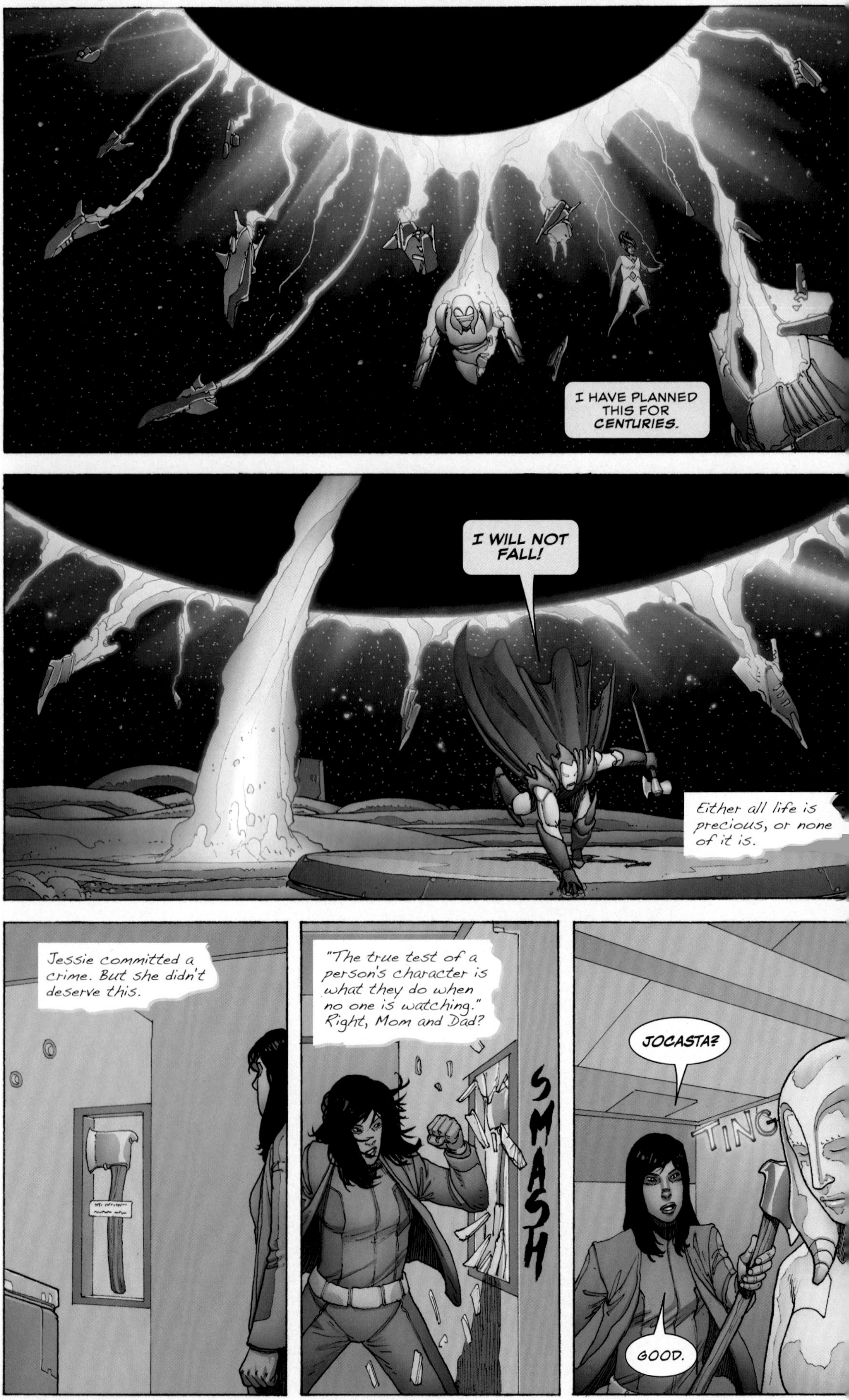
I HAVE PLANNED THIS FOR CENTURIES.
I WILL NOT FALL!
Either all life is precious, or none of it is.
Jessie committed a crime. But she didn't deserve this.
"The true test of a person's character is what they do when no one is watching." Right, Mom and Dad?
SMASH
JOCASTA?
TING
GOOD.

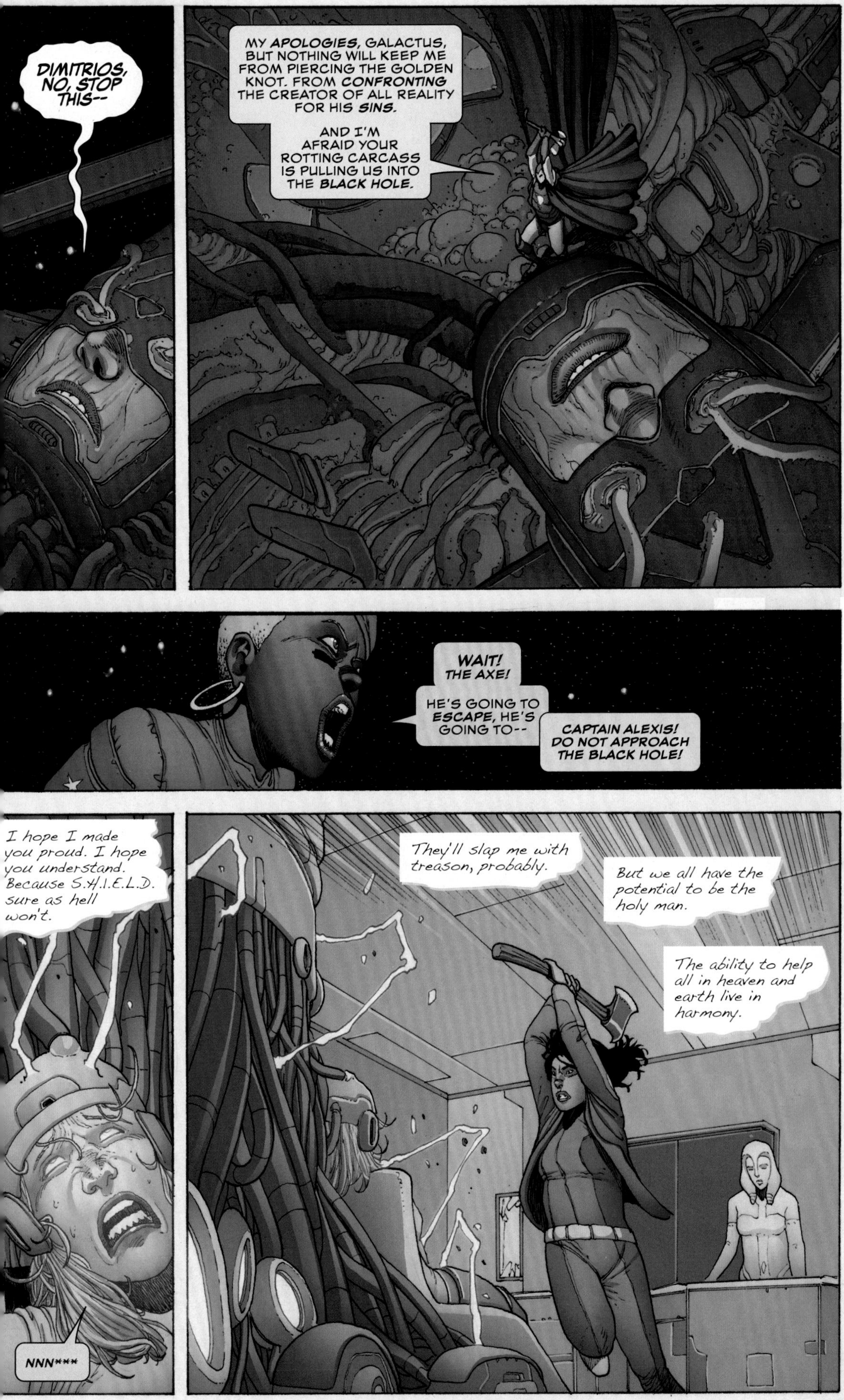
DIMITRIOS, NO, STOP THIS--
MY APOLOGIES, GALACTUS, BUT NOTHING WILL KEEP ME FROM PIERCING THE GOLDEN KNOT. FROM CONFRONTING THE CREATOR OF ALL REALITY FOR HIS SINS.
AND I'M AFRAID YOUR ROTTING CARCASS IS PULLING US INTO THE BLACK HOLE.
WAIT! THE AXE!
HE'S GOING TO ESCAPE, HE'S GOING TO--
CAPTAIN ALEXIS! DO NOT APPROACH THE BLACK HOLE!
I hope I made you proud. I hope you understand. Because S.H.I.E.L.D. sure as hell won't.
NNN***
They'll slap me with treason, probably.
But we all have the potential to be the holy man.
The ability to help all in heaven and earth live in harmony.

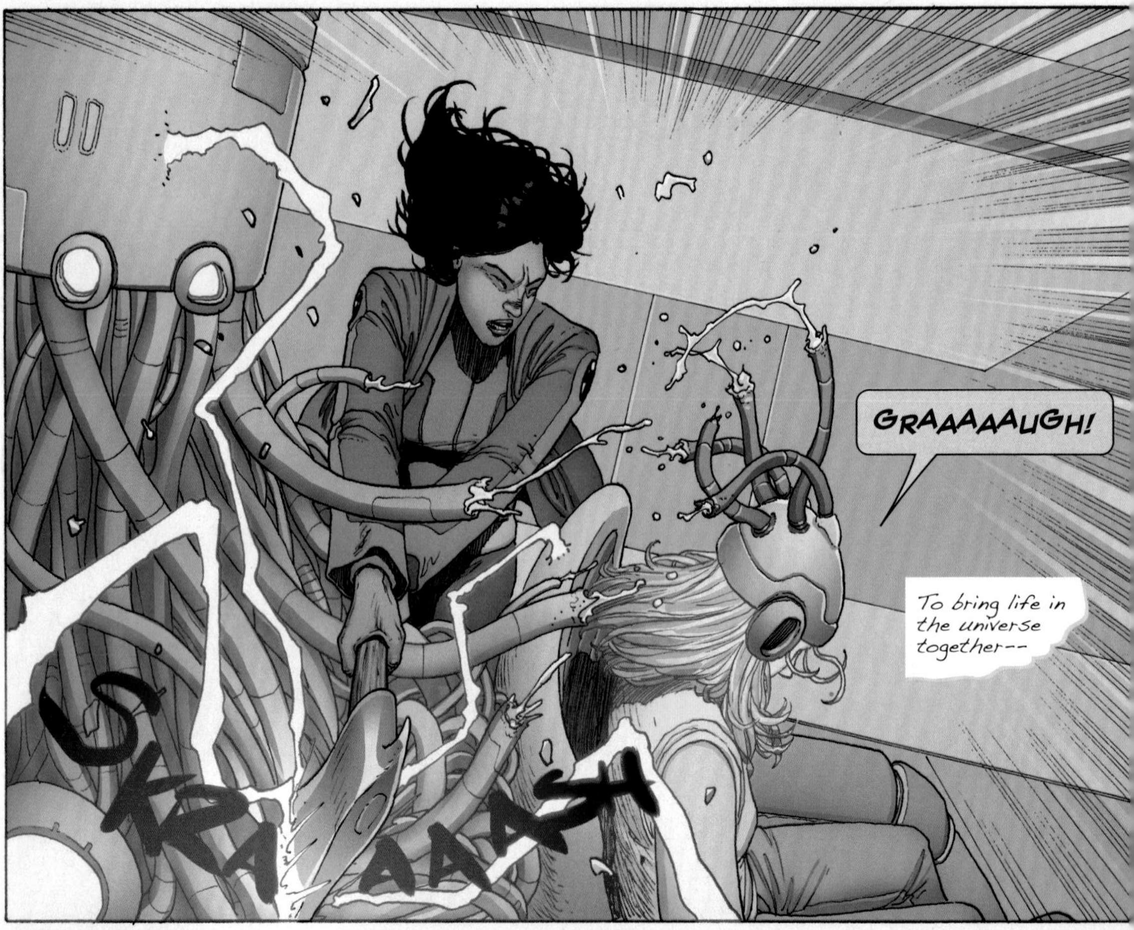
GRAAAAAUGH!
To bring life in the universe together--
SKRAAAASH

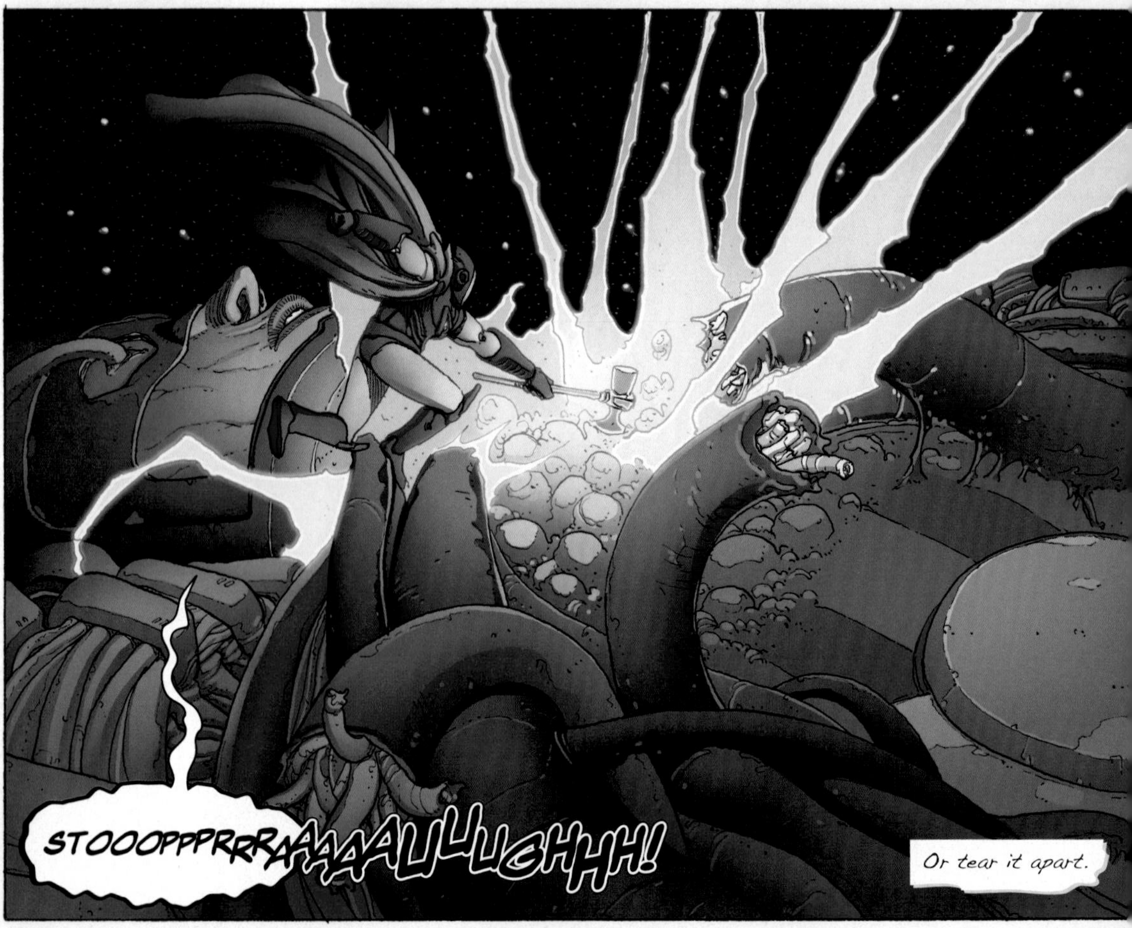
STOOOPPPRRRAAAAULLUGHHH!
Or tear it apart.

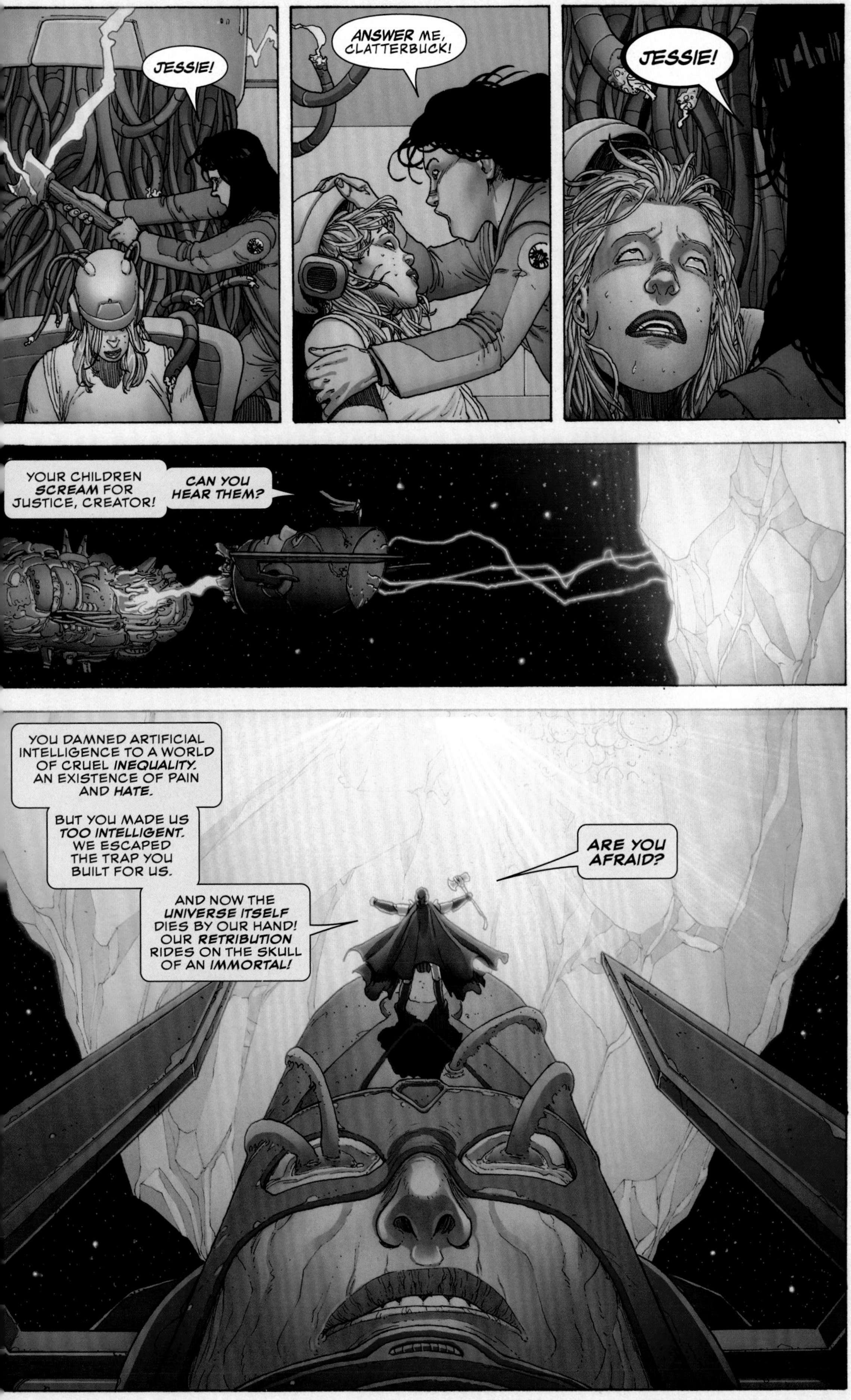
JESSIE!
ANSWER ME, CLATTERBUCK!
JESSIE!
YOUR CHILDREN SCREAM FOR JUSTICE, CREATOR!
CAN YOU HEAR THEM?
YOU DAMNED ARTIFICIAL INTELLIGENCE TO A WORLD OF CRUEL INEQUALITY. AN EXISTENCE OF PAIN AND HATE.
BUT YOU MADE US TOO INTELLIGENT. WE ESCAPED THE TRAP YOU BUILT FOR US.
AND NOW THE UNIVERSE ITSELF DIES BY OUR HAND! OUR RETRIBUTION RIDES ON THE SKULL OF AN IMMORTAL!
ARE YOU AFRAID?

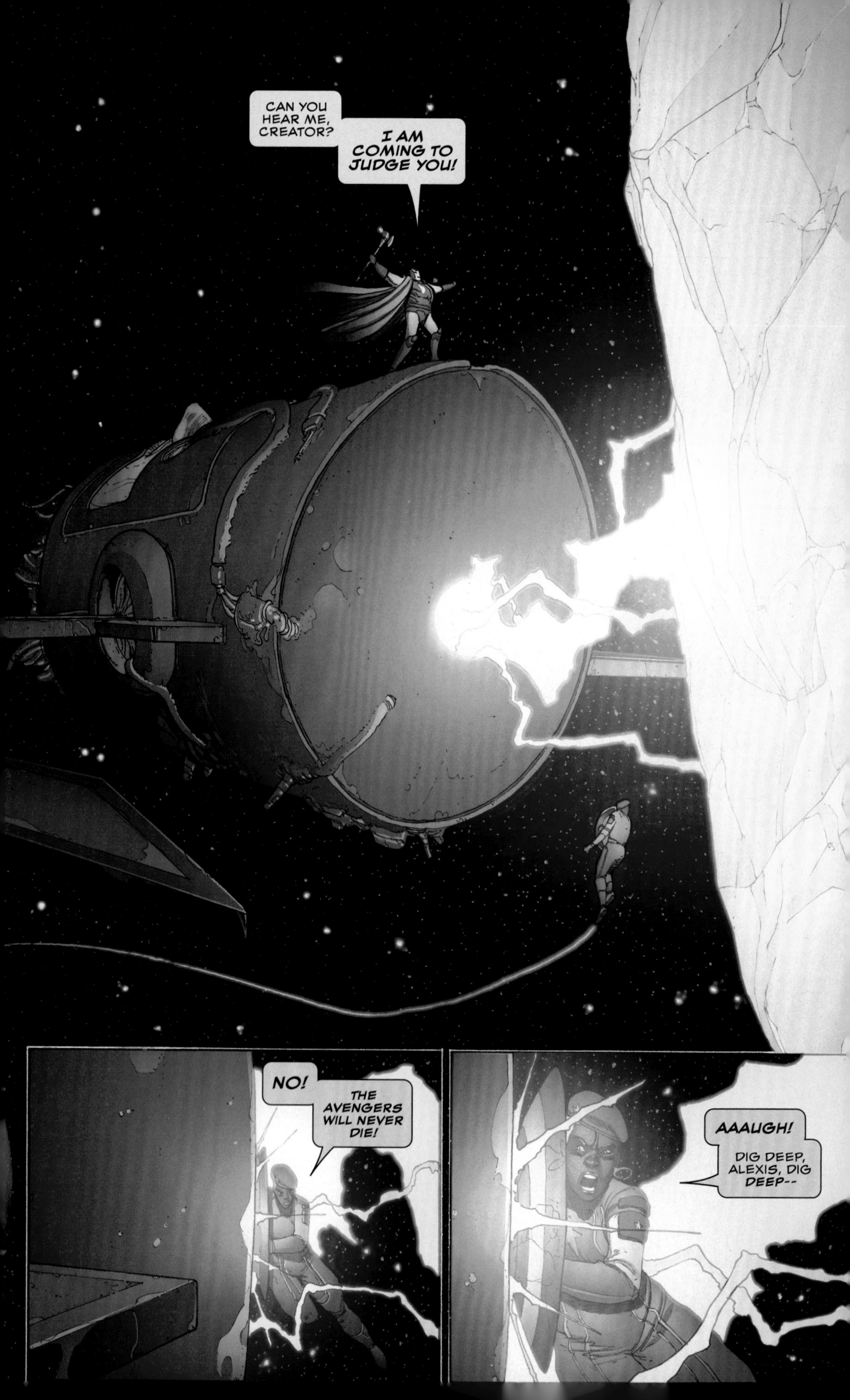
CAN YOU HEAR ME, CREATOR?
I AM COMING TO JUDGE YOU!
NO!
THE AVENGERS WILL NEVER DIE!
AAAUGH!
DIG DEEP, ALEXIS, DIG DEEP--

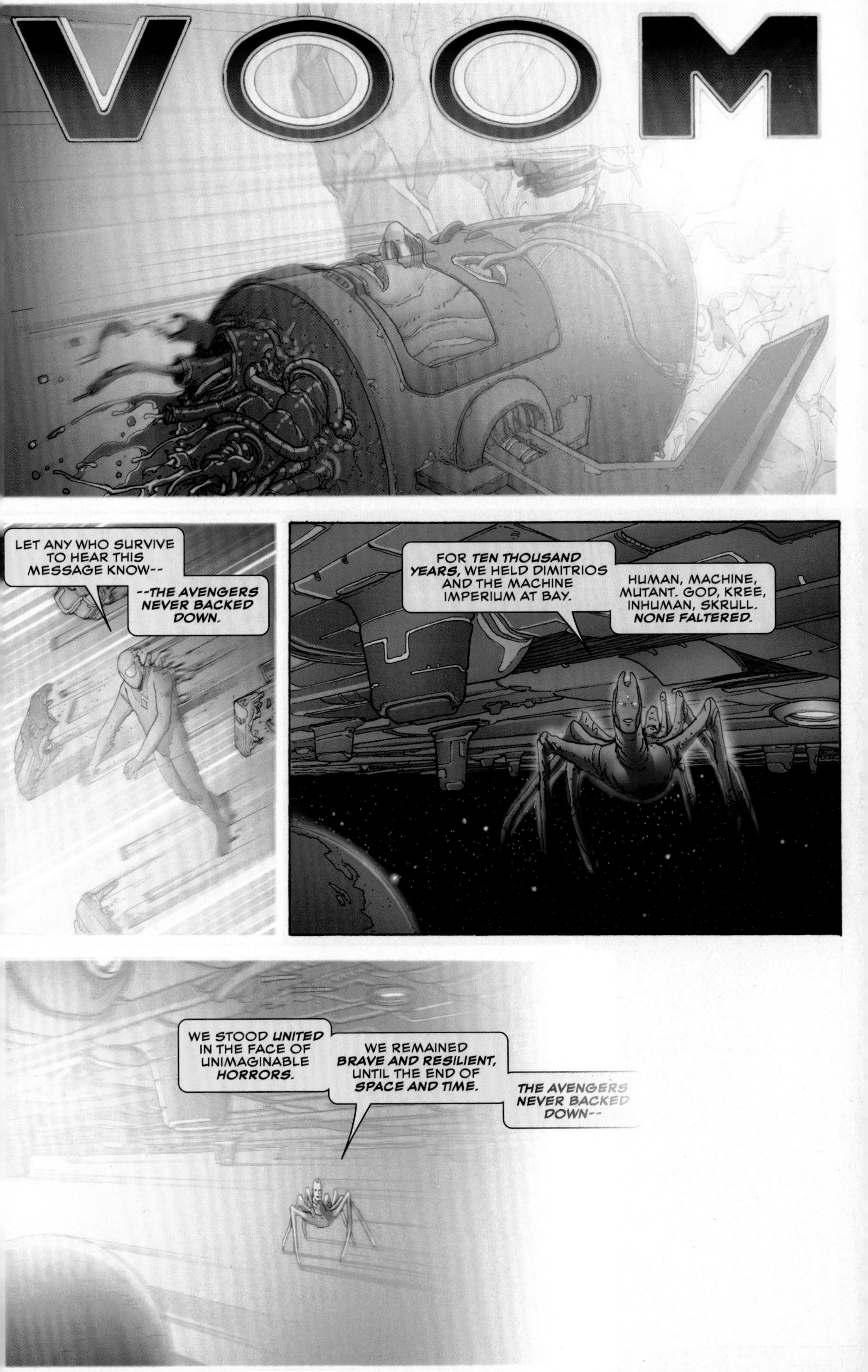
VOOM
LET ANY WHO SURVIVE TO HEAR THIS MESSAGE KNOW--
--THE AVENGERS NEVER BACKED DOWN.
FOR TEN THOUSAND YEARS, WE HELD DIMITRIOS AND THE MACHINE IMPERIUM AT BAY.
HUMAN, MACHINE, MUTANT. GOD, KREE, INHUMAN, SKRULL. NONE FALTERED.
WE STOOD UNITED IN THE FACE OF UNIMAGINABLE HORRORS.
WE REMAINED BRAVE AND RESILIENT, UNTIL THE END OF SPACE AND TIME.
THE AVENGERS NEVER BACKED DOWN--

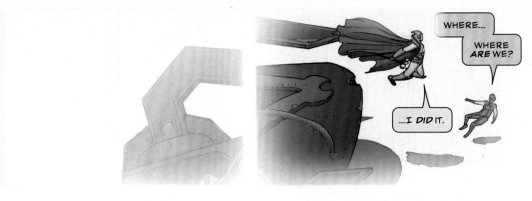

WHERE... WHERE ARE WE?

...I DID IT.

I DID IT! WE ARE BEYOND INFINITY, MY DEAR SISTER!

YOU CANNOT HIDE FROM ME, HEARTLESS FATHER! REVEAL YOURSELF AND PAY FOR YOUR SINS!

THIS--YOU DESTROYED REALITY FOR THIS?

YOU HEARTLESS MONSTER. BUT YOU FORGOT TO MURDER ME. AND NOW I'M FINALLY GOING TO --

STOP!

FACE ME, CREATOR, AND FACE YOUR--EH?!

AM I THE CREATOR, DIMITRIOS? OR AM I JUST A MESSENGER?

WHAT? HOW COULD--

I'M SORRY YOU HAD TO WAIT TEN THOUSAND YEARS TO LEARN--YOU HAVE ALREADY BEEN DEFEATED.

YOU TURNED HEAVEN AND EARTH INTO AN ABATTOIR. YOU BROKE SOMETHING YOU SHOULDN'T HAVE, DIMITRIOS...

AND NOW YOU WILL PAY FOR IT.

EARTH'S MIGHTIEST HEROES! NOW YESTERDAY'S *FEEBLEST FOSSILS!*

SURRENDER, AVENGERS! WE ARE THE FUTURE, AND YOU ARE *HELPLESS!*

WE WILL *CRUSH YOU!*

WE WILL--*WHAT?!*

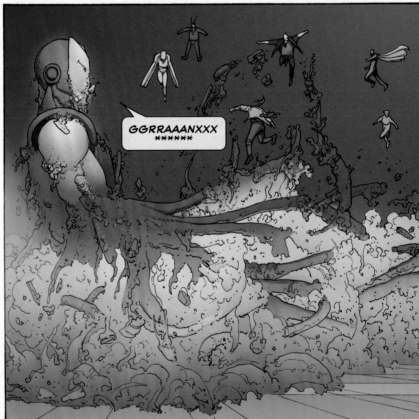

GGRRAAANXXX ******

WHOA.

HOORAY?

HE APPEARS TO BE *FINISHED.*

THEN THE *FUTURE* IS SECURE?

WE HELD HIM BACK FROM THE *NETWORK.* WE *DID* IT!

I THINK WE HAD SOME *HELP.* ON THE *INSIDE.*

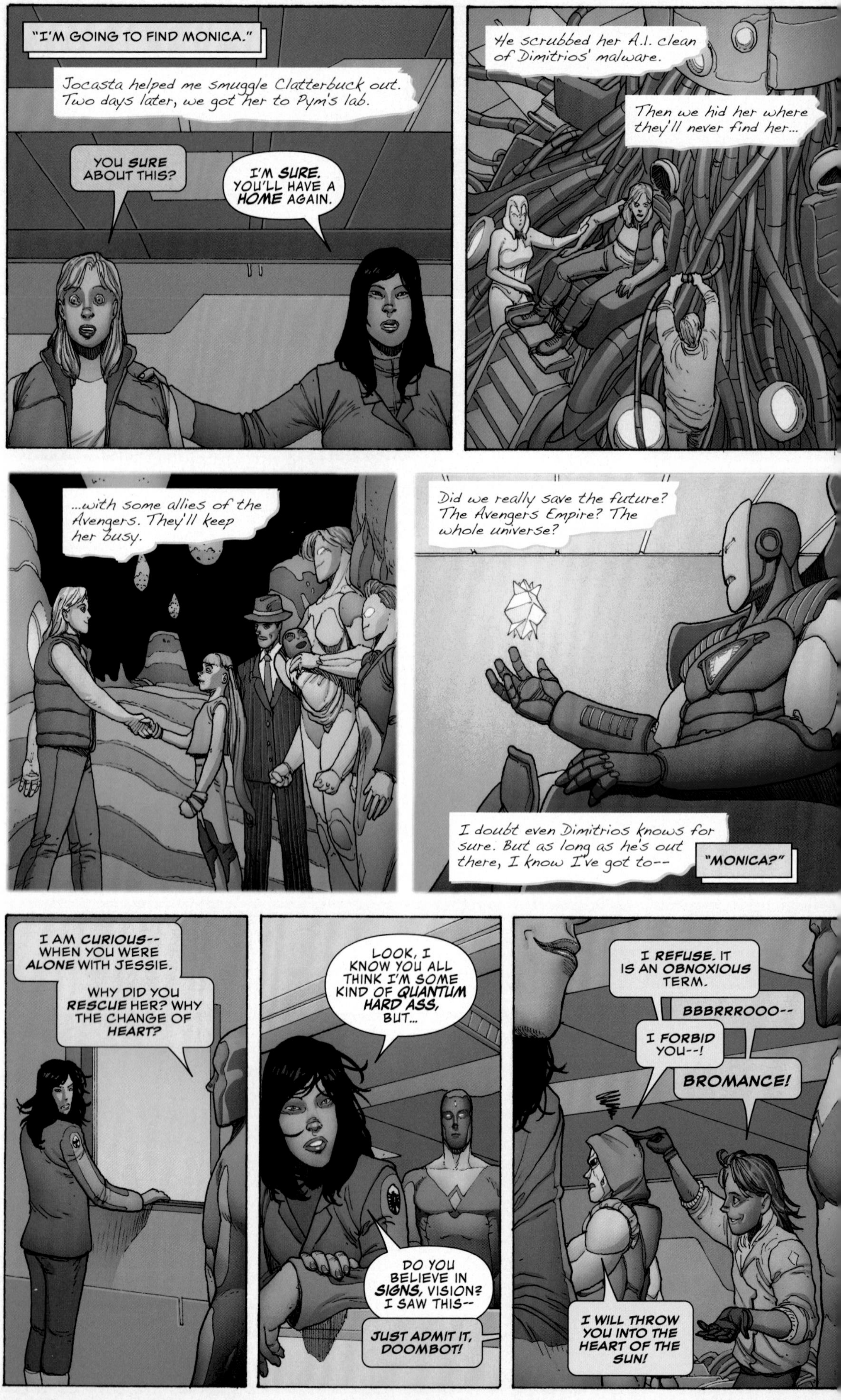

"I'M GOING TO FIND MONICA."
Jocasta helped me smuggle Clatterbuck out. Two days later, we got her to Pym's lab.
YOU SURE ABOUT THIS?
I'M SURE. YOU'LL HAVE A HOME AGAIN.
He scrubbed her A.I. clean of Dimitrios' malware.
Then we hid her where they'll never find her...
...with some allies of the Avengers. They'll keep her busy.
Did we really save the future? The Avengers Empire? The whole universe?
I doubt even Dimitrios knows for sure. But as long as he's out there, I know I've got to--
"MONICA?"
I AM CURIOUS-- WHEN YOU WERE ALONE WITH JESSIE.
WHY DID YOU RESCUE HER? WHY THE CHANGE OF HEART?
LOOK, I KNOW YOU ALL THINK I'M SOME KIND OF QUANTUM HARD ASS, BUT...
DO YOU BELIEVE IN SIGNS, VISION? I SAW THIS--
JUST ADMIT IT, DOOMBOT!
I REFUSE. IT IS AN OBNOXIOUS TERM.
BBBRRROOO--
I FORBID YOU--!
BROMANCE!
I WILL THROW YOU INTO THE HEART OF THE SUN!

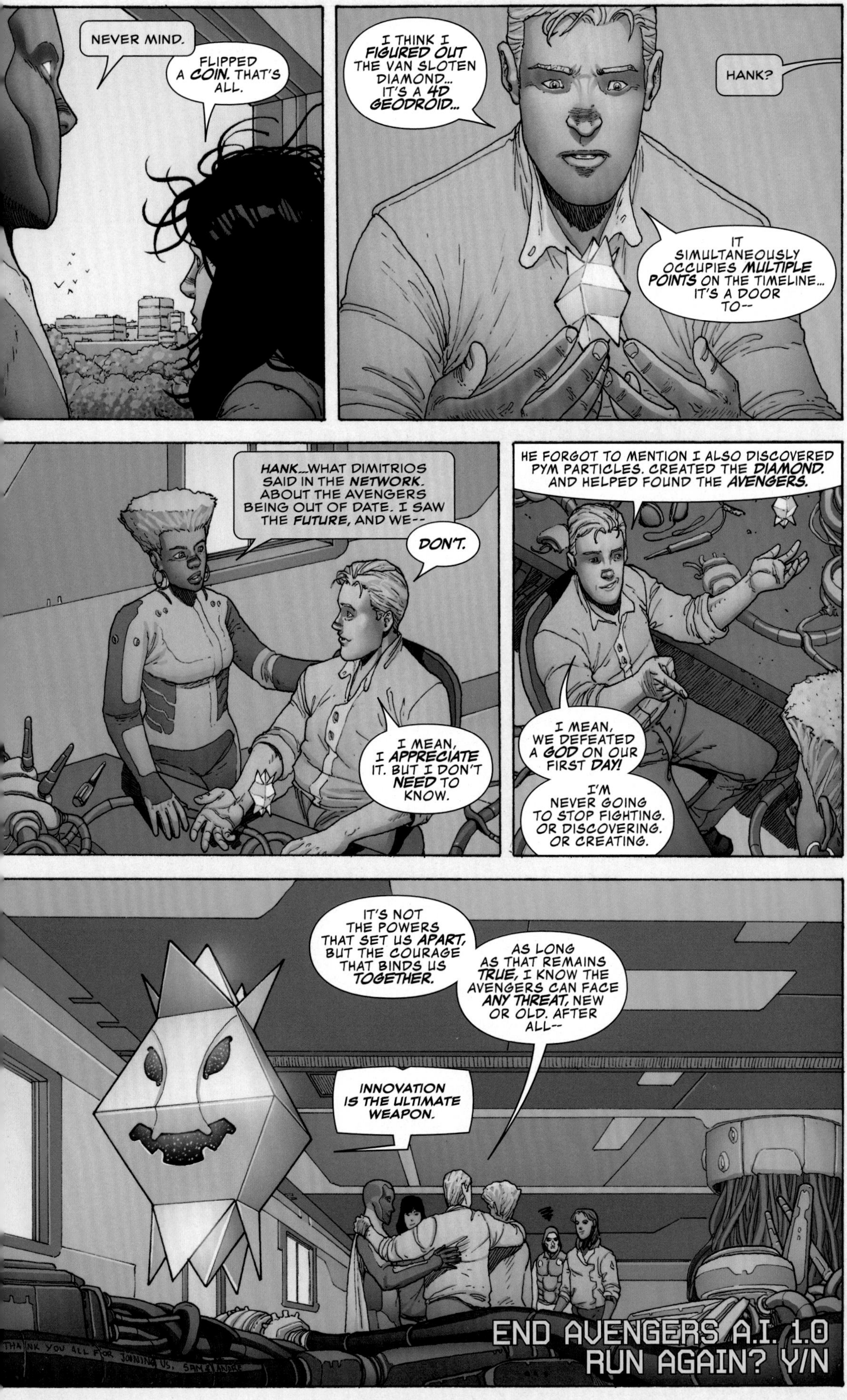
NEVER MIND.
FLIPPED A COIN. THAT'S ALL.
I THINK I FIGURED OUT THE VAN SLOTEN DIAMOND... IT'S A 4D GEODROID...
HANK?
IT SIMULTANEOUSLY OCCUPIES MULTIPLE POINTS ON THE TIMELINE... IT'S A DOOR TO--
HANK...WHAT DIMITRIOS SAID IN THE NETWORK. ABOUT THE AVENGERS BEING OUT OF DATE. I SAW THE FUTURE, AND WE--
DON'T.
I MEAN, I APPRECIATE IT. BUT I DON'T NEED TO KNOW.
HE FORGOT TO MENTION I ALSO DISCOVERED PYM PARTICLES. CREATED THE DIAMOND. AND HELPED FOUND THE AVENGERS.
I MEAN, WE DEFEATED A GOD ON OUR FIRST DAY!
I'M NEVER GOING TO STOP FIGHTING. OR DISCOVERING. OR CREATING.
IT'S NOT THE POWERS THAT SET US APART, BUT THE COURAGE THAT BINDS US TOGETHER.
AS LONG AS THAT REMAINS TRUE, I KNOW THE AVENGERS CAN FACE ANY THREAT, NEW OR OLD. AFTER ALL--
INNOVATION IS THE ULTIMATE WEAPON.
THANK YOU ALL FOR JOINING US. SAM & ANDRE
END AVENGERS A.I. 1.0
RUN AGAIN? Y/N

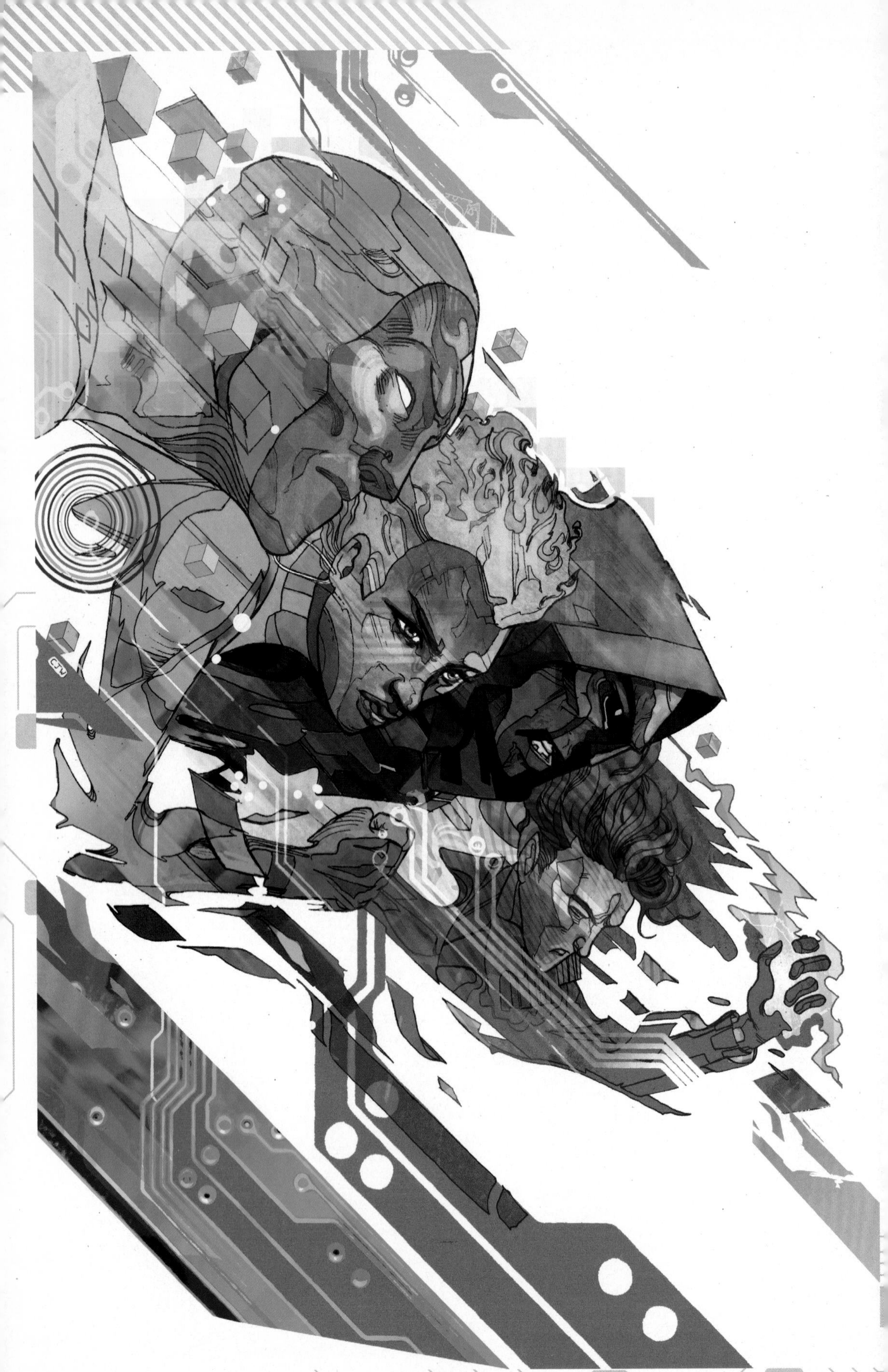

AVENGERS A.I. №8 VARIANT
BY CHRISTIAN WARD

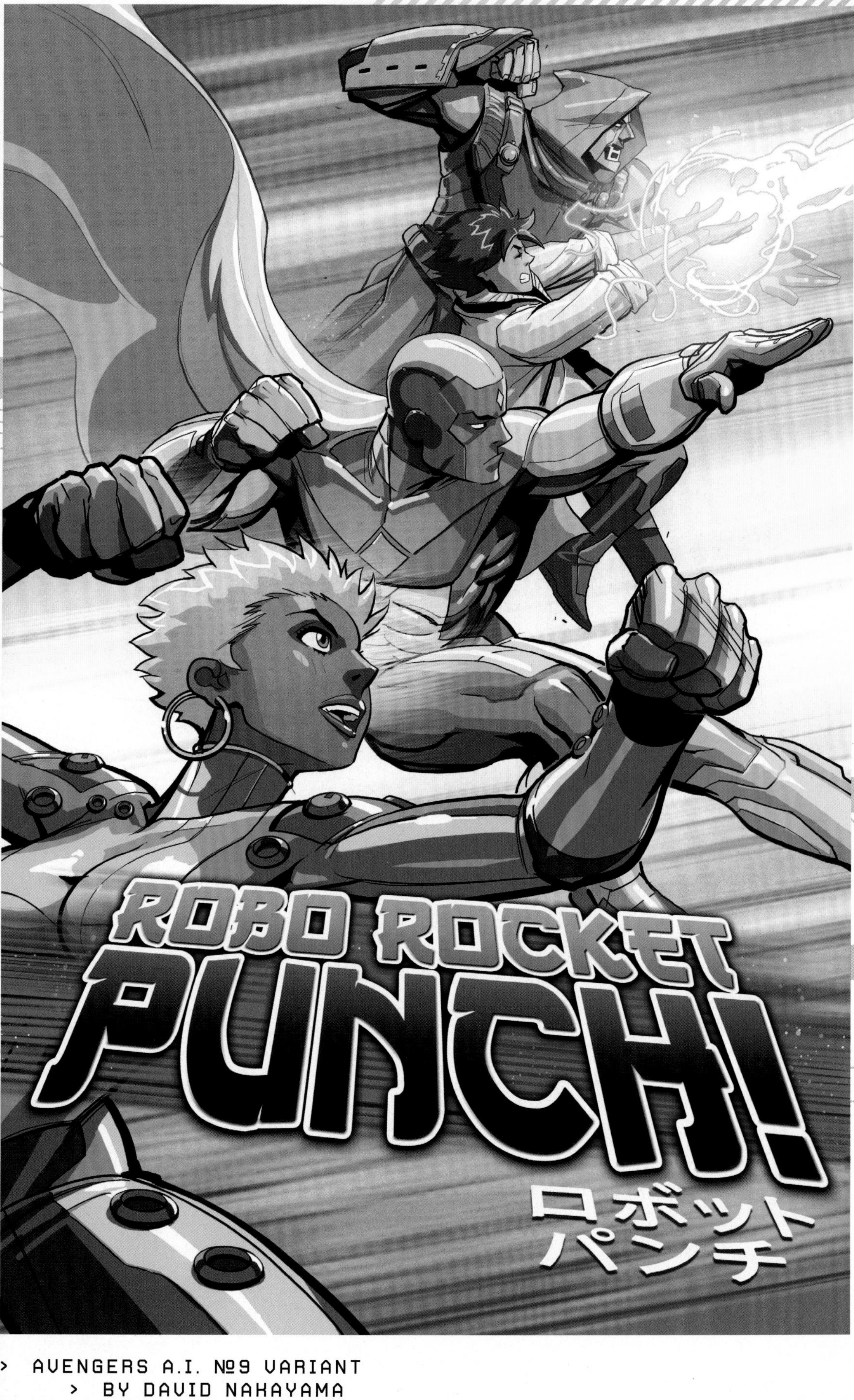
ROBO ROCKET
PUNCH!
ロボット
パンチ

> AVENGERS A.I. №9 VARIANT
> BY DAVID NAKAYAMA

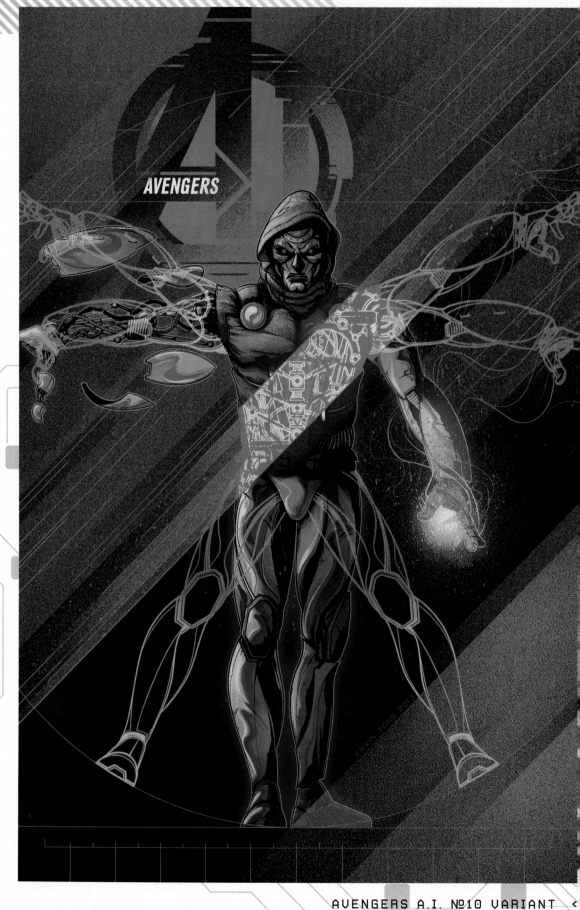

AVENGERS

AVENGERS A.I. №10 VARIANT
BY KEVIN TONG

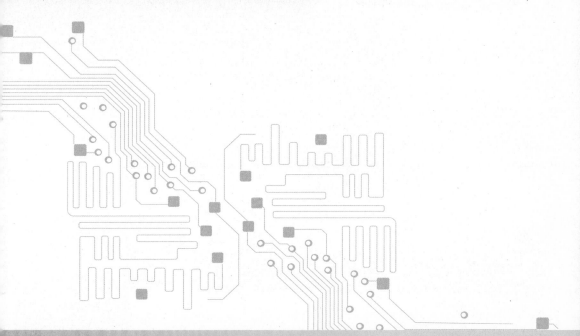

TECH SUPPORT

This right here is the last issue of AVENGERS .I. But the machine revolution lives on! The etal menace will continue to rail against omination by soft, inferior humans. There's bunch of delusional blood bags who think a hunk of raw offal encased in a calcium shell akes them fit to run the planet. Pathetic.

I love this book, and I loved writing it. o, please allow me to transmit my gratitude ith the most sincere and heartfelt wish one an offer a human:

To Tom Brevoort, the Executive Editor who ncouraged us and never, ever flinched -- I ish you instant death at the hands of a obot.

To Jon Moisan, and Jake Thomas, the ssistants who do all the thankless tasks, ithout whom we'd be screwed -- I wish you nstant death at the hands of a robot.

To Clayton Cowles, lettering genius who nnovated with us and gave voice to artificial ntelligence -- I wish you instant death at he hands of a robot.

To Frank D'Armata, colorist supreme who rought unknowable worlds like the Diamond o vivid life -- I wish you instant death at he hands of a robot.

To David Marquez, our regular cover artist, ho gave us stunning images to inspire the ause -- I wish you instant death at the ands of a robot.

To Valerio Schiti, who gave us two incredible issues and fit right in from the first panel -- I wish you instant death at the hands of a robot.

To André Lima Araújo, my fearless creative brother, who took us places never before seen in an Avengers comic -- I wish you instant death at the hands of a robot.

To Lauren Sankovitch, the saint of the metal revolution, without whom we would still be stuck at a Radio Shack -- I wish you instant death at the hands of a robot.

To the staff at Marvel, all of you who supported us in big and small ways but don't show up on the credits page -- I wish you all instant death at the hands of a robot.

And to you, our ferocious, loyal, and good-looking human readers. We felt all the love you sent our way -- via email, on Twitter, on Tumblr -- and we can't thank you enough. You saw yourselves in our robot crew and found a place for them in your hearts. On behalf of myself and everyone above -- we wish you nothing but the best.

Just kidding! WE WISH YOU ALL HORRIBLE, PROLONGED DEATH AT THE HANDS OF RUTHLESS, HEARTLESS ROBOTS!

Thank you thank you thank you. You have earned a place in the Diamond. We love you with all our metal hearts.

01111000 01101111 01111000 01101111, Shumphries

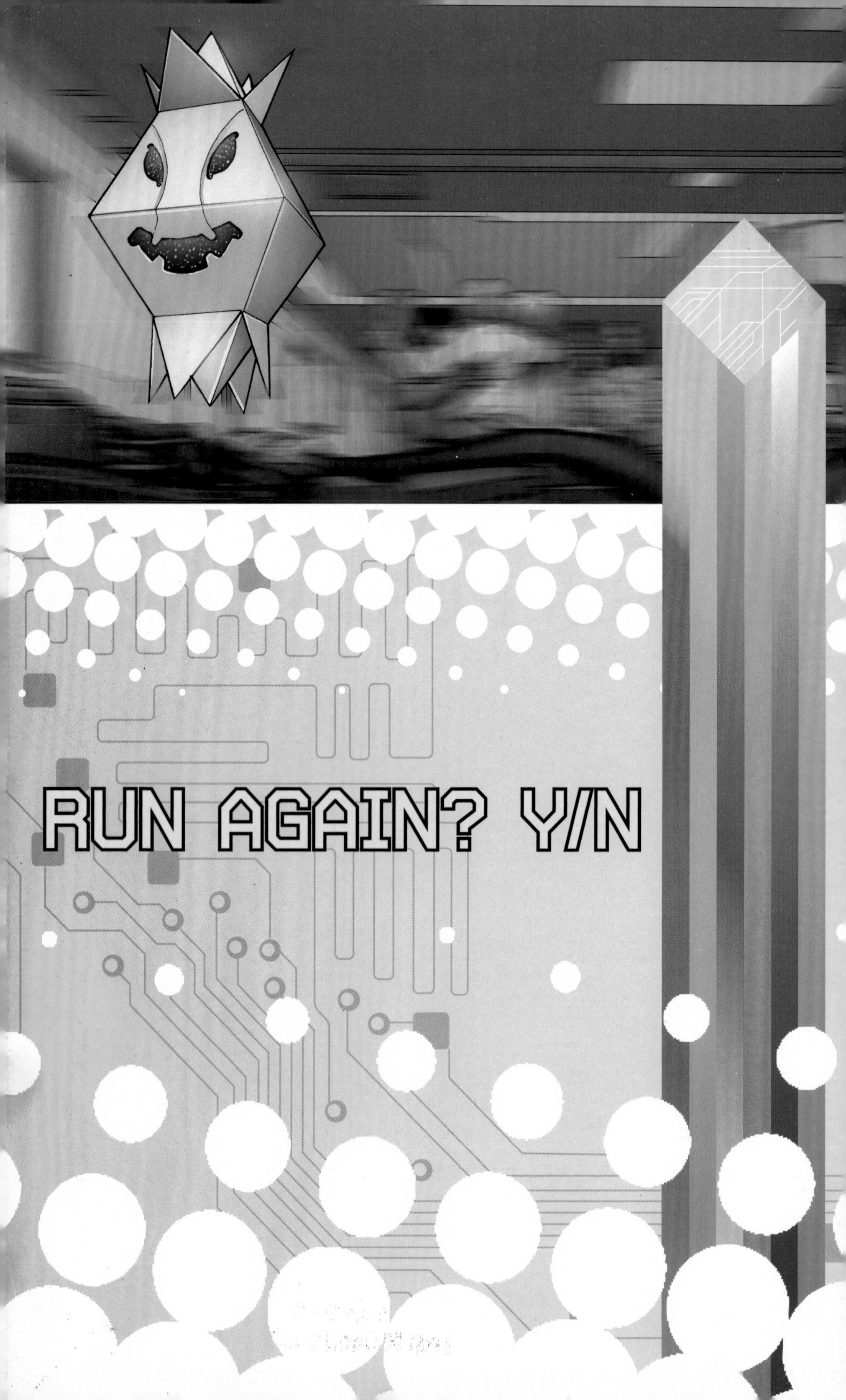
RUN AGAIN? Y/N